PRAISE FOR SOUTH FROM ALASKA

A book that speaks to both sides of the brain simultaneously and without contradiction...prose so beautiful, and with such a dose of self-deprecating comic relief, that you yearn to be there with them.

Cruising World

Litzow is a talented writer... evocative and powerfully visual.

The Age (Melbourne)

Eminently readable.

The Sydney Sun-Herald

As a sailor who raised his daughter aboard, I was touched by this book. Litzow writes from the heart.

Cap'n Fatty Goodlander, sailor and writer

Mike writes well and with utter honesty about the sometimes overwhelming sense of responsibility he feels when he and his partner Alisa take a toddler to sea. He clearly shows the stress this places on their marriage and how it is balanced by the rewards they and their slowly maturing son reap. Essential reading for anyone contemplating voyaging with very young children.

Lin Pardey, author of *Storm Tactics Handbook, Self Sufficient Sailor* and *Bull Canyon*

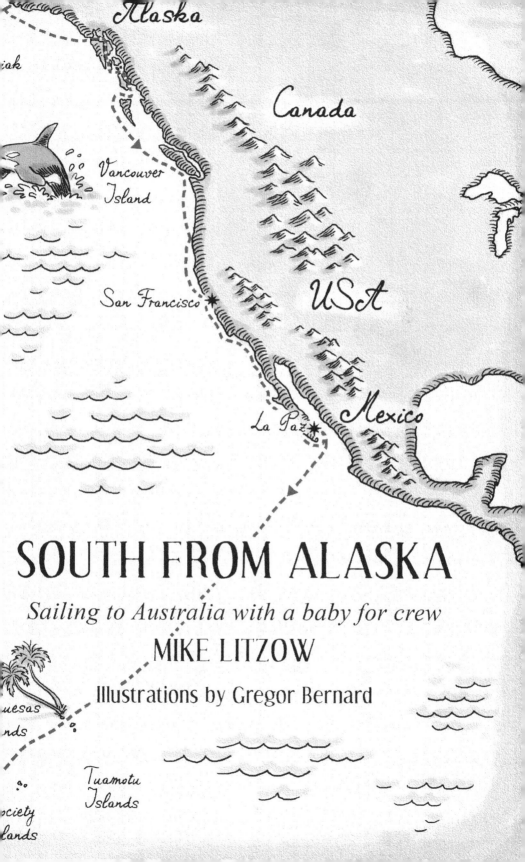

SOUTH FROM ALASKA

Sailing to Australia with a baby for crew

MIKE LITZOW

Illustrations by Gregor Bernard

South From Alaska: Sailing to Australia with a baby for crew

ISBN: 978-0692029268

First published 2011 by:
NewSouth Publishing
University of New South Wales Press
Sydney, Australia

Second edition published 2014 by:
Blue World Press
Kodiak, Alaska
blueworldresearch.com/blueworldpress

Editing by Tim Fullerton
Cover design by Damon Za
Illustrations by Gregor Bernard
Design by Benjamin Carrancho
Photographs by Mike Litzow and Alisa Abookire

Mike and Alisa have a new boat – and a new kid.
Follow the continuing adventure at TheLifeGalactic.blogspot.com

This book is for Alisa.
Of course.

There is no life like the sea where reality falls so short of romantic expectation.

Joseph Conrad, *Lord Jim*

CONTENTS

FORTUNE FAVORS THE BOLD

I CONSULTED OUR chart for the umpteenth time and steered us through the marked channel through the flats north of town. After a dewy-eyed start of checking the oil in the engine and coiling dock-lines, *Pelagic*, our somewhat elderly sailboat, was leaving the coastal town of Cordova before dawn and heading out towards the open Gulf of Alaska. Even as I followed the channel, my senses were half given over to *Pelagic*, listening, and feeling, for any irregularity that might be the first sign of something going wrong. That boat was our home, the repository for nearly everything that we owned and, literally, the vessel that carried our dreams, the 37-foot boat that we had decided to sail from Alaska to Australia. Everything depended on the boat, and even on this calm morning in protected waters, I was constantly attuned to *Pelagic*.

When I did sense something going wrong it wasn't the sound of the diesel engine hesitating, or the feel of the steering cables slipping.

What I heard was the sound of a baby crying.

'I'll get him', I said to Alisa. Leaving her at the wheel, I went below and retrieved ten-month-old Elias from his bunk. A good-natured baby, he stopped crying as soon as I picked him up, and smiled a three-toothed grin at me as I changed his diaper. Elias wasn't walking yet, but he was active enough, and strong enough, to make a determined effort to get in the way of my job. We had a long standoff over who would get to keep the wet diaper that I removed, and only a determined bout of tickling convinced him to give up the diaper cream. I finally got the new diaper on him, and bundled him in all the layers of clothes that a baby might need to stay comfortable on a sailboat in Alaska. In the cockpit I handed him to Alisa for his morning nurse.

'I'm not sure how you change those diapers in rough weather', I said.

'I'm not sure either.' Alisa smiled.

So far on our trip we had followed the coast, sailing through fjords and straits and bays. Every day ended with a secure anchorage and a full night's sleep. But Cordova was the end of the line for that kind of sailing, at least for a while. Before us lay our first overnight passage with Elias, a 340 nautical mile crossing from Prince William Sound to the fjords of Southeast Alaska. During the first weeks of the trip, caring for Elias and sailing the boat had left us with our metaphorical noses just above water, and we relied heavily on the nightly recharge of anchoring *Pelagic* and sleeping soundly. Our passage to Southeast would give us the answer to one of the great unanswered questions of our trip – could we handle the double duty of parenting and sailing *Pelagic* continuously around the clock?

We knew we would have to eventually sail the boat, day and night, for weeks on end during the longer passages that awaited us in the South Pacific. But we just didn't know if we could do that with Elias. So, after all the work of severing our life on land and sailing away, after selling our house and quitting our jobs and overcoming our constant doubts to set out across the Pacific with our baby for crew, this three-day trip across the Gulf would give us a real idea if our dream was within our abilities, or if it was wildly unrealistic. We were both nervous about the test ahead of us, we both felt, but didn't say out loud, that we were approaching a juncture where our dream could either live or die. The night before we left Cordova, as we played cribbage in the cockpit, Alisa stayed characteristically upbeat. Holding her cards with fingers that were bandaged in gauze and electrical tape after an accident with the stove, she looked up at me and said, 'Well, at least in a few days we'll know what it's like, instead of wondering'.

We caught the morning tide out of Cordova and motored towards Hinchinbrook Entrance, our route out of Prince William Sound. It was a gift of a day: sunny, a luminous flat blue sea, fluffy white clouds sitting over the emerald mountains with their skirts of spruce forest spilling down to the water. Alisa and I were taut with the moment. Adventure doesn't have to do with spine-tingling thrills and narrow escapes; adventure exists when the outcome of a journey is unknown. So, on that flat-calm, brilliant day in the subarctic, as the three of us sat in the cockpit, we were at the height of our adventure.

The tide pulled us through Hinchinbrook Entrance, and out of Prince William Sound. Light west winds were forecast and we found no swell and no wind waves in the Gulf, just the pulse and swirl of the millions of gallons of water ebbing out of the Sound along with us. Now the clouds were cut from crystal, the water was turquoise. We motored along, me behind the wheel and Alisa feeding Elias his rice cereal. The mountains shrank behind us. The slightest motion of the open ocean began to rock *Pelagic*. We felt a sense of hope, optimism.

'We're pointing it south', I said. 'Warmer places. Australia.'

Alisa was jovial, Elias querulous. We put our faith in the notion that fortune favors the bold.

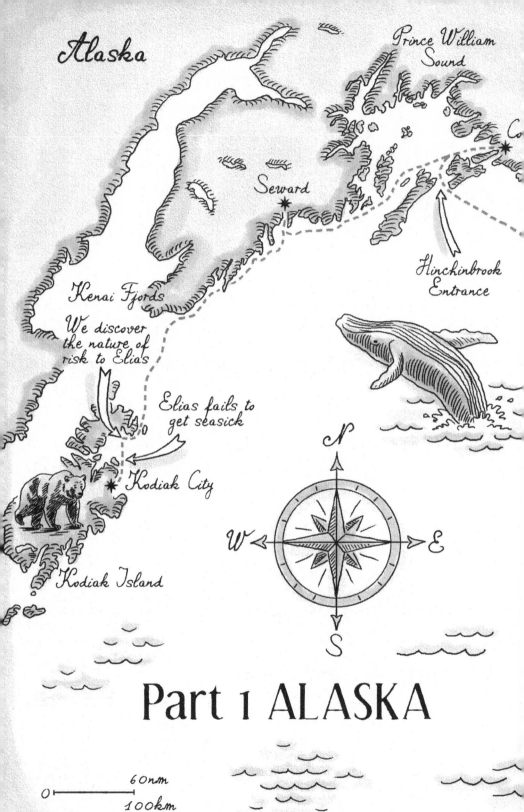

Alaska

Prince William
Sound

Seward

Co

Kenai Fjords

We discover
the nature of
risk to Elias

Hinchinbrook
Entrance

Elias fails to
get seasick

Kodiak City

Kodiak Island

N

W   E

S

Part 1 ALASKA

0   60nm

100km

Canada

Mt St Elias

Bay

Elias turns one   Haines

Lituya
Bay   Graves   Lynn
       Harbor   Canal

discover what it's
to sail for three days
raight with a baby

Tenakee Springs

Chatham Strait

Warm Springs Bay

Port Alexander

1

THE TOWN ALONG
THE SHORE

G ETTING THAT FAR hadn't been easy.

Three weeks earlier, in our hometown of Kodiak, Alaska, I had posted the news of our departure online.

'And this is the way a much dreamed-of day arrives', I typed, 'as a day like any other. Tomorrow we set sail for Australia.'

The dreamed-of day arrived, but it came in a guise I didn't recognize.

The day began with me opening the hatch to the cockpit to check the weather. The water was black and ruffled. A continuous layer of cloud was dropping rain on us and snow on the mountains above town. Sheets of mist swept through the harbor. Commercial fishing boats glistened at the dock. Deciding that the best course of action would be to keep the hatch closed and let the weather look after itself, I retreated down below, where the cabin heater was failing to keep the boat warm. Occasional gusts of wind pushed down the stack and filled the cabin with acrid diesel smoke. Condensation covered the insides of hatches and portlights, giving an underwater cast to the feeble morning light that managed to struggle below.

With the muted disappointment of experience I noted that the chaos in the cabin hadn't organized itself out of existence during the two minutes I had been elsewhere, looking at the weather. Piles of loose gear were still stacked everywhere, on settees and chart table and steps, threatening to slide to the sole each time a gust of wind grabbed hold of *Pelagic* and gave her a shake. A month after we had moved out of our house and onto the boat, we were still stuck with things that we neither wanted to get rid of, nor could find a place on the boat to store. The festive ribbons that we had tied on the overhead grab rails the night before in a successful bid to keep a gathering of friends from turning mournful were still there. They had been so successful in keeping things un-mournful that people had stayed until two. An impressive number of empty wine and liquor bottles were still crowded onto the little galley counter, and had failed to clean themselves up since I had last glanced their way. And, most incongruously on this 37-foot sailboat that was doing a poor job of providing enough space for even our pared-down version of the standard set of American possessions, the center of the cabin was still completely filled by a baby's playpen.

Alisa sat on a settee amid the clutter. I was used to her remaining effortlessly cheerful, and I realized as I looked at her now that I had, without thinking about it at all, decided that her constant cheer likely had something to do with being married to me, and was therefore a condition that I could take some pride in. Now, though, her face was uncharacteristically drawn, her eyes flat and somber. I noted these facts, briefly thought about how they didn't fit with my mental image of our departure day, and then decided to put off the question of whether taking mental credit for her up moods meant I also had to take the blame when she was down.

With one hand Alisa was apparently cradling our son Elias James to her breast, although I couldn't actually see any part of him past the cocoon of warm clothes that he wore to maintain life in the subarctic atmosphere of the cabin. In the other hand Alisa held our very last pre-departure job list. How many times had we dreamed of holding that final list! Now that the moment had come I just felt nervous, and desperate to get going. Our motivation couldn't be more romantic – we wanted to sail the world together, on our own boat, at our own pace, while we were still in our thirties. But breathing life into that romantic vision, it turned out, involved hundreds and hundreds of very mundane tasks. Alisa, the one of us who wasn't born with a complete lack of organizational skill, consulted the list of jobs and sketched out a plan that would allow me to execute them all. In order, I would fill jerry jugs with diesel fuel, buy spare anchor shackles at one store and fuses at another, replace the leaky pump that fed diesel fuel to our cabin heater, find a home on board *Pelagic* for the impossibly large assortment of gear that was still skulking in the back of my truck, lock up a few final possessions in a storage unit against the too-distant-to-imagine day when we would return, and drop off the truck with its new owner.

And then we would be ready to go.

Before I could get started there was a knock at the hull. I peered out of a rain-smeared portlight and saw our friend Zoya, her face pinched against the cold, hair blowing in her eyes, holding her five-month-old son in one hand and leading her two-year-old daughter by the other.

'Oh', she said when I slid back the hatch. 'I thought at first that I missed you, but then I realized you're probably not going in this weather, are you?'

'Yeah', I said. 'We're going.'

So Zoya came on board to say goodbye.

In my dreams, our departure day had been an event of joyous release, not a day filled to choking with goodbyes. All the long day as we worked in a frenzy to finish last-minute tasks while simultaneously caring for a ten-month-old child in the confines of a disorganized sailboat, we were prey to anyone who wanted to come down to the docks to say their goodbyes. We were exhausted from months of getting ready, months of selling the house and paring down possessions and getting our 25-year-old sailboat shipshape to the point where it could give us the illusion of being ready for whatever the sea might bring. We were exhausted from weeks of living the split life of being physically present in the little town that we loved but had decided to leave, while being mentally already far away in some palm-fringed anchorage. We ached with the feeling that the list of pre-trip jobs would go on forever. And then, on that last day as we worked at the home stretch of our marathon of preparation, our friends came down to say goodbye, one after the other, and made us miserably sad on top of it all.

Two doctors were the last well-wishers of the day. Like many of our friends that day they came with a gift, in this case some fillets from the rockfish they had just caught. The older doctor had been our next-door neighbor for seven years and he had delivered Elias. The younger doctor was the newest employee in the older doctor's practice, and he and his girlfriend had bought our house from us. That's how people's lives become enmeshed in small-town Alaska. One person is simultaneously your next-door neighbor, the person who delivered your child, and the employer of the person who bought your house. When you leave Kodiak, you say goodbye to people who have worked into the grain of your life.

The doctors left after handshakes and hugs, and I realized that I couldn't stand to say goodbye to one more person. I suddenly felt that if we didn't leave right away we would be fated to spend the rest of our lives at the dock, forever interrupted in the middle of some critical final job by the necessity of saying goodbye to another friend.

So, with Alisa occupied below feeding Elias his dinner, I started the engine and got ready to go.

After the diesel had warmed up I hopped onto the dock. Before I untied the lines I paused and looked back at *Pelagic*. From the dock I was at eye level with the pile of gear lashed to various strong points about the deck – a fiberglass dinghy, the mast and boom for sailing the dinghy, oars for rowing the dinghy, fishing poles, water jugs, diesel jugs, a boat hook, and diaper buckets. Yes – two buckets with screw-on lids, lashed to the stern rail, ready to soak dirty cloth diapers. All this gear cluttered the naturally sleek design of the boat, and she rested low in the water with the weight of supplies we had packed on board. But *Pelagic* still retained her purposeful look, with her long bow hanging over the water, with her canoe-style stern, pointed like a second bow ready to meet following ocean waves, with her bronze portlights gone green where a quarter-century's weather had passed over them. To a casual observer, *Pelagic* looked like a boat that would do the job.

To me, as I stood on the dock looking back at the boat, *Pelagic* appeared as a collection of problems: problems that were inconsequential and problems that could be serious; problems that were known, or suspected, or (worst of all) that were neither, and therefore might take me unawares far out to sea some day. For the three years we had owned the boat, *Pelagic* had been the medium through which I had struggled to turn myself from a dreamer who wanted to do grand things and travel to distant shores into a practical man of the sea who actually did travel to distant shores. So as I stood on the dock, poised to step ashore and begin our voyaging, I didn't see the classic seafaring lines of our boat. I saw the dark recesses where wiring ran behind bulkheads, I saw the dirty bilge where I bashed my knuckles with a wrench in hand, I saw things I had meant to improve against some hypothetical threat of the high seas, but had never gotten around to. There is a maritime tradition of commingling the identities of captain and vessel, to the point of referring to a captain by the name of his ship. What did it say of me, either as a 'captain' or a person, that I looked at my 37-foot fiberglass *doppelgänger* and saw nothing but problems?

I untied the lines and gave the boat a shove. *Pelagic* glided away from the dock. I leapt aboard, then shifted the engine into reverse and backed out of our slip. The bow cleared the piling at the end of the dock. I shifted into neutral, then forward. Eight tons of boat gained momentum beneath me. I enjoyed the stately feeling of the boat moving through the water again. I was immensely relieved to be going. Alisa stuck her head out of the companionway, smiling with anticipation. But then she registered the moving scenery around us and her smile disappeared.

'Are we moving?', she asked.

'Um. Yes.'

'I thought you were warming up the engine. You just untied and started without telling me?'

I thought for a second, then settled for another, 'Um. Yes.'

Alisa was angry. Her eyes flashed and she communicated her displeasure to me in the devastating way that married people can, through things left unsaid. Beneath her heavy sweater I could picture her shoulder muscles bunching and the cords of her forearms flexing in frustration. I was surprised by the strength of her reaction, though it was a powerful moment – the first symbolic step of untying the dock lines that were the final connection between ourselves and home. It's rare to come across such an absolute demarcation in life. Up until that very last moment when I untied the boat, we were residents of a remote Alaskan fishing town who were working towards the improbable dream of sailing far away on a sailboat with our baby for crew. A second later, after the lines were untied and I had pushed *Pelagic* away from the dock, we had made the transition to being wayfarers who were seeing what lay on the other side of a dream enacted.

I felt bad about making that symbolic move while Alisa was below feeding Elias, though I was still surprised at the way that she was glaring about it. Alisa was my life partner, the woman who had taken on my dream and made it her own, the woman who when the idea of sailing away with a baby for crew began to seem so foolish that I started talking about cancelling the trip had said, 'If we don't go now, we'll always wonder.' Now, on our special day, she was staring at me with anger in her eyes. I wanted to explain to her that our dream life had officially begun and was all of two minutes old. Glares hadn't been a part of our marriage in our previous life, so surely they didn't belong in this new, better, long-dreamed-of life that we were now living? But I thought better of saying that.

Instead I explained that the doctors made me to do it.

Alisa put Elias in his snowsuit to fend off the drizzle and cold and brought him up to the cockpit. I steered *Pelagic* past the green marker at the entrance to the harbor and quickly glanced down at Elias to see how he was doing. This quick glance, this regular assessment of how things stood with Elias, would become an inescapable part of the sailing routine for Alisa and me, as automatic as breathing. *Where's Elias?* would be the question we had to answer a thousand times each day. I glanced down and saw Elias for the helpless baby that he was. At ten months old, he could sit up and grasp things and make interesting noises. But he couldn't talk, couldn't walk, and was still an awkward crawler, trying to shuffle along on two hands, one foot and one knee. His cherubic cheeks were chapped red in the cutting spring weather of Alaska. His head, now hidden by the hood of his snowsuit, was bald except for a natural mohawk of fine gold strands that were bravely growing in. His personality swung between the opposite poles of cooing delight and voluble outrage. The smells he gave off varied from the reassuring whiff of talcum powder and burped-up breast milk to the rank offence of a full diaper. And here he was, on the 322nd day of his life, setting out on a voyage that few adults would choose. He was doing this without choice, of course, because he wasn't even up to choosing what he would eat for breakfast. He had no concept of risk, and was at an age where exposing him to any was, in the eyes of most societies, a criminal act. Even in the safe confines of a house, he was helpless, dependent on us for every single thing he needed in life. In the far more rigorous environment of a 37-foot sailboat on the open ocean, he was simply out of place, like a kitten in a roomful of pit bulls, or a china cup balanced on a wrecking ball.

Or like a baby at sea.

Making Elias a home on board *Pelagic* had been a major focus of our preparations for the trip. We bought a playpen that would fit perfectly into the tiny open space in the cabin. We cut the legs off a crib so that it would fit into the cave-like space of the forward bunk. We lashed his little eating chair onto a settee in the very center of the boat, the place where there would be the least motion at sea. We padded sharp edges and put baby-proof latches on locker doors. We read reviews of infant life jackets and we bought a tiny chest harness to keep him tethered to the boat when he was in the cockpit. From a commercial fishing friend who had brought up her own two boys on the water we inherited an infant-sized neoprene immersion suit against the terrible-to-contemplate possibility of abandoning ship. We dedicated significant amounts of our limited storage space to a library of medical reference books and the drugs to treat an exhaustive list of potential illnesses. We read and re-read the only book that we could find about sailing with babies. But its reassuring outlook was spoiled by my fresh memory of the way our upbeat books about natural childbirth had completely failed to describe the reality of Alisa's 39-hour labor.

We had done everything we could think of. And now we were going. I glanced down at Elias. There was nothing to do but trust we were prepared. *Pelagic* motored along the waterfront and towards the open sea. Alisa called our friends John and Patty on the cell phone to tell them we were on our way.

While I had been busy ignoring it, the weather had failed to improve. The sun was still lost above a blanket of clouds. Only a sullen daylight was available, enough light to see things but not enough to make any detail sparkle. Ragged fishing boats unloaded their catches at the tenders anchored in the harbor. Bald eagles clustered on the metal roofs of the canneries, their feathers soaked from the rain and their white heads soiled from foraging in the dump. Alisa and I looked at everything. We drank in the sight of our friends' houses, the fishing boats we knew, the onion dome of the Orthodox church, the shape of trees and rocks that had become familiar through the years. Kodiak was the place where we had bought our first house and had our first child, the only home we knew as a family. By the time we reached the end of the waterfront, tears were running down both of our faces. Even little Elias was quiet, having absorbed the solemn mood.

We motored under the bridge and came to the stretch of houses past the boatyard. We looked, and there were John and Patty, who had come out of their house to wave goodbye. Patty's family lineage on Kodiak Island extended, literally, to the time when mammoths roamed the earth. The day before she had given us a tiny spirit pouch in the style of the Alutiiq, the Pacific Eskimos of Kodiak – a flat basket the size of a ten cent piece, which she had woven from the fibers of a local grass. Patty explained that pre-contact Alutiiq whalers used to wear the same kind of pouch around their necks, carrying a pinch of Kodiak soil to ensure their return to land when they set off in their kayaks to hunt whales. Our own spirit pouch was now hanging from the radio over the chart table, filled with a little piece of Kodiak soil to guarantee our safe return some day.

Now John and Patty waved, and we waved back as we turned past a buoy and *Pelagic* felt the first motion of the open sea. John and Patty kept waving with their hands held high over their heads as we got farther and farther away, our little farewell crowd of two. We waved back, watching them even when they were two dots on the shore. The clouds behind us pulled back and we got a last glimpse of the mountains above town, and the town itself, lost in the vastness of the North Pacific, sitting on the edge of the island where its Russian founders had chosen to leave it. Then we followed the channel behind an offlying island and lost sight of the town, so that there was nothing to do but turn away and look forward, where we were heading, and savor the fresh memory of our last look at home, with the mountains above so big, and the town along the shore so ramshackle and small, and our two friends waving until they couldn't see us any more.

2

THE *HUSBAND* PROMISES
TO REFRAIN

'THAT'S WHAT YOU get for meeting guys at mountaineering skills seminars.'

For years that had been my response when Alisa mentioned the oddities of our shared life. The trip to Europe before we were married, for instance, which was centered on a week of −30°F winter camping in Spitsbergen, halfway between Norway and the North Pole. Or the secure, remunerative and rewarding job as a fisheries research biologist that she found herself walking away from when she bought into her husband's dream of living on a sailboat that was always cramped, occasionally damp, and a quarter-century old.

We met when I was teaching the session on ice axe technique on the first day of the annual alpine club course at the University of Alaska. Alisa showed up, her Levantine face framed by the wool hat and down parka that she wore against the brutal cold of February in Fairbanks, her Mt Ararat nose and full-moon cheeks isolated against the backdrop of unblinking white snow. The lock of hair that spilled out from beneath her hat repeated the onyx of her eyebrows. Somewhere beneath the pallor of her sun-starved existence in the subarctic winter her skin was olive. My eyes hesitated on her face, searching, and she smiled back. We looked at each other, and without knowing it, each looked into our future.

'Check out the cute Jewish girl,' I thought to myself, making an error of identification that I would repeat to Alisa, *sotto voce*, at gatherings of Lebanese-Arab in-laws for years to come.

We fell in love and together we took one long cross-country ski trip every year, towing our gear in sleds and camping in a different spot every night. We skied up isolated river valleys in Alaska where whiteouts made sky and mountains blend together in a landscape of vertigo, where the bare branches of willow shrubs reached their supplicating fingers to the sky, waiting for the subarctic summer to return. Our trips grew in length from days to weeks, and they became the annual milestone in a shared life that was leaning towards adventure.

One year our trip began with the propeller roar and avgas fumes of a skiplane that carried us into a remote airstrip on the north side of the Alaska Range. After we unloaded our gear and waved goodbye to the pilot we were suddenly just *there*, in the still perfection of a late winter day in Interior Alaska, with the highway that would mark the end of the trip 90 miles away. Alisa began breaking trail through the snow and I followed, willing myself into a rhythm by concentrating on the icy rasp of ski on snow. We looked up from our toil to stare at the ice-cream castle wonder of the highest mountain in North America, close by and high above. I had known Alisa for years. I knew her no-nonsense graduate student side; I knew her go-out-dancing-on-a-Saturday-night side. I knew the side of her that woke up in the tent on a winter morning in Alaska and refused to move until chocolate had been handed down through the tiny breathing hole in her sleeping bag. Now, skiing behind her with the vista of the Alaska Range before us, I said to myself over and over, 'Just do it. Do it now.'

I felt like a fifteen-year-old boy failing to work up the nerve to call a girl on the phone. Later I learned that Alisa was skiing ahead of me and thinking, 'This is perfect. If he doesn't do it now, he'll never do it.'

A week later I did propose, halfway up a mountain trail on Kodiak Island. But first I asked, 'Um, do you still think that you might like to live on a sailboat some day?'

In one of those essay assignments in a high school English class where you are asked to reveal something interesting about yourself, I might have written that I dreamed of someday sailing the world in a small boat. Or, I might not have written that at all. I might have thought of those sailing dreams as being so integral to me, like one of my arms, as to be unremarkable. Ever since my parents went to sailing school and bought a 19-foot boat when I was seven years old, I have been convinced that one of the fundamental upsides of being alive is that it gives you the chance to do things like sailing across oceans. In my adolescent imagination, living on a boat meant living life at the correct pace, the pace of swell and squall and tide. Living on a boat meant visiting far-distant shores that were clad in castles of glacial ice or rimmed with living reefs. Living on a boat meant really living, meant treating your life as an opportunity and not a chore.

In our thirties, Alisa and I were married and the phenomenon of salaries that increased much more rapidly than our spending meant that we had enough money to buy a sailboat. We took stock. We had jobs as marine biologists that we enjoyed very much about three-quarters of the time and not at all for the remainder. We had a little house that we loved, on the ocean on the outskirts of a remote town in Alaska. We had all those wonderful friends who would eventually make us miserable with their goodbyes. We were happy.

But the dream wouldn't be quiet. It stirred when we looked at our friends who had come to Kodiak thirty years before and stayed and we said to each other, 'That's not us. Not yet.' It stirred when we looked at our colleagues at work, passing their lives with days, and years, that were identical from one to the next. And it stirred when we looked at the broader society and wondered what people were doing in America with all the wealth that was available to them, besides working themselves frantic. Gradually, Alisa adopted my dream as her own.

If we sailed, we would need a goal. Being aimless would bore us in a week. My Australian father had lived in America for thirty-five years, dreaming all the while of returning home. We could join our dream with his, and sail to Australia. I could get an Australian passport. Alisa could get a resident visa.

All one long winter we talked it over. What did we want out of life? What could we afford to do? Having travelled all the way to Alaska from the lower forty-eight States and found a place that we loved, were we wise to sit put or should we range even more?

Those questions were important, but abstract. There would also be a baby, which was something important, and very concrete. Could we sail with a baby? We had no idea. We heard rumors of people who had sailed across oceans with their babies, but of course we had never met them. Would it be fair to the baby? Could we find answers to each problem that might come along? Before Elias was even conceived, we talked at great length about how a young child might fare at sea.

All one long Alaskan winter we talked around the biggest question of all. Would we act on this dream, in spite of the completely inconvenient, new-parent phase of life we found ourselves approaching, or would we leave the dream in its perfect, unrealized state, and look back twenty years later and wonder what might have been.

Then, one spring night, we drank a bottle of wine and Alisa wrote out a contract:

> I, Alisa Abookire, being of sound mind and hot Arab body, do hereby agree to quit the job, sell the house that I love, and sail to Australia with my loving husband and child, even though I am still 10 percent unsure that I want to go and am 90 percent sure that I don't like heeling. In return, said loving husband agrees to the following conditions:
>
> The *sprout* will be at least one year old before we go.
>
> The *husband* promises to refrain from putting up too much sail until the *wife* gets used to heeling.
>
> We can have at least X dollars in the bank when we leave.
>
> The *wife* reserves the right to place additional conditions at any time.
>
> Signed: Alisa Ann Abookire (*wife*)
>
> Signed: Michael Andrew Litzow (*husband*)

We lived up to that agreement, though in the actual event we were too impatient to let Elias turn one before we left.

3

PELAGIC

YOU CANNOT CHANGE your everyday life into a dream. No matter where you might go or how dramatically you might change things, there is no escape from the familiar frustrations of the everyday. Therefore, in order to live a dream, you have to change the dream into your everyday life. This is a process that no dream can survive. For people who dream of sailing across oceans, the act of buying an actual boat, on an actual budget, ends the romantic part of sailing. Everything that remains is practical.

We bought a 25-year-old boat. A design called the Crealock 37, made from fiberglass, this boat was a particularly elegant expression of the accepted thinking, in a certain time and a certain place, about what would make an ideal boat for a couple sailing the world. Later we would meet a Frenchman who told us how his nation's sailors described boats like ours: 'It's so American, if it were any more American, it would be dead!' So it turns out that there are other expressions of accepted thinking about what would make an ideal boat for a couple sailing the world. But, considering that we had never lived aboard a boat, and we spent 'only' 75 grand in 2004 US dollars, we did quite well in the choice.

The Crealock is narrow, with a stern that pinches off like a second bow, which means that the interior space for people and supplies is less than that of a similar-sized boat of more modern design. The stern and bow each overhang the water, which again reduces the interior volume. But those overhanging ends and that narrow beam also give the Crealock a motion at sea that isn't comfortable, since no small boat is comfortable at sea, but rather much less uncomfortable than it could be. In nearly every aspect of the boat, designer Bill Crealock seemed to hit the same golden center that he did in this tradeoff between interior volume and seakindliness. For almost every characteristic you can measure, the Crealock 37 falls precisely halfway along the continuum between an America's Cup racer and a coal barge. And in all that moderation Crealock worked a tiny bit of alchemy. He produced a boat that in many situations can exceed what you would expect of it. In light wind it sails a bit faster than you'd expect, in steep waves it rides a little more smoothly. This is the sort of *je ne sais quoi* that puts a twinkle in the eyes of people who work in the practical world of boats. And the Crealock is also one of the more beautiful fiberglass boats out there. If your sailboat cannot be a little beautiful, what is the point?

We found our boat after going through a long search, with a fixed number of dollars in hand, that had revealed few good options. The boat we found began her career with a succession of three owners who were content to let her sit in various marinas. Then a couple bought the boat and sailed around the world. To get ready for their trip they put on all the gear that people put on boats when they are going to sail them around the world – things like a powerful windlass for pulling up the anchor, a ham radio for talking to people at great distances and a sea anchor for riding out a storm. They began sailing, and they began replacing gear when the original versions broke. By the time they had returned home, nine years later, the major systems were on their third or fourth incarnation. Every locker that I peered into showed the history of nine years of maintenance in harbors around the world. The interior of the boat appeared calm and pleasing, but lifting up cushions and peering into crannies revealed thickets of electrical wiring, half of it abandoned. When I peeked behind the wiring I found a maze of water hoses that seemed all out of proportion to the number of sinks on the boat (two). Nothing was labeled, I knew where nothing led. But, conveniently, a number of very important parts of the boat had just been replaced. So for our purchase price we got a nearly new engine, rigging, lifelines, winches and sails. *(Those unfamiliar with nautical language are referred to the helpful glossary.)*

The interior of our boat was laid out to be a home any place in the world there was water enough for us to reach. There was one bunk in the stern that we would use to store the spinnaker in its big blue bag, and our three neoprene survival suits, and an ever-increasing grab-bag of miscellaneous gear to support family life afloat. There were two bunks along the sides of the boat, in neither the bow nor the stern, where we would sleep at sea. These bunks were short enough that we could brace our heads and feet against the ends and narrow enough that we wouldn't roll from side to side. There was a double bunk forward for sleeping in port. There was a galley. It had an oven with a three-burner stove that was gimbaled to stay level as waves rocked the boat. There was a stainless steel bar that kept the cook from being thrown into the hot stove when the weather was rough, and where Alisa mounted a strap that went right around her body and held her in place so that both hands could be free to cook. There was a double sink and a fridge that you reached down into. There was a galley counter that could neatly be covered by a handkerchief. Between the two sea bunks there was a table that folded away. There was a bookshelf. There was a chart table where the two radios and the radar and the autopilot and the GPS were mounted. There was a head with a fold-out teak seat and a drain so that we could take a shower sitting down. There were three drawers. There were two lockers for our clothes.

The four owners before us gave the boat four different names. We gave her a fifth name and put it on the stern for all the world to know. My early favorite, *Arab Rose* ('We'll name it after you!'), was vetoed by the eponymous life partner. We agreed on *Pelagic*, an adjective meaning 'of the open ocean'. In marine biology the word takes on a more formal definition, referring specifically to that part of the world's oceans beyond the continental shelves. It was a word we brought with us from our old work studying the life of the oceans and is, I still maintain, one of the more beautiful words in English. It is also a name freighted with our hopes for the kind of sailing we would do. We would not dwell in marinas. We would not hug coast-lines. We would sail grand voyages. We would visit the albatross in his realm, where the ocean carries unguessable depth. We would live at sea for weeks at a time. We would set our lives to the metronome of the waves below us that would rise and fall, rise and fall.

But first we had to leave.

4

FIVE MILES AWAY

I SET OUT FROM the safe harbor of my sleeping bag, across the uncertain waters of the cold cabin sole, to the far shore of the VHF radio for the weather forecast. The news wasn't good. The announcer droned through an endless loop of pessimism, painting a picture of unfortunate winds and inconvenient wave heights that spelled a change of plans for anyone who had hoped to be pleasure boating on the Gulf of Alaska over the next few days. Eager to start our trip and put an end to the leave-taking, we had been willing to depart Kodiak in weather that was already bad and meant to get worse. Now the really bad weather had arrived, and no impatience would get us moving again until it had passed.

With the boat shut tight against rain and cold during the night, the moisture of our three breathing bodies had first condensed on every available surface, then gathered together in rivulets and dripped back onto us in our sleep. Elias had slept in a cocoon of modern fabrics: a polartec sleeper layered over a fiberpile sleeper layered over a polypropylene hoody. His sleeping face had clenched in a tiny frown over the work of keeping the little spark of his body warmth safe against the pressing cold. When he woke his face went red with the passion of his squalling, and he would not be content until he was pressed against Alisa's breast. Things had taken a sudden turn towards the unpredictable in his young life, and he was clearly putting his bet on the constancy of the basics.

I slid open the companionway hatch and looked out at the world beyond the cockpit. Wind-driven wrack of cloud came pouring over the trees around the anchorage. Fog blocked any view of the world outside the entrance to our bay. The tide was low, the beach a bowl of black pebbles and brown kelp. *Pelagic* shied against the anchor chain with every windgust that found its way into the anchorage.

We always knew that Long Island would be the first stop on our trip across the Pacific. Only five nautical miles from the dock in Kodiak, Long Island offers a perfect natural harbor that can be easily reached at the end of a day mostly given over to last-minute preparations in town. We knew, given how hard it would be to sever our ties with Kodiak before the trip to Australia, that we would find ourselves limping out of town late in the day weeks after we had meant to leave, with just enough energy left to get ourselves to Long Island and regroup. Which, of course, is exactly what happened.

Alone and weather-bound, we had no distraction from the enormity of what we had just done, and from what we were about to attempt. The boat, still disorganized, crammed with baby gear and running with condensation, was not conducive to more hopeful thoughts of tropical anchorages ahead. So, in the interest of crew morale, I declared a day ashore.

To get ashore we would have to launch the dinghy, which meant we would get our first indication of whether one of my great ideas for the trip would or would not actually work. Almost everyone out cruising the world in a sailboat uses an inflatable dinghy to get between the anchored mother ship and shore. Not us. I spent five summers studying seabird biology on the Alaska mainland, a job that entailed daily use of outboard-powered inflatable skiffs. I ended every day with my ass numbed by the whack of pontoon against flesh, my spine out of column from the jostle of the rubber boat slamming over waves. So, we decided to get a hard fiberglass dinghy for *Pelagic*. It would be a salty little dinghy that could be sailed across the calm waters of some palm-fringed lagoon, that could be rowed in whatever weather we found, and would get us from anchorage to beach without the nerve-shattering racket of an outboard motor.

The catch was that a hard dinghy has to be a reasonable length to row well – say, ten feet. There was nowhere where we could store such a big boat on the decks of *Pelagic*. The solution, suggested by sailing writers – that industrious group of people dedicated to solving other people's problems – was a nesting dinghy. A nesting dinghy comes apart into two halves, bow and stern, which can be stacked one on top of the other, allowing a long rowboat to be stored in a short space. A nesting dinghy is both a neat idea and an indication that you've become enough of a boat nerd to know what a nesting dinghy is.

When we left Kodiak the sails for the dinghy were tucked away in hard-to-reach locker corners. The mast and boom were lashed awkwardly to the grab rails on deck. The dinghy itself was nested just aft of *Pelagic's* mast. And now, in order to go ashore for the first time on the trip, we would have to un-nest the dinghy and launch it.

In the cabin, Alisa carefully explained to Elias that we were leaving him in his playpen for just a few minutes while we put the dinghy together. He stared up at her trustingly as she spoke, giving every indication of understanding what she said. And then, as soon as we climbed the steps into the cockpit and left his sight, he began screaming. It was a viscerally unpleasant sound, this scream of his, and something I had completely failed to get used to over the ten months of his life, despite frequent experience. It was a scream perfected over evolutionary time to be so impossible for parents to listen to that they would drop anything to get back to the child's side and make the scream stop. Alisa and I gritted our teeth and leaned away from the companionway steps, willfully fighting the forcefield of our baby's scream, a sound that took physical effort to ignore. 'Let's just get this done', I said.

As we stood on the cabin top, about to launch the dinghy from the decks of *Pelagic* for the first time, a serious flaw in the nesting dinghy concept became apparent. Putting the dinghy together meant dealing with a ten-foot boat on the decks of *Pelagic*, where the longest available space was a little more than six feet long. This was a problem. Not an insurmountable problem for two people working in tandem. But a problem that was compounded by Elias' impossible-to-ignore screams.

'Oh God', I said after a few minutes of fumbling effort. 'It sounds like someone is cutting off his toes.'

Alisa didn't say anything. She just concentrated on the skiff as we tried different ways to align the two halves.

'Cutting them off slowly', I said.

'With a butter knife', I added.

Elias kept screaming. Alisa kept working.

Elias let loose an extra-loud scream, clearly indicating that his little body was ripping apart with anger and frustration.

'They're starting on his fingers', I said.

Alisa dropped her half of the dinghy and stood up straight to look me in the eye. She banged her shoulder, hard, on the boom on the way up. Her face showed a quick window on the pain she felt until she hid the pain and concentrated on giving me a stern look. In my mind's eye I remember her standing with clenched fists on hips. But I'm sure she wasn't.

'I don't think that kind of talk helps', she said.

After a few more moments of whispering instructions to each other and jockeying the awkward shape around, we finally lifted the assembled dinghy clear of the decks, checked to make sure that it was tied to the mother ship, and half-lowered, half-threw the heavy dinghy into the cold North Pacific water.

'Ouch', I said. 'There goes my back.'

Alisa went below and picked up Elias, stopping his crying as quickly as if it were controlled by a switch. The dinghy bobbed placidly by the side of *Pelagic*, ready to take us ashore. Everything was under control. Putting the dinghy in the water had been one more pain in the ass associated with learning the tricks of our new life, but now, I thought to myself, it was over. I didn't appreciate at that point what an enduring pain in the ass the dinghy would be, nor how an enduring pain in the ass could act as an enabler for bad feelings between two otherwise-happily married people who were perpetually confined with a baby aboard a 37-foot sailboat.

We put Elias in his life jacket for the first time on the trip and set out for the beach. We were dressed in typical clothes for early summer on the Pacific Ocean at 58 degrees north latitude: polypropylene hats, polypropylene pants, wool sweaters, wool socks, long neoprene boots. Once ashore we relaxed into the familiar feeling of just being outdoor-loving Alaskans having fun in Kodiak's back yard. With Eli in the backpack carrier we hiked the roads left over from the army base that had sprung up on the island during World War II. We walked through the old bunkers and gun emplacements on the clifftops, 65-year-old preparations against a Japanese invasion that lost its momentum in the Aleutians, a thousand nautical miles to the west. We tried to walk all the way out to the northeastern tip of the island, a narrow isthmus of cliffs, and were turned back by the untimely appearance of a herd of feral cows, attended by an aggressive-looking bull. The lupine were blooming in the meadows, making great blobs of purple against the greenest green of the oceanside grass. The fireweed, which would eventually count down the end of the too-brief summer as its flowers bloomed one by one, was still a string of pink buds on a green stalk. Guillemots trilled to each other on the water, and male song sparrows staked out territories with torrents of song from perches high in the grass. We ate strips of smoked salmon for lunch, and forgot for a moment about any problems of boat and travel. When we came back to the beach and saw *Pelagic* alone in the little bay, looking majestic and purposeful, I felt sudden elation at the giant chance we were taking.

The next morning we were still weatherbound, and the cabin heater refused to light. I fiddled with it all through breakfast, but succeeded only in souring my own mood. So, no heat for us. Alisa, forgetting a lesson I had learned when we first bought *Pelagic*, put too much toilet paper in the head and clogged it. This necessitated taking apart the head pump and cleaning it out by hand, easily the most foul job on the boat. The cabin interior was still cluttered with two diaper-changing pads (one for on the boat and a smaller one for excursions ashore), with the crib and the playpen, with the backpack carrier and bundles of diapers and various brightly colored toys designed to stimulate the baby intellect – the collection of standard-issue middle-class American baby gear that had followed us aboard in spite of our resolve to leave behind the land dwellers' stuff and excess. There was no space left over for us to move around. The hatches and portlights were still all closed against an insistent drizzle. The interior was damp and stifling. And then Alisa started carrying what she had dug out of the head pump through the cabin to dump overboard from the cockpit. Because she could only fit a small container under the pump, it took a lot of trips through the cabin to get it all overboard. Elias meanwhile was crying and, in spite of my best attempts, would only be consoled by his mom, who wasn't going to be doing any baby consoling until she was done cleaning the head.

The day went on from there. What we needed, more than anything, was to move. We needed to weigh anchor and raise the mainsail. We needed to trim the sails and pencil our course on the chart and find beautiful new Alaskan anchorages where our solitude would be complete. But the weather was bad and we weren't going anywhere. It was cold, Elias was crying most of the time, we were lonely for the town that we had just left behind, but that town was also just around the corner. Things got worse later that evening when the fog lifted, and we could see the town itself.

'Kim's birthday party is tonight', said Alisa. 'All our friends will be there.'

'It's only five miles away', I said. 'We could be there in an hour.'

'Do you want to go?', she asked.

'God, no.'

'Me either.'

Elias was asleep in his crib in the forward bunk. Alisa and I sat on the port settee, sharing the one bit of the main cabin not taken up by the playpen. We drank wine and talked softly, dodging the occasional drips of condensation from the portlights above us.

'We should just concentrate on getting to San Diego', I said. 'Australia is too much to think about.'

'I know', said Alisa. 'But right now even San Diego seems pretty improbable.'

'It does', I said. 'Improbable.'

5

SMART IS RETROSPECTIVE

I F I HAD known then something of what I think I know now, I would have taken a piece of paper out of the chart table and written a few things down:

Dreaming is easy, acting is hard.

Acting on the dream changes the dream.

Rewards come later, uncertainty comes first.

And I would have taped that piece of paper up over the chart table, where we could see it all day long as we lived the routine of our new life in the tiny storeroom–sitting room–cooking room–eating room–sleeping room–baby room–navigation room–work room that was the interior of our boat.

But of course smart is retrospective, life is reactive, even the heavily planned life of two people chasing a dream, and rarely do the twain meet.

6

THE TRUE NATURE OF RISK

RATHER THAN JUMPING straight into the 2200 nautical mile passage from Kodiak to Hawai'i and thence to the South Pacific, we had decided to feel our way into family life afloat by first sailing the length of the west coast of North America, all the way to the southern tip of Baja California. The months of coastal sailing that this would require would, we reasoned, arm us with the hard-earned lessons of our own experience before we launched into the long trade-wind passages that would eventually take us to Australia.

Taking the west coast route meant that we would begin our trip with more than 2000 miles of sailing along the Alaskan coast, almost all of it in day trips that allowed us to sleep soundly at anchor each night. From our time on research boats we already knew a lot of that coast – a grand geographic arc from Kodiak Island, up to the Kenai Peninsula and Prince William Sound on the Alaska mainland, then across the unforgiving coast around Icy Bay and the St Elias mountain range, and over to the glacier-carved labyrinth of the Southeast panhandle. Along most of that coastline you expect to have every anchorage to yourself, you take it for granted that you will see more whales than people, and every day is enlivened by the chance of a once-in-a-lifetime wildlife sighting, like seeing a wolverine on the beach. It's a place where the glaciers of the last ice age are still receding, a place where salmon come teeming to wild, undammed streams to spawn, a place where, if you are a lover of wilderness, it's easy to forget the troubles of the world.

The Gulf of Alaska can also be a very unforgiving place. It is a place where accidents happen, a place where tidal currents are swift, the water cold and the weather poor, a place where help may not be at hand in your moment of need. In a sense, we would be doing our trip in reverse order. Before venturing somewhere like the Gulf of Alaska, most sailors first get years of experience in the gentle arena of temperate waters, where storms are rare and the friendly services of a marina are always around the corner. Alisa and I, on the other hand, would serve our apprenticeship in the north, and progress to more forgiving waters only as our skills improved. Along the way we could see if sailing with a baby was anything that a rational person might recognize as a good thing to do.

After two days the weather relented and we were able to leave Long Island. The interior of the boat was still disorganized, so we shoved loose items into corners where they wouldn't come adrift while we were underway.

'Sail now, figure out the details later', I said to Alisa.

Soon *Pelagic* was motoring out of the harbor entrance. We cleared the northern end of Long Island and encountered a developed swell running in from the open waters of the Gulf of Alaska, the legacy of the days of wind that had kept us at anchor. Our course had us travelling with the waves hitting us directly from the side – in the parlance of Kodiak commercial fishermen, we were 'in the ditch'. *Pelagic* swam along the trough, with a wave on either side of us, before she was lifted up to the crest of the next wave to sweep in from the Gulf, where she balanced for a moment before falling down that wave to the next trough, over and over and over again, in the direction of travel relative to the swell that gave us the maximum side-to-side roll. More than any other factor, the motion of the sea is what makes living on a boat so different from living ashore.

Once the boat was all set up, with the sails properly trimmed and the windvane keeping us on course, Alisa and I both took a moment to look at Elias, who stood happily in his playpen lashed in the middle of the cabin. It was our first real day of travelling. And it looked like we were going to get an early answer to one of our most pressing questions.

Before we left, there had been naysayers. One of the real surprises from acting on our dream was the number of people who felt obligated to tell us that chucking it all to go sailing wasn't a smart thing for us to do. Doubtless the fact that we would leave with a child less than a year old increased the naysayer turnout, but there is also just a certain slice of humanity that cannot help but try to tug down anyone who is about to step away from the general crowd. Our preparations had taken a long time, so the naysayers had ample opportunity to make their reservations known to us.

The most difficult naysayers to handle were those who framed their objections in the guise of an innocent-seeming query. At their most naked, these were just annoying – 'Do you really think your boat is strong enough to sail across the Pacific?', an acquaintance asked me. But at their most subtle, the naysayer's questions are equally motivated by honest concern and veiled criticism. Those were the questions that had the power to get under our skin, to make us doubt ourselves, to make staying at home look like the essence of wisdom.

The best example of this sort of question-cum-criticism was, 'Do you know if Elias gets seasick?'

We were asked that question, by conservative estimate, about once every fifteen minutes after we announced our plans to friends. The short answer was that we didn't know – Elias was born in August of the year before we left, which didn't give us a lot of time for shakedown sails before the bad weather began in September. The longer answer was that we figured there were a lot of very important questions about the trip, including the question of whether Elias would get seasick, that we wouldn't be able to answer before we left. And we felt strongly that taking on an adventure meant living with that kind of uncertainty. But still, we wondered. Nothing would frustrate our plans like the experience of watching Elias vomit every time we hoisted sail. Maybe, we realized, those people asking if Elias got seasick were asking an honest question, and it was only our unease that suggested an impure motive.

So, as *Pelagic* moved out into the gray-green Gulf of Alaska and began to roll with the swell, we both found ourselves looking at Elias to see how he would react. He smiled a drooling, three-toothed grin back at us, gripping the top bar of his playpen to stay upright through the unaccustomed motion of the boat.

So far, so good. The real test, though, came at lunchtime. Being able to eat is the true sign of not being seasick. So, when we lashed little Elias into his eating chair, with *Pelagic* still bobbing up and down on the six-foot swell, and Alisa mixed up a batch of fresh rice cereal, the parental tension on the boat rose once again.

I started spooning the cereal into Eli's waiting mouth, and he responded just as always, with vigorous demonstrations of joy. The trouble, it turned out, was on my end. Fixing your eyes on an object close at hand tends to make motion sickness worse. That's why so many people can't read in a moving car. And that's why being on deck, looking at the distant horizon, tends to make seasickness disappear.

I was faced with a problem in three-dimensional dynamic

geometry as I concentrated on steering each spoonful of rice cereal to Elias' mouth, which was pitching up and down and back and forth with the boat. Staring at his open mouth and trying to hit it with the spoon produced the same effect as reading. I started feeling sick. I willed Elias to be full so that I could escape to the cockpit. He kept eating. Finally I had to call for Alisa to give me a spell. She only lasted for five minutes herself, and we spent the rest of his meal like that, feeding him in five-minute stints before retreating to the fresh air and distant sight lines of the cockpit.

Elias, meanwhile, had a triple helping.

That evening, at our second anchorage of the trip, the true nature of risk that Elias faced while living aboard first became apparent.

For weeks I had been wondering why the pull rings in the cabin floorboards had been so clean. These bronze pull rings lie flush against the cabin sole, above a little recess for your finger to reach into and grasp the ring, and they are normally the spots where everything nasty on the boat accumulates. Lint, stray hair, dinner crumbs, soot from the engine – all naturally collect in those recesses. In the midst of the madness after we moved on board *Pelagic*, I looked down one day and noticed that these recesses (there are four of them in the saloon) were all sparklingly clean. Distracted by a hundred critical tasks that I had no chance of ever finishing before we left, I didn't think anything of it, except to wonder if the constant use the boat was receiving now that we were living aboard somehow kept dirt from accumulating in those spots.

But then, in that second anchorage of the trip, as Alisa and I were savoring a quiet moment after dinner and Elias was enjoying the freedom of the cabin with his playpen put away, we were shocked to watch him, all snuggled up in his sleeper and ready for bed, crawl over to one of the rings, and, with a look of connoisseur's delight that could scarcely be credited in someone less than a year old, lower his head to the sole and lick clean the recess behind the pull ring.

The hazards of early childhood at sea were not as we had expected.

7

THE STRETCH OF TIME

AFTER WE MADE the eighty-mile hop to the Alaska mainland, we spent a week winding through the deep glacial fjords of the Kenai Peninsula coast. We motored past granite islands where thousands of seabirds nested in chattering colonies, we marveled at sheer mountain walls and glaciers that tumbled direct into the sea. We counted the white dots of distant mountain goats feeding on rocky points jutting over the tossing Pacific waves. The whole time we were blessed with a high northern sky that stayed robin's egg–blue and stormfree, and days, so close to the summer solstice, that knew little of the night that divided them. We were welcomed by full daylight when we awoke at six am, and there was always another hour of sunlight at the end of the day if we needed more time to make our anchorage.

Fifty miles to the north of us were highways and towns and the epicenter of summer tourism in Alaska, with endless streams of people from all over the world arriving to stare at country that was remarkable wilderness when their grandparents were young. We, on the other hand, were sailing a coast that was lonelier now than it had been twenty years before, as a shift throughout the Gulf of Alaska meant that the fishing boats that formerly plied this coast in search of shrimp and crab were now elsewhere, in grounds more productive of the salmon and groundfish that dominate modern fisheries. We sailed for days and saw only one or two fishing boats. Along the whole length of rockbound coast between Kodiak and Seward, our first port of call on the trip, we met not another sailboat.

When Outsiders think of Alaska they think of wilderness, and the vast roadless spaces that dominate the state. When Alaskans think of Alaska, we think of the people. Alaska is a place that collects interesting people, and a surprisingly intimate social landscape inhabits the huge spaces of the state. With a population of only about 700,000, it's amazing how often you run into people you know as you travel around. So it was no surprise that the only time we shared an anchorage on the trip to Seward, we shared it with good friends.

We knew that the research vessel *Alaskan Gyre* would be somewhere along the Kenai coast, but in the rush out of Kodiak I had lost their itinerary. When we motored into Moonlight Cove, our fourth anchorage of the trip, and saw another vessel already at anchor appearing out of the fog, Alisa immediately said, 'It's got to be them!' Sure enough, it was the *Gyre*, a converted salmon seiner with the clean, unworried look of a boat that enjoyed an annual government maintenance budget, a look that contrasted with the peeling linoleum interiors and scarred fiberglass hulls of the Kodiak seiners that worked for a living in an era of deflated salmon prices. We were greeted by waving friends on the deck of the *Gyre*. In twenty minutes we were tied securely alongside, where we shared a great night catching up with those friends, biologists from the US Geological Survey who were working their way along the entire Kenai Fjords coast, counting Kittlitz's murrelets, the little seabirds that are the most mysterious bird species in all of North America.

These birds feed around glaciers and nest in isolated spots on barren mountainsides, and almost nothing else is known about them except that their numbers in Alaska are plummeting.

Elias was at the peak of cherubic cuteness in these first weeks of the trip, a little round-faced lump of a boy who smiled easily and whose mohawk of fine blond hair sent strangers into cooing paroxysms of baby appreciation. We had followed the fad of teaching our little one some key words in sign language, giving him the ability to communicate with us before he could speak, and this had backfired to some degree, with Elias mastering the sign for 'milk', the motion of pulling at a cow's udder. He flashed the sign at Alisa all day long, with no consideration given to the patience of his audience.

The contrast between his tender body and the rough-and-tumble world of sailing the Gulf of Alaska filled my head with dark thoughts of what could go wrong. After we left the *Gyre* I found myself missing the company of friends, who had distracted me from the endless contemplation of my doubts. Alisa and I both struggled to shake off the feeling that first visited us during our forced stay at Long Island, the feeling that the desperate efforts we had put into making the switch from a land life to a life at sea had bought us nothing but uncertainty and a kernel of fear in our stomachs. Overwhelmed by the number of tasks that demanded completion every day, we fell into a division of labor. Alisa spent her days feeding Elias, and changing his diapers, and holding him on her lap when the motion got rough, while my days were spent reacting to windshifts, swinging the whisker pole across the foredeck, tweaking the windvane to keep us on course, and plotting the distance to our next anchorage. We each helped out when the other became overwhelmed – I changed diapers, Alisa navigated on the chart. Still, we found ourselves exhausted by the double duty of learning to cruise while we learned to be parents. That it was hard to do both of these things at once didn't surprise us. Thinking about how hard it would be almost made us call off the trip before we began. What did surprise me was the concrete, unyielding way some hours of those early days were hard. One of the shocking realizations that comes from parenting an infant is how honestly angry you can get at a completely helpless little one who won't stop screaming that particularly awful scream just when you are too tired to care much why they might be unhappy. That's normal parenthood, something that most people weather with nothing more than a self-deprecating tale about how easily sleep deprivation can alter what you thought were the bedrock qualities of your personality. In that first week afloat, I was amazed at how foul a mood I could reach from being tired by the physical and mental requirements of navigating that unforgiving coast, while at the same time I was cooped up on our little sailboat with a ten-month-old. Occasionally the dam burst, and I found the way to my inner Neanderthal. Then I would have to endure the moment of self-realization that followed as I sat alone in the cockpit, calming down after screaming at my little son.

The week from Kodiak to Seward also gave us experiences that were like bright scraps of tile set into a blank wall, the first bits of color that we hoped would spread over time into the rich mosaic of a new life sailing. The three of us sat in our cockpit in a lonely anchorage and listened to a loon's calls echoing off granite sea cliffs. We threaded a narrow passage between two islands and found puffins cavorting in the spray of a humpback's blow on the other side. We began to feel the stretch of time that was the part of the sailing life that I most looked forward to. The same week spent in the office would have slid complacently into the irrevocable past, travelling swiftly down the ruts of our routine. But our first week spent travelling the Alaska coast as a family drilled down to an endless series of little moments. Time became granular with the texture and richness of everything that happened – the flash of low sunlight from behind a mountain as Alisa handed me a bowl of peanuts from the companionway and I steered into a new anchorage, holding the Coast Pilot in one hand and the chart spread out in the cockpit before me. Or the hum of wind in the rigging, rising and falling in a cycle of changing pitch when I woke in the middle of the night to check on Elias in his crib. Or the shy, moist smile that Elias gave us when he spilled a spoonful of rice cereal on his head and saw how that made us laugh in spite of ourselves. It became a week that Alisa and I, together, could recall with satisfaction for the rest of our lives.

In that week we also came to grips with the immediate challenges of living with Elias on the boat. Alisa changed a score of diapers while *Pelagic* was underway and nothing – neither baby nor dirty diaper nor diaper rash cream nor baby wipes – could be trusted to stay in one place. We figured out the basics of feeding Elias on board and getting him to sleep, and we came up with a long list of improvements for the way we had set things up for Elias before we left, when the challenges of taking care of him on the boat had all been hypothetical. And I had gotten through the rigors of the first week of sailing *Pelagic* mostly alone while Alisa kept our son below, out of the Alaskan weather. So when we came to Seward, after a week of travelling past pristine spruce forests and beaches that collected the debris lost from fishing boats, we were immensely relieved to be done with the preparations and to be actually off on the trip, and we were also mildly pleased with how things had been going, almost proud that we had gotten through that first week without incident.

But travel is nothing if not a roller coaster of emotions, especially travel with your family in the confines of a small boat. Just as the toxic wastes of floorboard pull rings had never occurred to us as a baby hazard until we moved on board, there was a hazard awaiting us in Seward that could only become apparent after we began travelling on *Pelagic*. After our week of working together to overcome fears and misgivings, after a week when we never once set foot on shore because getting the nesting dinghy together was too much of a chore, and the waters between us and land looked a bit much for a baby in a ten-foot boat, after a week of quiet games of cribbage in the cockpit when Elias had gone to bed, after a week of taking our marriage to sea on a floating cushion of mutual trust, after that week we got to Seward and Alisa and I began to fight.

We fought the way that married people fight, with no rational motivations, but with a visceral desire to hurt back when being hurt by someone symbiotically close to us. I fought because the galley lockers were incredibly cluttered when I tried to find a can opener. I fought because the boat was too crowded, with Elias' crib and playpen and backpack carrier and Baby Björn carrier and diaper bag and Johnny Jump-Up all competing with me for space. I fought, in other words, for no reason at all, just that we had arrived in a new town and the magic quiet moments of that first week of self-reliance on *Pelagic* were somehow forgotten, and we were suddenly left with nothing but the physical discomfort of living on a crowded boat and the insecurity that came from having left behind home and jobs and friends and nearly everything else in our lives but Elias and each other. We were in a town we didn't know and had a list of things to do before we could leave and there wasn't a moment of peace to be had on our boat that was completely dominated by Elias' presence. Alisa and I weren't used to getting sour with each other; the glare she had given me when I pulled away from the dock in Kodiak unannounced really was an almost novel event in our marriage. So, after a couple days in Seward, as we started to cool off, we looked at each other in surprise, wondering what might have happened.

We slowly regained our equilibrium by concentrating on making practical improvements on board. We adjusted our system for housing Elias, identifying bits of baby gear that we could get off the boat so that there might be a little room for people. His crib made the one-way trip to the harbor dumpster and was replaced by a section of netting that I strung up to block off a baby-sized section of the forward bunk, at the cost of three hours I spent on my side in the bunk, working with my hands above my head to manipulate cordless drill and screwdriver and tape measure and scissors and netting and twine. The old saying that every boat job takes three times as long as expected was beginning to look conservative.

Suddenly cut off from any income at all, Alisa and I set ourselves a budget of ten dollars each for buying treats out on the town. One evening we ventured forth for ice cream cones and a walk in the endless midsummer sunshine of Alaska. Seward has become a town completely given over to tourism, a place that spends each summer catering to cruise ship passengers and sport fishermen looking to catch a halibut. The waterfront path that we followed took us by a campground filled with visiting RVs. Next to each parked vehicle sat a little group of people barbecuing dinner or drinking beer or watching TV as the end-of-the-day light played on the mountains on the other side of the bay. Looking at all these happy, relaxed people, I had an insight.

'My God', I said to Alisa. 'You know that dream that everyone thinks they'll achieve by sailing away on a boat? That dream of a carefree life?'

'Sounds familiar', she said.

'It's people on RVs who actually achieve it! Look at all these people – not a worry, everything uncomplicated. Meanwhile the sailors are all wondering why their autopilot isn't working.'

'You're right', said Alisa.

'God, they look bored', I said.

8

WHERE NO PERSON
HAD SET FOOT

WE COMPLETED OUR list of jobs and set out from Seward to the east, towards Prince William Sound, continuing along the arc of the Gulf of Alaska and leaving behind known cruising grounds for *Pelagic*. After a fits-and-starts beginning with fluky winds, the southwesterly wind promised by the forecast filled in and we had a brilliant reach with the spinnaker. Overhead we could clearly see the clouds curving out from a low pressure system centered south of Kodiak, two hundred miles behind us. The coast we travelled was so austere – cliffs to the water, glaciers unworldly clean snaking back into the mountains. Clouds hung low over everything – a nation of clouds building as the low crept closer from the south, their smooth shapes above contrasting with the jagged mountains beneath. Everything became gray, all color was inaccessible to my eye, even the summer green of the mountainsides became muted. It was a relatively busy coast, with a few other vessels making the daytrip between the Sound and Seward, but the land itself was remote, too rugged in most places to access from a boat, too rugged often to even walk. Untouched, untouchable. As my eye scanned the wall of summits following the coast, I looked at a hundred places where no person had ever set foot. Alaska.

The end of the day found us in a bay just inside Prince William Sound, a place where our solitude and our protection from the elements were both perfect. After the anchor had splashed and chain had rattled and the engine was shut down, we found ourselves in the midst of that rarest of phenomena in the twenty-first century, a perfectly natural sounds cape. The salmon jumping in the bay were startlingly loud, their slap against the water reverberating on the upland crags above us. Songbirds ashore competed against each other with their trills. Nowhere was there the sound of an engine, no matter how distant. Alisa and I found ourselves whispering as we took care of little jobs on deck. The place was completely wild. That we were the only boat in the anchorage didn't surprise us. That this obscure spot we had never heard of was possessed of a grandeur that would have made it legendary in a lesser place, like Washington State, we took as a given. Solitude and stunning beauty were things that we took for granted as Alaskans. We would have the chance to miss these things later, when we visited some of the more famous destinations of the Pacific.

After dinner Elias slept while we played cards in the cockpit. Coming below afterwards I smelled the typical boat smells – salt, must, oil. Then, going forward to check on Eli asleep in his little net pen, I came upon the sudden surprising smell of baby. His lips had parted in his sleep, showing me his upper left tooth coming in.

In the morning we motored through long fjords that gave us passage into Prince William Sound proper. Dall's porpoise joined us to bowride – catching a free lift in the pressure wave in front of *Pelagic*, playing back and forth in front of our bow just for the joy of it, cleaving the water, sucking perfectly timed breaths when they erupted from the water's surface. Dall's are black and white porpoises that have the couch-potato physiques of the cetacean world – their bodies are too thick to be called sleek – but they are reputedly among the fastest of all cetaceans, the tiniest flick of their flukes accelerating them to speeds that send sheets of water spraying up into the air. I left the wheel to look after itself and walked up on the bow to watch them darting back and forth across our track, and I decided then and there that any boat too fast for Dall's porpoises to bowride would be too fast a boat for us.

The weather changed and the day ended with bullets of rain sizzling into the sea around us. *Pelagic* sailed at a crazy angle of heel, the mast cantilevered out over the water, our three sails like blades thrown into the wind. I peered through the gathering mist at the mountainous island off our bow, trying to find the entrance to the bay where we planned to spend the night. But the rain was blowing hard enough that it hurt my eyes, and I had to look away. I glanced down the companionway at Elias, checking on how he was handling the angle of heel and sudden lurching of the boat against the choppy waves that had sprung up. I was wearing rain gear and neoprene boots and a winter hat, but he was down below in the snug cabin, wearing his baby sleeper outfit with the built-in slippers and the puppy face on his chest. He stood in his playpen, smiling at the motion, holding on with one hand and pointing up at me with the other.

If I wasn't paying attention at the wheel, and sometimes even when I was, we plowed the bow into a wave and took water on deck, water crystal clear and six inches deep, the motion of the boat sending geysers into the air where the lifeline stanchions blocked the water's passage. The boat was slow and a little pool of water collected on the cabin sole from a deck leak we didn't know about. The coast we closed on was lonely, racked by ragged clouds that tore themselves to pieces on the spruce forests above the water.

We pulled into a short, twisting fjord that gave us protection from the growing waves but turned out to be a blowhole – winds accelerated down the mountain slopes above the harbor and gusted into the thirty-knot range. For two and a half days we stayed put while the wind knocked us from side to side, heeling *Pelagic* over and sending us dancing around the anchor. I looked at the radar again and again to measure our distance from shore but our anchor held and it never did change. We watched through rain-smeared portlights as dizzy images of sodden green mountains spun past. Condensation dripped from bronze. Wind boomed in the rigging. After two days the trapped moisture had turned the back of every cushion wet and mould was sprouting in the lockers. We did everything in a watery half-light. Gusts of wind backdrafted the cabin heater and filled the saloon with diesel smoke. We went about the business of our days, the work of caring for Eli giving time its only structure, our little family surrounded by storm-bound seabirds and glacier-carved valleys that were hidden in the mist.

When the trip's second spell of bad weather had eased, *Pelagic* ventured out of the fjord and motored across the glassy inland sea of Prince William Sound. The diesel chugging in the stillness, we steamed under mountains perpetually covered in snow and past beaches still bearing the secret of buried oil from the *Exxon Valdez*. Swinging north to enter the channel into Cordova that evening, we crossed over 60 degrees, 38 minutes north latitude, our furthest-north point on the trip. On the general principal that each minute of latitude covers one nautical mile of distance, that put us 3562 miles from the equator and 1838 miles from the north pole. Everything on our trip from that point on would be to the south.

We arrived in the little town of Cordova and looked up Alisa's friend Erik, who had moved there with his family several years before. All grizzled beard and tangled blonde hair and shambling diffidence, he began his life in Cordova by teaching violin to support himself. In a town of 2500 people.

'Then I bought a gillnet permit', he said. 'And people suddenly seemed to know what to make of me.'

The commercial salmon fishery was open, but a mechanical problem with his boat was the chance event that had Erik in town for the day, present to receive our phone call. I helped him pull his boat out of the water to look for the problem. A stick was lodged inside the jet drive. Erik bent down and pulled it out. His boat was fixed. He stood up and gave me a shy smile that folded in on itself, laughing at a joke inside a joke.

'Ahh', he said. 'If I'd gone out fishing I would have just made money.'

Cordova is tucked into the eastern corner of Prince William Sound, a short boat ride from the mouth of the Copper River, a mighty sluice of water that is thick with the flour of rocks that have been ground to nothing under glaciers. The Copper is blessed with the first run of salmon to arrive in Alaska each year, a fact that is the basis of a very successful marketing campaign. Every year the first catch of Copper River red salmon is flown to Seattle among great fanfare. The combination of a healthy run and high prices gives the town the bustle and energy and working-for-a-living vibe that every coastal Alaskan town should have in summer, and which contrasts with poor lifeless Seward, tarted up for the flesh trade of processing hundreds of thousands of tourists every year. The boats that fish the Copper are bow pickers that deploy and retrieve their gill nets over the bow. They are worked by one-man crews in the shallow flats and sandbars of the Copper River Delta, directly exposed to the Gulf of Alaska. The few boats that were still in town during the opener throbbed through the harbor like stock cars, all engine and net, each with a clean-cut man standing at the steering wheel in the bow.

Mist hung in patches on the mountainsides. Fog spent the day gathering around the town. With evening, the hopeful sightlines of the summer opened to the north, showing us a patch of sunshine on a rocky island, and promising calm weather and long days that would continue for months to come. A monument in front of the grocery store, above the harbor, listed the names of fishermen who had come to grief on the shallow bars and sudden swell of the Copper River Delta. Erik came aboard to help us get *Pelagic* along the fuel dock, a treacherous spot where a relatively underpowered sailboat could find itself swept under the high dock by the river of incoming tide. He warned me to steer around the plume of ground-up fish guts coming from the cannery, for fear of blocking the cooling water intake for our engine. Alisa and I were only half-occupied by our visit to Cordova, distracted by what would follow.

9

THE SLATE-GRAY SEAS

NON-SAILORS OFTEN ASKED us if we couldn't just anchor up for the night when we were at sea, but that's never an option – the open ocean is usually far too deep for any small boat to anchor, and in the shallow areas it's too rough. While we sailed multi-day passages Alisa and I would have to take turns standing watch through the night, keeping a lookout for other vessels and making adjustments to sails and windvane to keep *Pelagic* on course. And because we found watching a child less than a year old on a sailboat to be a don't-turn-away-for-a-moment sort of job, there would be no chance for us to nap when Elias was awake – one of us had to watch the boat, and one of us watch him. That meant the only time for us to get uninterrupted rest would be the ten hours or so he was asleep each night, which we would have to share between us. Sailing the boat and raising a baby would no longer be enough; now we would have to do it on five hours or less of sleep every day.

After we left Hinchinbrook Entrance we motored southeast over the shallow continental shelf, past Seal Rocks and Wessels Reef, crossing water less than a fifty fathoms deep that makes the area so treacherous in a blow. Non-sailors hearing of our plans often asked about the size of the seas that we would meet in the open ocean, but in fact waves get higher and steeper as they enter shallow water, which is one of the reasons that sailors prefer to be far from land if the weather is bad. Waves also begin to break when they encounter an opposing current, which, with all the water that is drained out of Hinchinbrook Entrance with every falling tide, is another reason this area can be so dangerous. The Coast Pilot, our constant reference and guide to Alaskan waters, soberly warned us that 'With a strong S gale and ebb tide ... tremendous seas, steep and breaking, are encountered just outside the entrance ... During heavy weather, tide rips and confused seas are in the vicinity of Wessels Reef. Many halibut schooners have foundered ...'

Happily none of that was going on. Just outside the entrance we motored by an adult ancient murrelet and two chicks, paddling along the flat sea. Ancient murrelets are arguably the most marine of all birds – while the majority of birds raise their chicks in the nest until they have feathers and can fly, ancient murrelet chicks hatch out of the egg and go to sea almost immediately, as tiny balls of down only a day or two old, where they're fed by their parents until they're big enough to be independent. I had never seen ancient murrelet chicks before, and it felt, in a very small way, like one of the natural wonders of the world was slipping by us as we motored past the three little shapes.

All through the afternoon and into the long evening the St Elias Mountains ghosted by in the distance on our port side, slowly turning salmon-pink in the alpenglow. We took bearings with our hand compass and consulted the chart to pick out Mt St Elias, the highest coastal mountain in the world, and the landfall that Vitus Bering made in 1741 to start the era of Russian America.

The wind came up a bit from the west that afternoon, but nothing like the fifteen knots forecast. Concerned about momentum, and not wanting to slat along at two knots, we kept motoring. We put Elias to bed and Alisa and I took turns standing watch through the night, looking out at the mysterious sea as the sun sank behind the mountains to the north of us. It never grew completely dark through the whole crossing, since we were still close to 60° north and summer solstice wasn't far behind. *Pelagic* came equipped with a hydraulic autopilot when we bought her, but it had stopped working when we first sailed the boat up to Kodiak three years before. 'Fix autopilot' had been an entry on many a list of boat jobs since then, and I had put hours of fruitless effort into trying to get it working. Thinking about the fact that we were leaving home with a broken autopilot had given me a sweaty-palmed, what-are-we-thinking moment a few weeks before our departure. But Alisa and I reasoned that we had a windvane that would steer us while we were sailing, we didn't want to pay for a new autopilot, and we would never leave home if we insisted that everything on the boat be working perfectly at the outset. So we left with the autopilot still broken. And on the first night of this crossing, we paid the price. While we were motoring, all the freedom the person on watch could get was a minute or two away from the wheel for a quick trip below, and when we ran back up the companionway we were likely to find the boat well off course, merrily running down the meridian for Hawai'i. So for hours we were tied to the wheel, staring at the faint glow of the compass dial that told us where to point the bow as we listened to the slap of the waves on the hull. On that first night we fell into the watch-keeping schedule that we would follow for the rest of the trip. After dinner Alisa nursed Elias to sleep behind the lee cloth, the barrier that turned the settee into a snug bunk that would hold them tight if the boat rolled. I was left alone with my thoughts and the rumble of the diesel, with the green ghost glow of the compass light and the slowly fading mountains somewhere far to the north, like a cardboard diorama sliding by. After my five hours on watch I went below, an alien dressed in X-Tra Tuff neoprene boots and two wool sweaters and nylon rain gear. I turned on the red night light over the settee, waking Alisa to take her turn at the wheel. Once she was well awake I sloughed off my rain gear and eased into the bunk next to my son, where I fell asleep with the consoling little weight of his body pressing against me.

The next day the west wind did come up, and we made sail. This entailed a half-hour of me monkeying around with the sails and getting everything set up, watching all the while for sudden movements by the battering ram of the boom or the head-knocking whisker pole, both of which could at any moment be animated to sudden life by a roll of the boat or a shift of the wind. Once it was all organized, though, we were sailing wing and wing, the most beautiful and stable point of sail. The mainsail was flying on one side of the boat and the jib on the other, the wind was directly behind us, and the motion of *Pelagic* across the waves felt stately and inevitable. I shut off the engine, and our joy was complete. The engine had been running for an entire day and night, and the noise had been wearing on us in a way that we hadn't noticed – we adapted to the chugging and the vibration that filled the boat without realizing that it was an effort to do so. But once the engine was switched off, it felt like bricks had been lifted from our shoulders, and Alisa and I let out spontaneous sighs of relief. And this, we hoped, was what we were doing on a broader scale – leaving behind an office-bound, highly organized life that we had molded ourselves into without really noticing it, and relaxing into a different kind of life. Although we hadn't quite felt the relief of metaphorical bricks being lifted from our shoulders just yet.

The slate-gray seas passed under us one by one. Now that we were sailing, relief was also provided by the fact that the windvane could steer *Pelagic*. The windvane is a mechanical autopilot, a unit of stainless steel tubing and marine plywood joined together by lines and blocks and chains and bearings, that sat on the stern of the boat and, through a process that seems much too complicated to work as well as it does, kept *Pelagic* on a constant course relative to the direction of the wind. The vane only worked while we were sailing, so after we put up the sails and shut down the motor we suddenly had no need to attend to the wheel every minute. It's hard to overstate how big a difference that made. During the day I read, I drank cups of tea, and I gave Elias horsey rides on my knee while the windvane and the sails worked together to take us where we wanted to go.

We keenly felt the wildness of the patch of water we were crossing, its elemental non-humanness. During the three-day crossing we sighted four vessels: a tanker riding low in the water with the weight of crude oil it was taking out of Prince William Sound, a cruise ship riding high in the water taking tourists in, and two fishing boats, their sodium deck lights like welders' arcs on the horizon, working through the night over the shallow Fairweather Grounds just offshore of Southeast Alaska. At that point in our sailing careers, it felt like the essence of solitude.

Our days followed the rhythm of the sea, as the wind built and faded and the waves changed according to the wind. We watched Leach's and fork-tailed storm petrels flitting by, and more and more frequently we saw the grand shapes of black-footed albatross wheeling low over the waves. At one point on the second day the wind left us and we pulled down the sails to resume motoring. I looked up from the job of flaking the mainsail on the boom and saw thirteen albatross sitting on the still water around *Pelagic*, evidently mistaking us for a longliner about to set gear. Longliners are commercial fishing boats that set hundreds or thousands of baited hooks on individual fishing lines. Albatross and other seabirds are attracted to the baited hooks, bite them as the gear is being set, and drown when they are dragged down by the anchored line. Mediation measures are in place for most longliners working in Alaska, but global longline bycatch of albatross is an ongoing conservation tragedy, with nineteen of the world's twenty-two species of albatross at some risk of extinction as a result.

The black-footed albatross that gathered around us were giant, stately things. Alisa wondered out loud if we could feed them, and then she remembered the canned clams and mussels that had been sitting in a locker, failing to entice anyone, for the three years we had owned *Pelagic*. She opened cans and flung the bivalves one by one at the assembled albatross and even drizzled the enticing oil on the waves, but got no takers.

At times on this crossing our five-hour night watches dragged into battles against sleep, when it seemed that some irresistible force was pulling our eyelids downwards. But for the most part Alisa and I looked forward to night watch as our moment of solitude on the boat. We were both grateful for the chance to be alone with our thoughts while the others slept below, alone in the half-light and the ineffable peace of the sea, with the slap of waves on the bow ahead of us, and the gurgle of the wake behind. Alisa asked me one morning if we had a voice recorder on board.

'My mind just gets going', she said. 'It would be great to get it all down.'

One night, as the windvane steered *Pelagic* beneath the stars and the twilight on the northern horizon slowly ebbed from ember orange to blood red, I got to thinking about the differences between men and women when it came to adventure – specifically, why adventures attract more men than women. The sailing magazine that we subscribed to during our years of preparation, and that I occasionally wrote for, was forever carrying stories about the ways that women manage to cope with tagging along on an extended boat trip when the whole thing was their husband's idea. And Alisa and I were following that pattern – although she had made the dream completely her own, it had originated with me.

There are, of course, the mechanisms of biology and evolution to explain gender differences in adventure-seeking. But that night, with *Pelagic* rocking along on a steady swell, I thought less of the reductionist explanations that evolutionary behaviorists might invoke and more of the merciless need that some boys and men feel to be world-beaters, to find some way to rise above the crowd, to satisfy the ambition to do something notable. A friend from my mountain-climbing days once told me that he looked for storms in the eyes of potential climbing partners, some hint of inner turmoil that would get them to the base of a mountain with the determination to keep going up once they started, accepting along the way measures of discomfort and danger completely unknown in everyday life. And that's who we were, in my little circle of climbing friends around the University of Alaska, ten and twelve years before Alisa and Elias and I left home on *Pelagic* – awkward young guys with storms in our eyes who went out in groups of two, occasionally three, to try dangerous climbs of remote mountains that no one had ever heard of. We had found a way to write our own version of the classic adventure narrative – young men, unseasoned and untested, setting forth on our quests, enduring a series of improbable dangers ('It was thirty below on the ski out, and we took acid to stay awake!'), coming home transformed by their experience.

But the archetype of a young man setting out to tackle the challenges of the unknown couldn't apply to our voyage on *Pelagic*. My youthful dreams of sailing the world had always included the faceless figure of the woman who would accompany me, some perfect life partner. But they never included a baby. I sat there in the dark cockpit, listening to the murmur of our bow wave and the occasional slap of a sail losing wind with the swell, and thought about Elias sleeping peacefully below, too young to understand anything but his complete trust in us.

Our peaks of morale on the passage were transcendent, our valleys were choleric. On the second day, with sunshine, good boatspeed, and the windvane taking care of all the drudgery, Alisa and I reveled in each other's presence. Then came another long night, each of us standing watch with our solitary thoughts. Then the dawn of the third day, the morning made bitter by short sleep, the two of us working together to set the spinnaker and pole it out as the breeze died. I had stumbled out of the bunk when Alisa called for help with the sails and I found myself fuming at her, all for no reason other than the fact that I had been up three times during my off-watch and could feel a bucket of sand behind my eyeballs, where my brain should have been. Elias, meanwhile, had awoken in the bunk and, furious to find himself alone, was screaming. And screaming. And screaming.

The sails trimmed, our family regrouped over breakfast and took stock of our setting as we slowly grew reconciled to one another. We were within range to reach our anchorage by early afternoon. Our first crossing was nearly behind us. The morning light was showing the coast of Southeast Alaska to port, all sullen glaciers and impassable mountains. We had a first, tentative answer to our big question, and in spite of sleep deprivation and occasional sour feelings, it was an answer that we liked.

We sailed past the entrance to Lituya Bay. I had been there once before, on a work trip, and I knew that little fjord, six miles long and a mile and a half wide, as perhaps the single most impressive spot in coastal Alaska. In the summer of 1958 a giant rockslide from one of the mountains above the bay created a wave that crested at *1,720 feet* above sea level and swept away the three fishing boats that happened to be at anchor in the bay. One of the boats was lost, another was swept out to the open Gulf of Alaska where it sank, and a third successfully rode out the giant wave in the bay. Everything below the high water mark was swept clean, so today, sitting on an anchored boat in the bay, you can see the exact path of the wave as it ran down the bay – everything above the high water mark is mature spruce forest, everything below is first-generation alder, and the line between the two is so sharp that it might have been drawn with a pencil.

I had been thinking about visiting Lituya ever since we decided to travel down the west coast of North America, but now that it was in sight, we passed it by. The narrow entrance to the bay is subject to potentially dangerous tidal currents – the French explorer La Perouse lost twenty-one of his men when the tide swept them out of the entrance in small boats in 1786. We had the advantages of tide tables and charts that La Perouse lacked, and could surely have navigated the entrance safely. But the idea of anchoring *Pelagic* inside that remote bay and exploring in our little dinghy, with our little baby, wasn't very attractive. Our crossing felt like enough for two people who only a few days before had wondered if they could sail around the clock with a baby on board. Rowing and hiking around Lituya was a diversion for a different crew. So far our voyage had been internal, short on visits to spectacular places like Lituya, but rich in moments of self-discovery as we adjusted to the challenge of stretching our adventure to include the care of someone who was still in diapers.

Alisa asked if I minded passing by Lituya Bay, and I honestly didn't.

'I feel like I've had my visit to Lituya,' I said.

Instead we headed for Graves Harbor, another spot I knew from the decks of a work boat, a straightforward anchorage for the night before we would leave behind the open Gulf and move into the fjordland of Southeast Alaska. Just after lunchtime we passed through the granite islands on either side of the harbor and left the swell of the ocean behind. We motored through the flat bay, our bow cutting a path across the mirror-still water, our wake sending little packets of information to the spruce-clad shore. We anchored far in the back, past a hard right turn that would protect us from any weather from the Gulf. It was a beautiful spot, and no one else was there. Paradise. Sun came out and we dried our musty cushions on deck and broke out the solar shower to give the crew a much-needed scrub. Harbor porpoise breaths broke the stillness, common and red-throated loons swam by. The forest climbing the mountains above us was so static after the constant motion of the Gulf. The landscape of rock and spruce was possessed of a slow patience that spoke of the thousands of years since the glaciers had retreated from this place, so different from the ephemeral moods of the sea.

Alisa and I didn't comment on the fact that we had been able to handle everything successfully. There was still too much in front of us, it was too early in the game to celebrate a success. Instead we sat in the sun-drenched cockpit, drinking tea, and enjoyed the moment for what it was. I bounced Elias on my knee, and Alisa and I enjoyed the feeling of being tired in a place where we could rest. Everything was enlivened by the knowledge that we had just done something significant.

The first passage of the trip was over.

10

ANOTHER TOO-SHORT MIRACLE

I T WAS FOGGY as we motored along the few miles of open Gulf of Alaska coast to the pass that leads into Southeast, so foggy that even our thoughts were muffled in gauze. Visibility closed down to 100 feet, then 50. Seabirds sat on the water with beads of moisture gathering on their feathers, appearing off our bow as big as houses in the fog-skewed perspective until they shrunk down to their proper size as we motored past. Even with the aid of radar and the GPS everything felt claustrophobic. Commercial salmon trollers and charter boats carrying tourists called out their position on the VHF as they transited the pass blind. It all sounded a bit congested after the open horizons of the Gulf, so we decided to pull into the delightfully-named settlement of Elfin Cove to fuel up and let the fog burn off. But then the mist overhead opened to show us a glimpse of blue sky, and suddenly the curtain of fog lifted, revealing the rock and ice symphony of the Fairweather Mountains to the north.

Our goal was the town of Haines, two or three days' travel away. Our route carried us along Icy Strait, named by Russian explorers in the eighteenth century, when blocks of glacial ice were a common sight in the water. The British explorer George Vancouver travelled along the Strait in 1794 and noted the snout of a giant glacier on the north shore, disappearing into the far distance. John Muir came to this same place in 1879 and found that the glacier had retreated forty-odd miles northwards to create Glacier Bay. That glacial retreat continues, and the glaciers are now far enough away that Icy Strait has no ice at all.

Glacier Bay is a fantastic place, rich in wildlife and unsurpassed in scenery, but from our time working there as biologists Alisa and I knew it as a place that was first and foremost a National Park, a place thick with rules and permitting procedures and law-enforcement rangers in bulletproof vests. A place where everybody wants to know your business. A most un-Alaskan place. We continued down Icy Strait, leaving Glacier Bay to port.

One of the great recent developments in Southeast Alaska is the ongoing recovery of humpback whale populations following the cessation of whaling. In the summer of 1985, biologists used the unique pattern on the flukes of humpbacks to identify forty-one individual whales feeding in Glacier Bay and Icy Strait. By 2007, the summer we were passing through, the count was up to 161 whales – a four-fold increase in only two decades. As we motored by Glacier Bay we heard a sound that I was sure was a shotgun being fired on nearby Pleasant Island, but that turned out to be the sound of two humpback whales impacting the water a half-mile away. One lobtailed over and over, holding itself vertically with its head down and its tail out of the water and slamming the tail down with incredible violence. The other was breaching, launching its body almost entirely out of the sea and displacing vast sheets of whitewater when it came crashing back down. Occasionally there was a pause in the full-body acrobatics while one of the whales would lie on the surface and pec slap, smacking the water over and over with white pectoral fins that looked to be fully a third of the animal's total length. Humpback whales are *Megaptera novaeangliae*, with the generic epithet *Megaptera* meaning 'giant wing' and referring to those long pectoral fins. The two animals kept it up, slapping and crashing and booming into the water as we motored closer. Ancient murrelets are cool, but thirty – or forty-ton animals carrying on aerial displays constitute a much grander sort of wonder of nature. We watched the two whales cavorting for half an hour, then wondered what coastal Alaska would have looked like before whaling, when humpback and sei and fin and right and sperm whales were all many times more abundant than they are today.

'Every point of land on the coast would have had a display like this', I said to Alisa.

We spent the night in the village of Hoonah, then had two unbelievable days of sailing up Lynn Canal to Haines. Lynn Canal is an incredible fjord, a trench five miles wide and sixty-five miles long, bordered by mountain walls a three thousand feet tall. It's a place that fills you with awe at the sheer volume of ice that would be needed to carve such a feature into the earth's surface. But, because it was the Englishman Vancouver who first gave European place names to much of Southeast Alaska, and not some Norwegian explorer, fjords aren't called fjords in Southeast. They're 'canals' or 'sounds' or even 'inlets', nomenclature that is completely insufficient for the majesty of the geography being described.

As we sailed north up Lynn Canal, the wind built from the south past the forecast twenty knots to a steady twenty-five, gusting thirty. I looked around and realized that all the other recreational boats that had been sharing the water with us had gone home. I reefed the mainsail, and then reefed it again. The waves were steep and they built behind us one by one as we ran north up the canal. The wind sang in the rigging. The sky stayed clear but the outline of the mountain walls on either side of the fjord blurred perceptibly with the moisture that the wind was picking up from the water. *Pelagic* rode back and forth from wave to wave, the poled-out jib balancing against the pull of the reefed main. Whitewater built on the bow as we sailed faster and faster. Elias stood in his accustomed rough-sailing post, inside the playpen lashed into the middle of the saloon, holding on with one hand and pointing up at me with the other while he smiled a drooly smile.

Alisa stuck her head out of the companionway and asked, 'What's the tide doing?'

'We're right at high tide now,' I answered. 'But there's probably still some current behind us as the tide moves up the fjord. Why?'

'The GPS just showed us hitting 9.2 knots.'

That was news – even allowing for some favorable current, sailing at nine knots was seriously fast for *Pelagic*. Of course, nine and two-tenths knots is ten and a half miles per hour, so any discussion of cruising sailboats as being fast has to be kept firmly in perspective. Still, I always liked to try to sail the boat at her best, and I could feel the quick smile that Alisa's news brought to my face.

That night, when we were safely at anchor, Alisa said, 'I knew I shouldn't have told you how fast we were going – now you're going to want to do it again.'

Our second day in Lynn Canal brought us to Haines, a little town at the end of the fjord that is as close to the interior of the continent as you can get while still being on salt water. Haines lies in an uncommonly spectacular corner of North America, infested with majestic peaks and recumbent glaciers. We pulled into the harbor in the afternoon and called two friends who had rented out their house in the ski town of Girdwood, near Anchorage, for a year and came to Haines for a change of pace. Visitors are always an event in small-town Alaska, and within two hours Greg and Ann were on board *Pelagic* with an incredible Alaskan dinner to share – a king salmon fillet and more Dungeness crab than we could eat, both caught by them, accompanied by a salad from their greenhouse and beer from the local brewery. We listened to their news, and heard the travails of these two people who had lived in Alaska for more than twenty years but then found themselves playing the role of newcomer in the insular little town of Haines. Small towns in Alaska can be tough places to meet new people once the winter has set in, and the winter gone by had seen weeks on end when the wind blew hard enough to deprive Greg and Ann of their great solace in the winter, skiing in the mountains.

'And then, after we made it through the whole winter, and my brother came to visit', Greg told us, 'we were in a store in town and I hear someone say, "Oh, the summer people are starting to arrive." I couldn't believe it – *summer* people! I wanted to ask them where the hell they had been when we moved here in September and wanted to meet some locals.'

We spent a great month in Haines, visiting Ann and Greg, and Kelly, the very first friend that Alisa had made when she moved to Fairbanks for graduate school, and Jamie, who I realized was the toughest person I had ever known when I watched him walk down a mountain in Kodiak with the tip of his tibia fractured at the end of a mountain goat hunt gone bad, and Jen, who had been the third person on the week-long trip that began with me trying to work up the nerve to propose to Alisa as we skied across Wonder Lake, and Clint, her new husband and the answer to the long-standing question of 'who is ever going to be incredible enough of a person to land that Jen?' All of these people had moved to Haines from somewhere else in Alaska, and by that happy circumstance Haines was both a place we had never been to before and the place where we had more good friends than anywhere else in the world. These friends had just lived through the long winter when the winds come funneling through the narrow mountain pass at the head of the fjord and the blizzards rage. Now it was summer, the time of year for working outside and living with the energy and optimism that comes from days that are twenty hours long. Their lives were given over to building houses and getting firewood and checking crab pots and earning cash studying some aspect of marine biology at remote field sites. In between doing all that there was always time for another potluck dinner or another hike up a local trail. We helped Jamie and Kelly ferry a load of lumber across Mud Bay to the beautiful timber frame house they were building on a site off the power grid. When Friday afternoon came and they paid the two hippy carpenters who were working on the house we played horseshoes on the beach with the little group of friends who gathered, and helped them to drink gallon bottles of the local beer, while the mountains across the bay caught the evening sun.

One morning we loaded Jamie's subsistence gillnet on board *Pelagic* at the harbor dock and then, an hour later, Alisa and Jamie fed the long monofilament net out over the bow while I reversed *Pelagic* away from the shore of Lutak Inlet. The net set as an invisible curtain underwater, with floats holding the top at the surface, and lead line holding the bottom underwater, while an anchor at each end held the long net perpendicular to shore. Gillnets, either free-floating from a boat or set fixed to shore and tended by skiffs, are one of the primary gear types used in commercial salmon fisheries in Alaska. They are also used in the personal-use fisheries that provide Alaskan households with their annual supply of salmon, and going out to set a gillnet with friends is one of the rites of summer in coastal Alaska. So setting the gillnet with Jamie was a regular sort of Alaskan thing to do, but on this day we also had a particular reason for getting a fish.

We sat on *Pelagic* and waited for the telltale dancing of floats in the jade-green waters that would mean a sockeye salmon had been caught. Twice before the tide turned and the net was swept in towards shore, the floats danced into the water and Jamie and Alisa rowed over in the dinghy to pick a fish out of the net. Then the tide was too strong to fish and Alisa and Jamie struggled to pull the net in over the bow as I reversed into the current to keep the joined net and boat from being swept along onto the rocks. It was a hard half-day of work for only two salmon, but that night we were able to celebrate Elias' first birthday with a sockeye salmon dinner in the Haines harbor. For the event Alisa produced the first cake she had ever baked on board. I took a picture of her handing the cake down to Elias in his little eating chair lashed into the middle of the saloon and that's how I'll always remember the day he turned a year old, with his fine blonde hair growing out in a natural mohawk and his eye twinkling as he reached out to touch the shining delight of the single candle we were about to blow out.

Ever since we left Kodiak in tears, unsure of how things would go as we learned to live aboard a travelling sailboat with an infant, we had concentrated on just reaching Haines, where we could relax with our friends and take a break from travelling and get ready for the long stretch of coastline down to Mexico. We did all that and then we looked up one day and realized that the season was coming to an end. It was still August, but the fireweed, that beautiful magenta flower that marks the passage of every Alaskan summer with the progression of its blooms, was mostly gone. The trees and meadows were starting to change color, and people were getting serious about making sure they had enough firewood for the winter. Fall was suddenly everywhere creeping in, and another too-short miracle that is summer in Alaska was coming to an end. Alaskans live by the season more than most people, and all the signs told Alisa and me that it was almost time for another winter, the long season of skiing and close community, the time for saunas and potlucks and conversation to fill the long nights. But there wouldn't be a winter for us that year. We were leaving Alaska, even though I liked to think that we loved that place just as much as anyone. Our month in Haines was a great curtain call for all the years that we spent in the Great Land, a time with old friends that reminded us that while the country up north may put most any other place to shame, it's the people that make Alaska incomparable.

11

ONE BRAVE WOMAN

THE MASSIVE FJORD that is first known as Lynn Canal, then as Chatham Strait, led us 180 miles south to the open sea. We were making our way towards the exit, transiting a final stretch of the Alaskan coast, travelling through a part of the state where we knew no one. For hours and hours Alisa and I took turns reading behind the wheel, or playing cribbage if Elias was asleep, while *Pelagic* motored in light or contrary winds past the unspooling scenery of glacier-carved mountain walls. Looking at us on the boat, who wouldn't picture a dream-like, carefree existence? We were travelling through the beautiful fjords of Alaska, on our way to Australia! Who could imagine the thumping fear in my heart, the sinking feeling in my gut, that came almost every day when I thought something was wrong with the boat. A father's responsibility in our culture entails things like holding down a job to provide for the family, and being nurturing and caring and setting a good example. To those normal expectations I had added maintaining our 25-year-old boat so that it was seaworthy, afloat, and a safe place for Elias to live. Unfortunately, I knew my practical side well enough to be suspicious of my ability to do that. I kept private my gnawing fear that I would miss something important on the boat, so that not even Alisa picked up on how hyper-sensitive I grew to any perceived problem. As we travelled out of Alaska I developed a slow case of hypochondria, once removed, to any possible defect of *Pelagic*.

In Tenakee Springs, we chatted with the harbormaster, a heavy-set, gray-haired man sitting in front of the optimistically named Party Time Bakery, working on a beadwork project in his lap.

'The town's dying,' he said. 'The Mercantile's closing after a hundred years. Their inventory sits around so long that it's like a food museum. Everyone gets everything off the barge from Seattle.'

The town had entered a weird demographic-economic spiral, so that almost everyone who lived there was a retiree. We suspected that they were all from somewhere outside Alaska. Low-hanging, ripe blueberries were everywhere along the four-wheeler track that served as the main street. Alisa fished a gallon plastic bag from her backpack and started picking.

'No group of Alaskan grandmothers would leave all these blueberries unpicked,' she said after she filled the bag. Back on *Pelagic*, Elias made quick work of his share of the berries, smearing his eating tray and his little mouth with the rich purple juice that was the goodness of an Alaskan summer, condensed.

Our friend Jamie, who had been all over Southeast Alaska working for the state department of fish and game, had told us that Baranof Warm Springs was not to be missed. There was room at the state dock when we pulled in, and we spent two wonderful days there, keeping company with the *Republic*, one of the storied fleet of wooden halibut schooners that are the romantic heart and soul of Alaskan commercial fishing, and the *Kesia Dawn*, a modern steel boat that had spent the season as a tender, collecting salmon from individual fishing boats on the grounds and delivering them to the cannery. Between us, and the crews of the two fishing boats, and a few pleasure boats that filtered through, there were never so many people that we couldn't each have the springs to ourselves for a while, which is the joy of Alaska – the chance, every now and then, to have the very best spots all to yourself.

The springs were in a forest glen overlooking the rushing torrent of a river that flowed from an alpine lake above to a waterfall dropping into the bay below. The hot water was channeled through three pools, each one slightly cooler than the last, before it emptied into the river. The water was too hot for Elias, so Alisa and I took turns soaking, relaxing in the pungent, steaming water while we gazed at the frigid whitewater of the river below. Later in the day I gave Elias a bath in one of the three tubs on the dock that are supplied with hot springs water, each of them sitting in a private room with a view overlooking the bay. The water of the bay below us was still, the mountains above were serene and unreachable, and there was the perfect combination of solitude at the springs and people to talk to at the dock. You could try to beat this whole scene in terms of tranquility, and natural beauty, and northern-style outdoor nudity and decadence. But it would be hard.

We met April Smith at the dock when she saw Elias' little shirts and socks drying on a line and asked if we had a baby on board. April had spent the salmon season on board the *Kesia Dawn* with her husband, Joe, and their two-year-old boy, Ocean, and two deckhands. It turned out that Joe and April had cruised a 34-foot sailboat between Washington State, Mexico and Hawaii before Ocean was born. Along with the crew of *Shambala*, an Australian boat we had met in Haines, April and Joe were the first long-distance sailors we had met on our trip. Common experience and outlook made it easy to hit it off. Spending time with them didn't involve the burden of constantly explaining what we were doing, the way it did with non-sailors. They just took it for granted that sailing the world in your own boat was a very, very good thing to do if you could pull it off. And after the reams of useless, mostly unsolicited advice that I had gotten from people ashore and on boats, I found that Joe, and Keill from *Shambala*, could make valuable suggestions that I could actually learn from. Little Ocean, meanwhile, was a marvel to me because he could both walk and pee standing up. After a lifetime of treating children as a peripheral concern, best left to others, I now found kids slightly older than Elias to be fascinating indicators of the developmental milestones that were coming soon. We were glad to hear that *Kesia Dawn* was travelling in the same direction as us, towards the little outpost of Port Alexander, where Joe had grown up.

The next morning we watched Warm Springs Bay disappearing behind the solar panels on our stern rail and wondered out loud if we would ever be back. Alisa recounted a conversation with April. 'She asked if I got to sail much, or if I spent all my time down below watching Elias', Alisa said. 'I told her I was lucky to get into the cockpit for an hour while he was taking a nap.'

'We could try to get you more sailing time', I suggested.

'At this point I don't see any other way than me watching Elias while you're watching the boat.'

'Maybe it will get easier when Elias is a little older.'

'It has to, doesn't it?' Alisa smiled. 'And you know what April said to me before we left? She said, "You're one brave woman".'

12

WHO'S THIS CHAINSAW JUGGLER?

PORT ALEXANDER IS so small that we had never heard of it before. The settlement sits on both sides of a tiny natural harbor reached through a narrow cut in the rocks and kelp that guard it from the outside. The place used to make its living on the Columbia River run of king salmon, and was bigger than Sitka until the Columbia was dammed and the run failed. The town languished until the 1970s, when land grants were available and a new generation was attracted to this incredible spot. Today, the town hosts a fleet of small commercial salmon trollers and a few small lodges, and some very friendly people.

Our first days in Port Alexander were idyllic. They were late-August days that could pass for good summer weather anywhere, and were near-miraculous in the context of Alaska. Each day ended with a twilight that lasted for hours while the sky above us slowly turned from clearest blue to salmon orange. The trollers tied along the dock had their deckhouse doors open to welcome the warm breeze and chance visitors. Knots of young people drank beer on the dock and wandered from boat to boat, shouting with excitement at the slow transition from perfect day into promising night.

Then for one day a storm changed everything. It was a violent storm, a storm with a chip on its shoulder. Wind blew, rain flew. The world beyond the narrow harbor entrance was erased by fog. The blue sky was replaced by something the color of dishwater. It was the kind of August storm that warns coastal Alaskans how fleeting the summer will be, and how hopeless and dreary the winter that waits. On this day, being aboard a boat on the rock-girt fjords beyond the harbor would be a misery; to be on the open sea would be a mortal risk. The only people left on the trollers at the dock were fishermen unlucky enough not to have anywhere else to go. The younger guys all seemed to have someone in town they could visit. It was the older guys who were trapped in their deckhouses with the doors closed and the windows fogged over, guys looking ahead at sixty, or seventy, and looking back on another season spent alone on the water, trolling for king salmon.

Beads of condensation appeared on our portlights. Rainwater gurgled in the deck scuppers. Our breath made plumes in the cabin. Elias wore a knit cap and two fleece body suits, one over the other. I walked over to the *Kesia Dawn* for a cup of coffee and a chat. Joe would soon be going longlining for sablefish, a fall fishery more rough and tumble than tendering for salmon. We talked about the change of season and fall gales on the Pacific Northwest coast.

'I know delivery skippers on the west coast, very experienced guys, who won't round Cape Flattery after October first', Joe said.

Cape Flattery is the point of land at the very northwestern corner of Washington State that we would round before heading south down the west coast of the US. Alisa and I had been worried about getting out of Alaska before the fall storms began, but talking to Joe made me realize that the real hurdle before us was the passage down the Pacific Northwest coast. That night after Elias was asleep Alisa and I agreed that our goal would be to round Cape Flattery no later than September 15th. We got out the charts and checked our options for getting out of Alaska. The open ocean route from Southeast Alaska to the Strait of Juan de Fuca, our entrance to Washington State, was six hundred miles long. The Inside Passage route, which winds through the protected fjords of southeast Alaska and British Columbia, was seven hundred and thirty miles long. The outside route would take less than a week, but we would also be exposed to whatever weather came along. The Inside Passage would offer nearly complete protection, which was no small consideration if the unsettled weather of fall was beginning. But on the Inside Passage we would only travel during the day, when we could see the endless hazards of the shoreline on either side of us. Anchoring each night would double our transit time. The Inside Passage would protect us from the vagaries of fall weather now, at the price of a later start down the west coast, and a bigger chance of running into bad weather on that part of the trip.

Decision making. One of the most challenging skills for a couple out sailing the world in a small boat is decision making. Being masters of their own fate, operating independently in a challenging environment, cruising couples live a life of making constant decisions with potentially serious consequences: decisions about where to anchor, when to leave port, and which route to take.

We sat in the damp saloon, cramped by Elias' playpen, staring at the mute charts and willing them to give us some clue about what we might find in the actual world that was depicted in their tracery of shoreline and soundings of depth. I felt myself falling into the not-quite-rational pattern of decision making that I learned during my mountain climbing days, when the paucity of hard information about route conditions left me relying on instinct and emotion to guide my decisions. In those days before Alisa and Elias, as I sat in a little tent with my climbing partner on some glacier in the Alaska

Range, I often felt that my decisions were the result of a battle between the two personas of my inner mountain climber – the daring inner climber who wanted to throw himself at the mountains and thereby taste the success of the bold, and the cautious inner climber, who more than anything just wanted to come back from the mountains alive.

And so it was now. I didn't know which way would be best. Should we throw ourselves at the offshore route, or should we be prudent sailors and, realizing we were still feeling our way into the dual grand adventures of child rearing and long-distance sailing, be grateful for the easy route of the Inside Passage?

'Well, we should see how many of the large-scale charts for the Inside Passage we have', I said. 'I'll start looking at the anchorages for the first few nights.'

'A lot of the inside will be playing the tides', said Alisa.

'That's true. We could pick up better tide tables and a cruising guide in Ketchikan.' We began talking over the details of the first few days of the Inside Passage, looking up anchorages in the Coast Pilot and plotting out the distances between them. As we mentally progressed through the early stages of the trip I could imagine my inner Adventurous Sailor, a gray-haired old salt wearing yellow raingear and an old-fashioned sou'wester hat, begin to walk away in disgust. My inner Responsible Parent Sailor, wearing a concerned look and a cardigan with leather patches at the elbows, leaned closer over our shoulders and nodded in approval at the short hops we were plotting out for each day.

After a minute Alisa said, 'There's going to be a lot of traffic on the inside.'

My inner Responsible Parent Sailor raised an eyebrow.

'True', I said. 'Tugs with log barges. Fishing boats. *Cruise ships.*'

'And there's a lot of stuff to hit', she continued. 'Look at all these rocks in Clarence Strait. And there will be deadheads from the log barges.' Alisa and I had long ago internalized what we consider to be the founding philosophy of any real sailor – the open ocean is a refuge, and the coast is a dangerous place where boats come to grief.

My inner Responsible Parent Sailor looked at Alisa with real alarm.

'Still', I equivocated. 'It's been blowing hard from the southeast for days. If we take the ocean route we'll have to take whatever weather comes along.'

'It's only been blowing twenty or twenty-five', she said. 'We're going to have to get used to rough weather sooner or later. We should just go for it.'

I thought to myself, where's the woman who used to get scared by the boat heeling? And who's this chainsaw juggler who took her place?

'I guess you're right', I said. My inner Responsible Parent Sailor threw up his arms and walked away. My inner Adventurous Sailor leered a grin, put a fresh wad of tobacco inside his lower lip and threw his salt-stained arms around our shoulders.

Three more days we sat at the dock, waiting for a break in the weather. The forecast for the offshore area that we planned to transit was for southeast winds blowing hard – all the way up to gale strength, thirty-five knots. Every day the forecast stayed the same, and each day we crossed off the calendar: August 26th. August 27th. August 28th. On the fourth morning Alisa sat on the settee, changing Elias' first diaper of the day, and said, 'We're just going to have to go *one* of these days'. And so, early the next morning, when the forecast was still for contrary southerly winds, but at least light southerly winds, we left.

It was another huge moment for us. So far we had been able to answer many of the unresolved questions of our trip, questions like:

Will Elias get seasick? (no), or: How will we change diapers when we're under way? (not very easily), or: Can you handle a three-day passage with a baby? (yes). But every answer also produced a new question. The passage from Prince William Sound to Graves Harbor was short, and fair, but it had still ended with us musty-headed through lack of sleep. The offshore passage to Washington would be twice as long, with the promise of uncomfortable weather thrown in. How would we handle that? How would Elias?

Loose items were stowed away below, the oil level in the engine was checked, and the cover was off the mainsail. Everything was ready for sea. Alisa joined me on the dock to cast off. Elias screamed from his playpen down below. *Pelagic* carried us past the tender in the center of the harbor where the trollers delivered, past the big mats of brown kelp on either side of the harbor entrance, past the beacon on the entrance rocks, past the gulls quarrelling over some scraps of food from town. Alisa retrieved Elias from the saloon and brought him upstairs, now mollified, to sit in her lap. We headed to the sea.

We motored just one more mile down Chatham Strait, one more mile along the glacier-carved rock wall of Baranof Island that we had followed for 100 miles from Cross Sound and Tenakee Springs. The vegetation on the cliffs was at the apogee of late-summer green, the waters of Chatham Strait were placid. But then we left the strait and entered the open sea. The tide was still falling and all the water of the inland sea behind us was pushing out to the open ocean, millions and millions of gallons of water implacably following the moon. The disturbance that resulted when that moving water hit the ocean swell seemed oversized for the forces involved, an over-reaction of nature. Waves stood straight up in the air and broke in place.

The confused water was nothing dangerous, but it was an unkind reintroduction to ocean sailing after our weeks on protected waters. As *Pelagic* entered the ocean swell, cormorants and murrelets and gulls gathered to feed in the swirling water around us. *Pelagic* lurched from side to side. I braced myself against the wheel. The bare mast drew a crazy arc against the sky. I was alone in the cockpit, Alisa had retreated below and put Elias in his playpen. The waves grew steeper. Her bow reaching for the sky with each wave, *Pelagic* rose to the challenge. The crew was slower to come back to form.

Working alone on the rolling deck, I managed to get the main halyard, the bright blue line that raises the mainsail up the mast, wrapped around the radar dome, 30 feet above the deck. Nothing I tried helped to free it. We could use the topping lift as a spare halyard, and climb the mast to retrieve the fouled halyard once we were in smoother water. But Alisa had just changed a stinky diaper down below, and was obviously worse for the experience, while I was working over my own background level of incipient nausea. It was easy to convince ourselves that anchoring up to untangle the halyard was the smart thing to do.

13

NO TIME FOR PERFECT WEATHER

A QUICK SCAN OF the chart showed Egg Harbor, in Coronation Island, to be our closest refuge. Once the anchor was down, I quickly freed the halyard, so quickly that I felt a bit sheepish that we had delayed our passage over such a minor glitch. But then the weather came up again and we were glad not to be at sea. Our overnight stop changed into another indefinite wait. While the winds blew, the three of us retreated to our home life below decks. Elias regaled us with his five words that we at least could recognize, though a stranger might have trouble picking them out: dog, ball, book, momma and dadda. Throughout the happier moments of the day he also muttered and shouted in his own vernacular, a beautiful, rolling vocabulary that was trill and vowel-rich, like the singing of a stream. I was sorry that those sounds had no place in English, and would soon disappear.

But during our second night in Egg Harbor he had a screaming fit at three-thirty in the morning. I woke musty-eyed to his cries, slid out of the zipped-together sleeping bags Alisa and I shared on the forward bunk, and felt my way back to the playpen in the dark, shivering in the cold cabin in only my blue polyester long johns. I picked up my crying son and cradled him in my lap, playing out a regular moment of fatherhood in the midst of this wilderness where our anchor light was the only sign of human life. During the first months of Eli's life I had mastered the trick of wrapping him tightly in a blanket and jiggling him in my arms until he went quiet. But now he was too old – the baby blankets weren't big enough any more, and his arms were too strong to swaddle. So I just held him, and rocked him on my knee, and shushed him, and that didn't help at all.

Alisa relieved me after a fruitless forty-five minutes. I raided the chart table for ear plugs, desperate for some physical barrier between myself and Eli's constant crying. There is nowhere to hide from a screaming baby on a 37-foot sailboat. I had few second thoughts during our trip, but I had one then. It took the form of a nearly sensual vision of walking out of our old house on Kodiak, fitting the key into the ignition of my happy green Toyota pickup and driving away up the hill. Such easy escape, compared with what seemed like a mad vision of travelling down the coast of North America with a sub-toddler in tow. Sitting in the pre-dawn black on our little boat off this island that appeared completely unchanged since George Vancouver named it for the English-speaking world in 1793, with a screaming toddler whom neither of us could placate, I felt how alone we were, how trapped within the world of this dream come mysteriously to life. How distant our past life on land was, and how impossible to return.

The quiet day that followed renewed my faith. Alisa baked bread and fixed the thermocouple on the oven. The iPod provided us with a varied and entertaining soundtrack. We both played with Eli, we changed his diapers and sang to him when it was time for his nap. We took turns going up on deck and looking at the spruce-clad mountain slopes above *Pelagic*, the anonymous wilderness landscape that was slowly revealed to us as a unique place, rich in detail and character, as we stared up at it from our weather-bound boat. In the afternoon the updated forecast promised reprieve. The winds were predicted to remain southerly, and so less than ideal, but they were at least meant to come down to fifteen to twenty knots. We agreed to go the next morning. So we would finally leave Alaska. The two passages ahead would take us all the way to Washington, and then to San Diego, thirty degrees of latitude from our northernmost point in Prince William Sound.

At dawn gusts of wind still pulled *Pelagic* against the anchor chain. We looked suspiciously at the steel-gray clouds that were flying across the mountain tops above us. We looked suspiciously, but then gave a mental shrug of our shoulders and went about pulling the anchor.

'The end of August is no time to wait for perfect weather to get south,' said Alisa.

For months we had been telling ourselves that we had to be out of the Gulf of Alaska by September first. We left Egg Harbor on the last day of August.

Like a kitten in a roomful of pit bulls, or a china cup balanced on a wrecking ball. Or like a baby at sea.

We marveled at sheer mountain walls and glaciers
that tumbled direct into the sea.

Keeping company with the *Republic,* one of the storied
fleet of wooden halibut schooners that are the romantic
heart and soul of Alaskan commercial fishing.

You could try to beat this whole scene in terms of
tranquility, and natural beauty, and northern-style outdoor
nudity and decadence. But it would be hard.

Gaunt and unforested in the early sunlight shining across from the
mainland, like a wall of the Grand Canyon set in the Pacific Ocean.

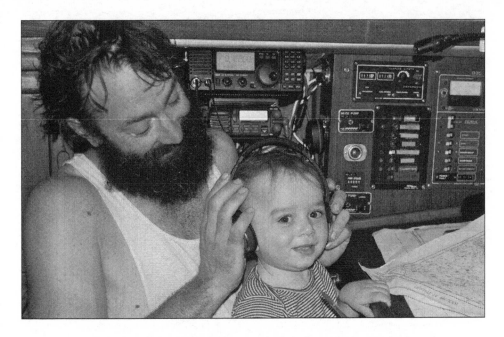

It might have just been something about how each day was built around the same schedule of meals and diaper changes and on-deck chores and ham radio nets.

We lacked a shellback, so Elias stood in, making his appearance in the cockpit after breakfast, wearing a tinfoil crown and carrying a tinfoil trident.

I was spending most of my time crammed into our tiny engine room, sweat pouring off me as I struggled to pry various pieces free from the engine.

Hakahetau as seen from the water was the tropical paradise that westerners have been idealizing ever since the days of Captain Cook.

I took a snap of A'tai holding his rifle with the
spires of Ua Pou in the background.

We found that moment when dream and reality contested
the field, and reality did not come out second best.

The patterns resolved themselves as stylized male and female
faces and marine animals: sharks, manta rays, moray eels.

Part 2 THE WEST COAST

Hawaii

Islands

The hardest passage
of them all!

Canada

Blocked by fog

Vancouver
Island

Neah Bay   ✳ Port Townsend

'll we want
to get South

Newport

Refuge from
weather here

Eureka

San Francisco

United States

San Diego ✳

Irrational fears over
entry requirements

Isla Cedros ✳

Punta
Abreojos

I spent the first moments
of 2008 upside-down

Bahia
Magdalena

La Paz

Mexico

Our first maki maki

14

WHAT THE SEA REQUIRED

'THE HARDEST PART is leaving home.'

That was the pre-trip advice we got from friends who spent five years sailing a small boat from Germany to Kodiak and back. Before we started our trip, the only actual full-time sailors we had ever met were two cruising couples who were adventurous enough, or bored enough with tropical sailing, to spend a winter on their boats in the Kodiak harbor. During our years of planning, Alisa and I treasured any wisdom we remembered from these four sailors. So in the depths of our pre-departure winter, as we systematically broke every tie between ourselves and home, we repeated those words. 'The hardest part is leaving home,' I thought on the day when we handed over the keys to the new owners of our house. 'The hardest part is leaving home,' Alisa told me when we were driving away from our goodbye party, trying not to think about the friendships we were walking away from. These six words of advice reassured us that the sorrow we felt would prove transitory. Once we left home and settled into life on *Pelagic*, everything would be better.

We might not have started the trip without that promise. And so we learned a central lesson of human striving: doubt is the deadliest enemy of any dream, and before we can explore the bounds of what is actually possible, we need the motivation of an idea, a perceived wisdom, to quiet doubt. We needed the motivation of an idea, for instance, before we could upend our entire lives, just when the arrival of our first child had every reasonable instinct telling us that it was time to nest and not to explore. And so, like many others before us, we worked under the aegis of an idea, and later we looked back with surprise at what we had managed to accomplish.

Even though, in this instance, the idea proved to be wrong.

We motored out of the harbor to the open sea, and found that the wind was still blowing – average windspeed was somewhere in the low twenty-knot range, right in our face. I started tacking the boat, sailing as close to the wind as we could travel. Steep waves swept down on us, pushing us back to the north. I ran around on deck barefoot, wearing full raingear and a winter cap and a chest harness to keep me tethered to the boat. Every tack required a one-man orchestration of lines to pull – in quick order I had to set up the new running backstay, center the traveler, turn the wheel, release the sheets for both jib and staysail, haul in the new sheets for both sails, bring up the traveler, check the wheel, take down the old backstay, and get the boat sailing again. Our weeks in the protected waters of Southeast Alaska had left me out of practice as a sailor. But I didn't hesitate in what I was doing. I didn't entertain any mental complaints about the sheets of cold spray that lifted over the dodger and landed on my head in the cockpit. I didn't worry about the angle of heel that had me working in shin-deep water when I took down the running backstay on the low side of the deck. I threw myself back into the sailing, I did what the sea required of us.

When the boat heeled over on each new tack water came pouring over the low side of the deck, achieving a mysterious transformation from the opaque green of the northern sea to crystalline transparency after it splashed aboard. The water gurgled out of the scuppers and back to the sea, but there was always another wave for us to bash through. The decks on the low side were always full to overflowing.

Alisa stuck her head out of the companionway. 'There's water coming in,' she said. 'Lots of it.' Elias started to scream in his playpen and she returned below. I couldn't leave the boat unattended, so I just stayed at the wheel and tried to imagine what it was like for Alisa, stuck below with a crying one-year-old on a leaking boat that was sailing into six-foot seas. I tacked us back and forth, trying to clear the Hazy Islands, a group of rock pinnacles seven miles off of Coronation Island. I sweated inside my raingear as I worked the lines, then I felt cold rain and spray seeping down my back as I sat steering in the cockpit. When our zigzag course took us in close to Coronation Island I was able to judge our progress by seeing how much further south we were along the high seaward cliffs. Twice when we came back to the island after an hour of sailing and I saw how little ground we had made I thought about just turning the barky around and sailing back to Egg Harbor. But I kept going.

Alisa came back up to the cockpit, having put Elias down for his nap. She slumped on the downwind side and I saw that her face was green. Not figure-of-speech green, but actual, pistachio ice-cream green. Being stuck below with Elias, in a boat shaken like a maraca by the endless series of waves, was more than she could take. She told me that water was coming in the forward cabin and the starboard side of the saloon, apparently from the seam where hull and deck meet.

'The forward bunk is soaked. It's like a waterfall up there', she said. 'You can just watch the water pouring down.'

'It must be the caprail', I said. Ever since we left Kodiak we had been noticing strange leaks. But this was the first time in the whole trip that we had buried the rail under water, and the leaks had gone from drips to cascades. I realized that the section of teak rail covering the joint between hull and deck, which had been replaced in Kodiak, must not have been properly sealed.

I cursed the shipwright who had replaced the caprail with the vehemence of those at sea who can blame their discomfort on someone who is dry and happy ashore. We agreed there was no way we could fix the rail until we were in port. Alisa went downstairs to nap with Elias. Aside from the relief from seasickness that lying down would give her, we would be taking turns on watch through night and day until we reached Washington. Any time that Elias was asleep was a chance for one of us to sleep.

The weather got worse. Line squalls appeared from the south, each one a black line of cloud trailing purple curtains of rain. When a squall passed over, the rain didn't just fall from the sky. It was thrown down to the sea, it was shot out of cannons. The rain beat on the sea around us with the sound of steaks sizzling on a grill. The impact on the hood of my jacket sounded like golf balls falling on a metal roof. The surface of the ocean absolutely smoked with rain. Water ran off the sails in great liquid sheets. Daylight faltered. The unblinking hazard of the Hazy Islands disappeared behind the purple curtain. I peered after the islands, willing the steep black rocks to stay in view, but the rain felt like a thousand needles pushing into the skin of my face. I had to look away.

15

HOW THINGS MIGHT
FALL APART

EVENTUALLY THE WEATHER did ease, and we did make it past the Hazies. I took over the watch from Alisa at five the next morning. The wind had died completely with the dawn. I was treated to one of my favorite recurring moments, sunrise at sea. Watching the pre-dawn light over a calm sea beyond the sight of land simultaneously convinces you that you might be watching the first sunrise ever, and reminds you how ancient the oceans are. After I took over, Alisa racked out with Elias for another hour of sleep. I started motoring south. The ocean around us was covered with *Velella velella*, or 'by-the-wind-sailors', little gelatinous zooplankton that floated with their vertical inflated sails out of the water, like miniature Portuguese Men-of-War three inches across but without the tentacles. There were hundreds of them, somehow all clumped together in that one patch of ocean. The morning sun lit them up like a field of diamonds cast carelessly across the ocean plain. It was a spectacular sight, made all the more precious by my feeling that it was a sight that so few would ever see, these ancient colonial organisms illuminated by the sun as they floated around the open ocean in their multitudes, with land nowhere to be seen.

The swell was low and long. The water's surface was like the flank of a vast sleeping animal, rising and falling with slow breath. I looked at the huge space surrounding the decks of our little ship, and I felt the ineffable peace that comes to people who sail oceans in small boats. The problems of the larger world were out of our reach, and we were equal to the task of steering our own course. The bad weather of the day before was already a memory. As the sun rose overhead and I pulled off my raingear and sweater, I thought that the worst was behind us.

That wasn't the case.

The day that followed, and the day and night that followed it, devolved into a pattern of headwinds interspersed by calms. *Pelagic* was never able to find her rhythm. I ran an endless treadmill of putting the sails up, trimming and tacking to respond to the variable winds, then pulling the sails down and motoring when the wind died. When we sailed we lived on our ear, with the barky heeling over and the sails sheeted in flat. Down below we struggled around the boat from handhold to handhold with Eli in one hand. It's hard to convey how uncomfortable sailing to windward for days can be. Alisa was stuck below caring for Elias, and never got over her seasickness. Gallons of water continued to come in through the deck leaks, making half of the already cramped boat unusable to us. Things didn't improve much when the wind died and we started motoring. Our autopilot was still down. The windvane could steer the boat while we were sailing, but motoring required constant hand-steering, for hour after hour, day and night. Eli too required constant attention, and he seemed to chafe under the restriction of living in just his playpen and the port settee. The rest of the interior was sopping in salt water for the duration of the trip, and Alisa and I found the cockpit too cold and wet and tippy for a one-year-old. Elias learned a new sound to convey his displeasure at being so confined, a high-pitched squeal worthy of a tortured kitten and completely inappropriate in the confines of a 37-foot sailboat.

By the end of the third day we were exhausted from standing watch around the clock and also caring for Elias. Alisa went to sleep right after dinner. I sat in the cockpit with one hand on the steering wheel, staring at the compass. The diesel pushed us southwards. The engine droned a two-note thump-a thump-a thump-a, reassuring in its persistence. A canopy of stars reached from horizon to horizon, demonstrating to me, the only audience, an unimaginable distance. Earlier in the trip that view of the celestial would have set my imagination free to wander over any topic. Now I was tired enough to just slip into a self-hypnotized state, letting the hours of my watch between eight pm and one am wash over me. Our little masthead light crept over the dark ocean, the only light showing that wasn't a star.

One am arrived and I woke Alisa from the port settee where she was curled up with Elias. She immediately got up, though her eyes were still dead to the outside world. She pulled on clothes that told the story of what it's like to sail at night in the Gulf of Alaska in early September: expedition-weight long underwear top and bottoms, two pairs of wool socks, two wool hats, a neck gaiter, two sweaters, raingear, gloves and neoprene boots. I peeled off my own stinking raingear and climbed into the bunk next to Elias, whose bunk forward was soaked and unusable. I fell asleep with the little weight of his body turning against me with every roll of the boat. At five am he woke me up screaming 'mama' and making the milk sign. Alisa came down from the cockpit to nurse him and I arose with eyes burning and head musty, and put the stinking raingear back on again.

After a few days of this we realized from the Canadian marine weather broadcast that we were sailing into a gale west of the Queen Charlotte Islands. We were in an area that wasn't forecast to get the worst of the weather, but travelling at our current rate of speed for another day would put us right in the path of the gale, with forecast winds of thirty-five knots. Even hearing the word 'gale' on the forecast was a little chilling, and for a ridiculous moment I found myself thinking how unfair it was, that it wasn't really fall yet and that the gales shouldn't be starting. Alisa and I had both been out in gales and worse on commercial fishing boats in Alaska. But we had never been in a gale on *Pelagic*. Tired as we were and with the soaked interior already making life aboard miserable, we didn't feel like starting just then. Luckily, there's a great sailing trick for this situation: heaving to. I rolled up the jib, and set up the staysail and a heavily reefed main so that they were pulling against each other. I then tied the wheel all the way over to point us up towards the wind, so the waves were hitting *Pelagic* at an angle of about fifty degrees from the bow. Our speed over the ground fell to less than a knot, and the boat looked after herself, so that we didn't have to steer. The motion was much better once we hove to, with the ten-foot seas taking us from the most comfortable direction. Down below we could hear each wave hissing by the hull as it lifted us up. After dinner Elias went to sleep. We were so completely alone; we hadn't seen another boat since the *Miss T*, back at Coronation Island. We agreed that getting rest was more important than keeping a lookout. So our little family slept the night through, Alisa and Elias together on the port settee and me on the quarterberth. *Pelagic* bobbed slowly along and the masthead light warned the empty ocean of our presence.

The next day the worst of the weather was past, but *Pelagic* jerked back and forth, the sails slapping violently as they tried to hold the light winds from our stern while we were climbing the swell on our bow. By noon the wind came back into our faces. We went back to sailing on our ear. Things got even less comfortable.

We continued caring for our one-year-old son in a soaking sailboat, far from anywhere.

That afternoon I silently entertained the thought that this particular passage was turning out to be harder than anything that we had expected for the entire sail to Australia. Elias wouldn't stop screaming. With the windvane steering us, Alisa and I both sat on the settee while Elias gripped the top of his playpen, two feet away, and squealed his wounded-kitten squeal. Alisa had been trying to soothe him for twenty minutes, but nothing had worked. I picked him up, put him back down, offered a toy – nothing.

'Do you think he's too cold', Alisa asked.

'I don't think so. His cheeks are warm.'

'Maybe he's just tired of being stuck in the cabin.'

'Maybe.'

We stared at our unhappy child, and could not escape the conclusion that he was unhappy because we had brought him along on this sailboat trip that was completely inappropriate for a one-year-old.

After Elias finally went down for his nap, we did something that we almost never did before we moved on board, and hadn't done in the weeks since Seward. We fought. Imagine our situation: two married people stuffed into the confines of a 37-foot sailboat with no privacy, and the marriage and their one-year-old as their entire social universe. Now imagine those people shocked to find themselves thinking that they might not be caring for that one-year-old child properly, that they might not be meeting the bedrock requirements of keeping their child warm and safe. And finally, imagine those two people full of self-recriminations over giving up everything to put themselves in that position: home, friends, jobs, possessions, all cast away. In that situation, would two people share their concerns openly, would they calmly speak their fears and start a dialogue in search of a solution?

Like hell they would.

We had given up all those things even though leaving home to chase a dream by definition meant that we had no guarantee on how things might turn out. We believed that we would be able to figure things out as we went, we believed that adventures were always conducted with an inescapable element of improvisation. But now we had arrived at a point where we were getting an answer that we didn't like, where we were finding that there were some things in this new life that we weren't figuring out very well. And so we lashed out. Tempers flared, pointed comments were made. The dream was threatened right before our eyes. Of course, we thought. Of course all those people who said we couldn't sail across the Pacific with a baby were right. And so, coming to that realization simultaneously, we fought, and made things worse.

After our tempers had calmed, I said, 'If I had known it was going to be this hard, I never would have asked you to leave home and come'.

'I'm so glad to hear you say that', said Alisa.

So, you might ask, if you were sailing past the British Columbia coast, why didn't you just stop in port somewhere and take a breather?

Well, we considered it. In Egg Harbor we had talked about stopping to cruise the Queen Charlotte Islands, an out-of-the-way archipelago that enjoys a reputation as one of the jewels of the earth. But after the squalls on our first day out, and the gale that we dodged off the Queen Charlottes themselves, it was obvious that the bad weather of fall was starting, and that the season for dinking around at high latitudes was over. Once we realized that, we were determined to get south as quickly as we could. We were safe on the passage, even if we were sleep-deprived wrecks and uncomfortable. We could have pulled in to a port somewhere in British Columbia, overlooking for a moment the complicating factor of the limited number of ports where vessels from overseas are allowed to check in to Canada. We could have dried the boat out and rested up and given Elias the treat of a few days ashore. But then we would have had to go back out, the leaking rail would have soaked us again, and we would have been right back where we started. So we figured that until we took the time to fix the rail properly, we should just keep going. And we weren't going to take the time to fix the rail until we were at least as far south as Washington State, where we would have some breathing room before the change of season caught up with us again.

Later, when we started to meet other rookie cruisers setting off on their trips of a lifetime, we would be grateful for our 'get south now, figure out the details later' attitude. Endurance is a characteristic that is always rewarded for people who go to sea.

After our nadir, the next day dawned sunny, and we were at last blessed by a continuous day of downwind sailing. The windvane steered us, the waves met us from behind, and all day we gently made progress towards our destination. The crosses we drew on the chart every four hours to mark our position were finally offshore of Vancouver Island. The Strait of Juan de Fuca, and the end of the passage, waited for us at the south end of the island. The whole family sat in the cockpit and enjoyed the September sun. Two sharks, maybe spiny dogfish, swam for a moment in our wake, their dorsal fins exposed. Cassin's auklets swam away from us as *Pelagic* approached, concern showing from their ceramic dolls' eyes set amid charcoal feathers. Two black-footed albatross, our old friends from Alaska, wheeled above the waves. Alisa and I agreed that the passage had been particularly hard because of the windward sailing and deck leaks, and that it wasn't representative of what we would face in the future. We also took consolation in the idea that after we reached San Diego we wouldn't have any long passages until March, when we left Mexico for French Polynesia, and when Elias was that much older things could only be easier.

A school of northern right whale dolphins appeared. They were black, slender animals without dorsal fins that looked like sea serpents as they came charging up from behind us, bursting out of the waves and exposing their thin backs. They stayed with us for half an hour, occasionally erupting in exuberant acrobatics, throwing themselves clear of the water again and again to show us their white bellies, then swimming forward to catch up with us and criss-crossing over and over before our bow. One swam right up next to the cockpit, showing itself above the waves as it came up to breathe. Elias leaned forward and pointed, his face lit up with a grin of recognition.

'Dog!' he said.

We were close to the end. That afternoon we sailed into fog off the Vancouver Island coast. I flipped on the radar to look for other boats. The screen showed circles of gibberish. This had happened before.

'The belt that turns the radar must have come off the drive sprocket again', I said.

So 'fix radar' was added to our list of jobs to complete before we left Washington, and we had some anxious moments that afternoon dodging fishing boats that suddenly appeared out of the mist.

Morning found us outside the mouth of the Strait of Juan de Fuca, twenty miles from Neah Bay, Washington, where we could finally drop the hook in a secure anchorage and sleep the night through. We would be only three or four hours from the end of the trip – if it weren't for the fog. Sunrise had revealed a wall of fog across the mouth to the Strait. It was incredibly well defined; *Pelagic* bobbed on a quiet sea in brilliant sunshine, while a mile away an impenetrable cloud of cotton sat on the water. The fog by itself wasn't the problem – the problem was the ships. Getting into the Strait meant crossing the shipping lanes that served Vancouver and Seattle. As we sat on the placid ocean we were treated, every fifteen minutes or so, to the sight of a vast steel ship, nine hundred feet long or more, charging out of the wall at twenty knots. Without our radar we'd have no warning of those ships in the fog – they'd just loom into view a half – or quarter-mile away, with the chance of a collision unacceptably high. I pictured *Pelagic* as a frog hopping across a highway in the fog, hoping that no trucks came along at the wrong time. Trying to shake that image from my mind, I suggested that we wait for the fog to burn off. We started sailing back and forth in the sunshine.

I dozed off and on in the cockpit, even though I was trying to stay awake to keep a lookout for ships. The week-long passage was catching up with me, and I could feel how low my reserves were. From our vantage off the side of the shipping lanes, we watched the giants come and go all morning long. It's an incredible insight into our appetite for material goods to watch the volume of shipping that leaves a big urban area like the Pacific Northwest on any given day.

'I don't know how much longer we can wait', I said to Alisa an hour after lunch.

'Is it burning off at all?' she called up from the settee where she was nursing Elias.

'Not at all.'

'I guess we'll have to go for it at some point?'

'I think so. The last thing I want to do is stay hove to out here all night, riding the tide in and out and dodging ships without radar to help us.'

I plotted a course that would take us towards the Vancouver Island shore at right angles to the shipping lanes, so that we would spend as little time in the danger area as possible. Our course plotted, I fired up the engine and took down the sails. The wind was light, and we would want to motor as fast as we could across the shipping lanes.

The sails down, all that was left to me was to put the engine in gear and start to follow a compass course. But as I shifted into forward and pointed us towards the fog, I couldn't shake a feeling of real unease, almost dread. If we crossed the shipping lanes at a right angle, I knew that we'd be exposing ourselves to a pretty small risk. But still, I couldn't shake that image of a frog getting ready to hop across the highway. We had been uncomfortable for much of the week since we set out from Egg Harbor. But we hadn't been in danger, and it felt a little foolish to run a risk now, with the end so close. What does that frog really know about trucks? I thought to myself.

Just on the one in a thousand chance, I went below and switched the radar on. It warmed up for a minute. I pressed the transmit button. And then, instead of the patterns of gibberish that we had seen before, the screen showed me the invisible world behind the fog. There was the range-finding circle, just where it was supposed to be. There was the surface clutter around our position, just where it was supposed to be. And there, within sixteen miles of us, were the shapes of five ships on the screen, invisible before, but now clearly revealed, and therefore easy to miss.

I have been around complex electronic devices on boats long enough to know that things turn on and work after they have been broken, oh, about once every lifetime.

I'm glad our turn came when it did.

A few hours later the anchor chain rattled over the bow roller in Neah Bay. *Pelagic* came to rest. Alisa held Elias on her lap in the cockpit. He pointed at the seagulls that had gathered around us in hopes of a handout. It was four o'clock on a gray September afternoon at the tip of the Olympic Peninsula. The town of Neah Bay was spread out before us around the harbor. We'd check it out in the morning. For now we just needed to sleep.

The whole family went downstairs. Half the boat was still soaked. Dealing with that could wait. Alisa folded up the playpen and put it away on the bunk up forward. Elias could finally crawl around the saloon without us having to worry about him getting hurt by the boat's motion.

I thought about a celebratory beer. The settee looked like a better idea. I stretched out and closed my eyes, let myself slide into the relaxation of finally having nothing to do. No sails to trim, no wheel to attend, no ships to plot on the radar. No need to worry about the chance accident that might befall a one-year-old at sea.

I felt myself relaxing into sleep. And then I was sick. After a week of living at sea, unconcerned by seasickness, I found myself suddenly retching and running for the sink.

I lay down again, aware of the pain that permeated my body. I tried to figure out how many hours of sleep I averaged each day during our week at sea. The answer I came up with was four.

Alisa was standing over me with a look of concern. Elias, able to walk only by shuffling along with his hands on the settee in front of him, wandered over and planted a sticky hand on my chest. I dully wondered how I could have been fine right until the moment we dropped anchor, and then suddenly become so incapacitated.

I spent the afternoon asleep, waking only to vomit. My teeth ached, my ribs felt like they were out of place. I slept for sixteen hours. In the morning I was fine.

'I was worried about you', whispered Alisa. Elias was still asleep.

'I'm all right now', I said.

'We made it, we're here.'

'Yep, we made it. Looks like we have a few things to figure out.'

'I'm so glad you didn't get sick while we were still sailing.'

And so, together, we started planning the work to get the boat ready to sail down the West Coast. Stopping the leaks and fixing the autopilot were top priorities. Beyond that, we would have to figure out what it had meant to be so miserable on a passage, to find ourselves doing something much much harder than selling our house and breaking off friendships and leaving home. During our months of sailing in Alaska every hiccup, every difficulty of adjusting to our new life, was met with the equanimity of knowing that the hardest part of the trip was already behind us. The passage to Washington had robbed us of that self-assurance. We realized that things could get much harder than they had been when we were closing out our life on land. We realized that we had no idea how hard a life afloat might prove to be. We realized that we didn't know where this dream was taking us. On that beautiful September morning in a protected harbor in Washington, whispering in the morning light to keep from waking Elias, we each internalized the new knowledge that the dream of chucking it all to build a life afloat was still a tenuous undertaking, and that failure, something we had never really considered, was a possibility. That morning we looked at a new world where we no longer had the certainty of sailing to Australia together with Elias, and where we were each free to imagine on our own how things might fall apart.

16

AN UNHAPPY SHIP

EVERYONE KNOWS ABOUT seasickness as one of the challenges of a life afloat. At the end of our tough passage from Alaska we discovered another bane of the sailing life, an ill much less obvious than seasickness, but one that would over time bring us more misery than seasickness ever would. You might call it port-sickness.

During our week-long passage, tempers had flared on board exactly once. At the low point of the trip we each realized that the challenges of caring for Elias while we sailed might be too much for us, which of course meant that the whole trip might be too much for us, and for a moment we cracked. But when good sailing conditions returned it was easy to take on a more nuanced view of the trip's shortcomings. We had never been in danger, and we had never been scared. What made us unhappy was how uncomfortable and difficult the passage became. Once we were comfortable again, and sailing with the wind behind us, it was natural to just think about ways to make things better for the next trip, and to stop worrying about problems that were no longer immediate.

In port, though, things were different.

From Neah Bay we set out for Puget Sound and the oasis of Port Townsend. Fixing the autopilot and the leaking caprail were must-do jobs before we tackled another passage, and we needed a good base for that work. When we first bought *Pelagic* I worked on her for two months in a Port Townsend boatyard. We knew Port Townsend as one of the great sailing towns on the west coast, a place where we could get whatever supplies or help we might need. And having spent our early days with *Pelagic* in Port Townsend made the place seem just a little bit like home, a place where we could get away from the feeling of being complete strangers everywhere we went.

After working the tide and motoring the entire length of the Strait of Juan de Fuca in seventeen hours, we rounded Pt Wilson in the teeth of a growing ebb tide with the pink of sunset fading from the sky. On the other side of the point two communities appeared: Port Townsend, which we expected to see, and a mirror community of hundreds of anchored sailboats off the town, which we did not, their white masthead lights a temporary galaxy low in the night-time sky.

'The wooden boat festival is going on!' I called down to Alisa, who was feeding Elias in the cabin.

Completely without trying, we had arrived at the time when Port Townsend shines most as a sailing town. For the next couple of days, instead of being a family alone on the wild sea, we reveled in the company of crowds of people who shared the sailing passion.

'Look at that!' I said to Alisa on the last day of the festival, pointing at one of the classic yachts sailing back and forth in front of the Victorian architecture of Port Townsend's main street. 'Four headsails. You don't see that very often.'

'So do you still think wood is the worst material for building a boat?' asked Alisa, as she scanned the crowded waterfront for an open spot to change Elias' diaper.

'I do. Every time I walk around a harbor and see some wooden boat slowly rotting away at its slip, all I can think is, 'what an out-moded technology'. But it sure is nice for all these people to go to the work and expense of maintaining their wooden boats all year long so that I can watch them sail this one day.'

The next day the wooden-boat owners went back to their jobs in the city. The temporary swarm of boats anchored off Port Townsend was reduced to a handful of holdouts. We moved *Pelagic* from the anchorage to the harbor for the convenience of being able to walk to the chandlery when a project suddenly required some new part. We were blessed by hot weather, and *Pelagic* bloomed with cushions and clothes drying in the sun.

I spent two days on my knees resealing all of the caprail that had been replaced in Kodiak. As with every boat job, this entailed more steps than you might expect. First I meticulously scraped out every bit of old caulking that I could reach beneath the broad teak board that covered the hull-to-deck joint, then I rubbed down the wood with acetone to give the new caulk an oil-free area to grip, then I put masking tape the whole length of the rail to catch dripping caulk, and then I finally got to the step where I pumped three tubes of very expensive marine caulk under the rail and crossed my fingers that this might give our family a dry home at sea. Meanwhile we paid $600 for a new fluxgate compass, betting that it would set our autopilot right. In between jobs we caught up with some very good friends who had made the move from Alaska down to Washington. And, without noticing when it happened, we found ourselves cast as characters in an absurd new play, one that required us to play very different roles when we were out with friends and when we were on the boat alone. With our friends we were our old chipper selves. When we were alone on the boat, the despair of the lowest point of the passage revisited us, stronger even than it had been in the depths of our discomfort at sea.

A big source of the foul mood on *Pelagic* was the difficulty of living aboard with Elias while we were also trying to work on the boat. Replacing the compass for our autopilot sounds like a simple enough task. But before I could even guess that the compass was the problem, I had to test all of the electrical connections between the various component pieces of the autopilot, something that involved me digging around in all sorts of hard-to-reach spots with the multimeter, my mood slowly going south. Then, after I had tracked down what appeared to be the only replacement compass that was available in the United States for our fifteen-year-old Australian-made autopilot, the real job began. Installing the new compass involved snaking a wire from the brains of the autopilot in the stern of the boat to the compass, in a locker in the middle of the boat, between the galley and the chart table. That meant lifting up every cushion and emptying every locker in the after part of the cabin, even dropping an overhead panel or two as I found a circuitous route for the wiring to follow. Suddenly, our chronically too-small living space was impossible – every spare surface was covered with loose screws and electrical tools and butt connectors and zip ties and rolls of wire and cans of paint and anti-corrosion spray from lockers I had emptied, all of it too delicate or too potentially dangerous for a one-year-old to handle. There was nowhere for Elias to safely be on the boat, so Alisa gamely put him in the stroller and took long walks. But of course a one-year-old needs the comforts of home quite often, so they would return, and I would halt the job and clear up a little space for them in the saloon. Dinner time found me lying across the galley with my head in the bilge, trying to thread the compass cable through a dirty hole that I couldn't see. Meanwhile Alisa sat in the cluttered saloon, waiting for me to clear out of the galley so that she could cook, holding on her lap a fussing Elias who didn't understand why he couldn't be free to crawl around.

The next time you're out of sorts with your life partner, try the experiment of staying together in the smallest room in your house, a space so small that you're nearly touching as you go through the routine of the day. Throw in a fussy one-year-old, and clutter the space up with all the junk that you can carry in from other rooms in your house. See how hard it is to regain your equanimity. See how the petty discomfort of being crowded together keeps bad moods alive.

After Elias went to sleep that night, I resumed the task of re-wiring the compass, and contemplated how much of our new life afloat I spent working on jobs that took three times longer than I would think possible. Alisa took a break from going through our food lockers, drawing up a shopping list for the big re-stock before we headed south, and looked down at me laying on the cabin sole, my head under the galley sink, still trying to thread the compass cable to its destination.

She said, 'We worried so much about safety, and dealing with diapers, and whether he'd get seasick. But the big problem with sailing with a baby is how hard it makes it to maintain the boat.'

All the while that we were working through the challenges of fixing up our floating home while we lived on board with Elias, we were beset by doubts over the larger picture. In our comfortable marina slip in Port Townsend, it was easy to worry about the wisdom of sailing with a baby, to wonder why we were working so hard at the details of caprail and autopilot when the larger goal of sailing all the way to Australia might be doomed. When we met our friends we rediscovered our smiles, but when we returned to the boat we sunk effortlessly into gloom. *Pelagic* was an unhappy ship, and we were in the unfamiliar position of being an unhappy couple, concerned with keeping up appearances to hide the depths of our dissatisfaction.

I had long known from my climbing days that psychology was the crux of adventure. Now we were learning that joint psychology – finding the knack of lifting each other up instead of bringing each other down – was the crux for two people taking their marriage on an adventure.

We agreed to sail as far as Baja California, and then to reassess things.

'If it's not working', I said, 'we can just sail back to Kodiak next summer, and pick up where we left off.'

Our boat repairs finished, we left Port Townsend, on track to sail past Cape Flattery before our self-imposed deadline of September 15th. Consoled by the freedom that comes from being away from the dock, we started to digest the lessons of our recent passage during the two-day trip back to Neah Bay. We realized we were at a turning point, a place where it would be easy to decide that sailing the world with Elias was tackling one challenge too many. We talked about taking the bad with the good in our new life, and what the trip down the Washington and Oregon coasts might bring.

An early morning start from Neah Bay saw us rounding Cape Flattery and pointing the bow south. The swell of the Pacific brought *Pelagic* alive after weeks on inland waters. Elias was down below, playing by himself, and Alisa and I were in the cockpit, warmly dressed in the cold fall sunshine. The wind filled from the northwest. *Pelagic* chased her own bow wave down the seas.

'You know,' Alisa said from behind the wheel, a smile on her face. 'That trip from Baranof feels like it happened to someone else.'

17

THREE DREAMS

THE BOAT WAS dark, with just the glow of the GPS and
the red light over the chart table to throw suggestive shadows
around the cabin. *Pelagic* was defined by sounds – the swish of water
past the hull, the slap of a halyard against the mast, and by motion
– the long up and down of each swell, the pull of gravity as I rolled
against the leecloth that kept me from tumbling out of my bunk,
and by smell – the clean iodine whiff of the sea all around us. Those
were the sounds and the motions and the smell of any boat at sea.
But then there was a sound that was unique to *Pelagic* – the sound
of Elias, awake before dawn, crying for his mother.

I had been off watch from one in the morning until five, but
that didn't mean I had slept for four hours. I had woken three times
– once to the beep of the radar display as Alisa adjusted range and
gain to track a passing ship, and twice because images of *Pelagic* in
danger invaded my dreams so that I dashed up to the cockpit, not yet
fully awake, unable to articulate the source of trouble to Alisa, who
was jolted from the reverie of her book to see me, wild-haired and
incoherent, appearing in the companionway and mumbling something about the anchor. When I was awake on passage I was calm,

my psyche soothed by the simplicity and beauty of sailing *Pelagic* out of sight of land. But the psychic monster of worry that was created by taking a young child to sea was always there, and in my bunk, with my guard down, the monster struck.

With the three interruptions to my already brief rest, the idea of getting up before dawn was a painful one. But Elias, lucky for him, was impossible to ignore. Alisa came down and undressed, I got up and dressed. I retrieved the little fellow from his bunk up forward and handed him to Alisa, who had settled into the sleeping bag that was still warm from my body. There Elias latched onto a nipple, and the two of them slept for another hour.

I, meanwhile, got to enjoy the sensation of being immediately involved with the world upon awakening. No slow morning routine for me – there was a horizon to scan for ships, a position and course to be plotted on the chart, and sail trim to be adjusted in the dark. Soon the pre-dawn light was silhouetting the coastal hills of Oregon. The pastel shades of dawn found me with a cup of coffee in hand, the sails down, motoring across a mirrored sea to the speck on shore that would prove to be the breakwaters of the Yaquina River mouth, with the town of Newport just behind.

Before we left home, we had planned on transiting the west coast of the United States in one mighty whack, all the way from Cape Flattery to San Diego. But now, with the length of the coast actually before us, it seemed wise to stop in Newport, Oregon, where we could visit friends. We pulled into the transient dock at the municipal harbor and found a handful of boats already there, the northern hailing ports on their sterns telling us that we had joined the seasonal migration of sailboats heading south. But talking with the other crews, instead of inspiring us, showed us that we were at the end of the season for easy travelling, and that the more experienced or more organized crews had left weeks before. And the back of the pack was a place where dreams of sailing the world seemed to end almost as soon as they were set in motion.

The three other southbound boats in the harbor were all ship-shape-looking, all about the same size as *Pelagic*. Peter and Ann, an older couple two slips over from us, had their boat built in Port Townsend. They put a huge amount of their own labor into the project, living aboard for two years in Port Townsend while they worked to get the boat ready to head south to Mexico and beyond. Ann sewed all the canvas for the boat herself, all of the awnings and fender covers and winch covers and sail covers, and sewed her own sails, which is such a difficult job that almost no sailor does it themself. After those two years of work they set off to sail the world. Along the Oregon coast, they lost all electrical power in the boat for an unknown reason. So they found themselves with no lights and no radio and no chart plotter and the paper charts they carried as backup proved too small-scale to be much good. Then Peter fell down the companionway stairs and broke two ribs. They turned on their emergency beacon. The Coast Guard towed them to Newport. A doctor said there might be blood clots and that Peter should wait one month before sailing again. By then the winter would be well started. Gales would rage along the coast and only the steel fishing boats with their high bulwarks and heated wheelhouses would go to sea.

I met them as they were walking back from the doctor's office where they had gotten the news of their month-long lay-up. 'Well', Peter said to me, as he pointed at the brewery next to the harbor, 'Looks like our winter of palm trees is turning into a winter in Oregon, staying warm in the brew pub.'

At first theirs seemed like an isolated story. But then Alisa checked the cell phone and got a garbled message from Sally on *Rhoda*, who we had last seen in the harbor at Neah Bay. Alisa listened to the message twice, frowning.

'It's hard to make out', she said. 'But Sally said something about getting beat up on the Washington coast and now they're in Willapia or somewhere like that, re-thinking things.'

'That's weird', I said. 'They left Neah Bay the same morning we did and we had good weather the whole way.'

Later that day I was in a chandlery, looking unsuccessfully for a chart of San Francisco Bay. A woman came up and introduced herself.

'I couldn't help but overhearing', she said. 'We saw you at the transient docks. We're reassessing things and we might have a chart of San Francisco that we could give you.' Her name was Veronica. She and her partner, who was also in his early thirties, were, improbably enough, wearing their combination deck harnesses – inflatable life jackets in the chandlery. Presumably the chandlery itself and the sidewalk they had walked from the marina were not places where you might need a deck harness to keep from being swept away by a huge wave, or, that failing, a life jacket to keep you afloat afterwards. Their boat, *Tenacious*, was a Cheoy Lee ketch with lovely varnished wooden spars. Veronica told me they were from Astoria, Oregon, on the Columbia River. For three years they had been getting *Tenacious* ready to sail down to Baja California. And now, after sailing the one hundred miles to Newport, they had changed their minds.

'It's just too slow', Veronica explained. 'We only have seven months off from our jobs. So we're going to leave the boat here and fly down to Baja.' She kindly gave us a roll of charts for harbors to the south.

Alisa and I took stock of the three dreams that we had just witnessed crashing into pieces. How could working for years to get ready to sail the world result in only a few hundred miles of sailing? We were glad to see another southward-bound boat, a double-ender with some unpronounceable Irish name emblazoned on the stern, also crewed by two rookies, gamely head out a few hours later to tackle another chunk of the voyage down the coast.

We spent a few more days at the transient dock as southbound boats continued to trickle through Newport. Every conversation at the dock turned to the South, an idyllic place of sunshine and warm waters. So late in the season, with the fall gales right behind us, the conversation was either wistful, for those who realized this wouldn't be their year, or determined, for those who still hoped to escape winter's gray skies and tedious days. None of us particularly wanted to be transiting the unforgiving Oregon and Northern California coast with its few harbors and its headlands stirring up diabolical currents and its river bars that denied refuge when it was needed most. But it was our only route to the South, and the time for moving was almost at an end.

Once we were at sea, the coast of Oregon looked like it could be Spain, or North Africa. Brown lines of hills, one behind the other, disappeared into a brown horizon. We found a 25-knot northerly blowing, with almost no swell behind it, and I soon had both main and jib reefed and set. A wave of foam built at the bow and we surfed southward down the little waves. A herd of Pacific white-sided dolphins joined us, riding the pressure wave before the bow and breaking free of the water to grab quick breaths. That night the full moon rose on our port as the sun was sinking to starboard, into the open Pacific. Alisa and I had spent our whole adult lives identifying with Alaska, and the northland. Now all we wanted was to be further south.

18

A CIRCUMNAVIGATION
OF SORTS

WE FOUND OURSELVES poised for a night-time arrival in San Francisco, but entering that busy, unfamiliar harbor in the dark was clearly out of the question. We knew that the seamanlike thing to do was to heave to outside San Francisco and wait for dawn, but spending the night floating around amid the concerns of nearby land, unpredictable currents and abundant ship traffic sounded like no fun at all. So instead we decided to pull into Drake's Bay, twenty-five miles north of the Golden Gate and named for Sir Francis, who was meant to have anchored there in 1579, if you can imagine that. Our standing rule was to not enter unfamiliar anchorages and harbors at night. But Drake's Bay is a broad bight, easily entered, and pulling in seemed much the safer option for the remaining dark hours. I had slept five and a half hours the night before, and had been on watch the whole of the following day with only a twenty-minute nap while Eli was eating dinner. The allure of deep sleep in a secure anchorage was strong.

Elias woke up screaming a one-year-old's desperate screams as we were making the final approach into the bay. Alisa nursed him and he calmed down, but after we were anchored he wouldn't go to sleep for either of us. It was after one am at this point, and I had been in the cockpit for eighteen of the last twenty-four hours. I was bushed, grumpy with Alisa and cross with Eli. He finally fell asleep on top of me, behind the leecloth in the port settee. I woke up at three o'clock with Elias completely zonkers and my right arm asleep from cradling him. I carried him up to his forward bunk, had a look around outside and then fled back to the solace of the bunk. My alarm went off at five thirty, before there was any suggestion of dawn on the horizon, in time for us to catch the morning flood tide through the Golden Gate. It was clearly an unreasonable time to be awake. I briefly consulted with Alisa about the necessity for an afternoon flood to follow that of the morning, and what an excellent idea it would be for us to catch the later tide. Without completely waking she agreed.

We all had a wonderful sleep-in, and woke happy to see each other. It qualifies as one of the 'no-duh' lessons of our trip, but it turns out that my state of rest had everything to do with the way that I reacted to the experience of living with my family in the ridic-ulously small space that was *Pelagic* while I underwent the routine stress of navigating that small space across the vagaries of the ocean. Refreshed and eager for what the day might bring, I was amazed to look back at the scowling beast that I had so successfully imitated the night before while Elias acted the screaming one-year-old.

The wind was blowing hard, gusting as high as thirty-seven knots with whitecaps pushing us against our anchor chain. After pan-cakes and coffee we enjoyed a great rip-snorting sail down the coast, effortlessly making seven and a half knots with a double-reefed main and poled-out hundred per cent jib. After a few hours of this great ride we pulled down the sails and motored through the disorganized waters of the Bonita Channel into San Francisco Bay. The waves steepened as we picked our way through the buoyed channel, only forty feet deep. *Pelagic* swung from side to side without any sails up to counteract the pendulum instincts of keel and mast. I stood on the seat behind the wheel and steered us past giant balls of floating kelp. A pilot boat steamed out the main channel, its hull completely hidden from us by the seas and only the superstructure showing. A tractor tug followed, bound for the same inbound ship, which was a silhouette on the horizon. The tug was throwing sheets of spray into the air that were carried clear over its wheelhouse by the northwest breeze. We passed close by the Bonita lighthouse, the surf sending whitewater shooting up the cliffs at its base. Then we were around the corner and steaming straight at the Golden Gate. The name has become synonymous with the bridge, but 'Golden Gate' predates the bridge, and actually refers to the entrance to San Francisco Bay. We had hit the flood tide just as good mariners should, but a wicked eddy on the north side of the entrance had us in ebb conditions – tide working against wind, with waves jumping straight out of the water, possessed by the laws of physics. The boundary between the eddy and the main flood current was remarkably distinct, and once we were across it we were in smooth water, able to concentrate on the treat of entering one of the great harbors of the world, watching the City appear under the brick-red bridge, the towers of the financial district in the background and the appealing jumble of low buildings, the human-scaled streets that are the heart of the City, spread over the hills in the foreground. (People who live in San Francisco take the liberty of referring to the place by capitalizing 'City' as a proper noun, denoting their faith that it really is the only city of note west of New York and east of Tokyo.) From the north, San Francisco looked, as always, like some white-walled Spanish village grown to a vast size.

We pulled into Aquatic Park, a little anchorage protected by a curving seawall off the north shore of the San Francisco penin-sula. Safely anchored, we stared at the apartment buildings marching up Russian Hill above us. San Francisco! It was suddenly hard to believe that we had sailed all that way from Kodiak, and that night in Aquatic Park was the first time that it felt like we were seeing the wider world from the decks of *Pelagic*. San Francisco would turn out to be the place where I took a break from my constant worry over the state of *Pelagic*, where I forgot the unexpected difficulty of re-learning our marriage in the confines of our little ship that we shared with a baby. San Francisco was the place where the rewards of our new life first showed themselves, minute specks of gold we had gleaned from the work of re-ordering our life around a dream.

In the morning we pulled the dinghy up the beach in Aquatic Park and found ourselves in the heart of the tourist district, a place completely unfamiliar to me as a former resident. We brushed the sand off our feet, joined the crush of sightseers, and set off into the City. Our destination was North Beach, the heart and soul of what has made San Francisco so unique through the decades, and I was pleasantly surprised at how easily I found my way there. I was quickly showing Alisa landmarks from my life seventeen and eighteen years before. We saw Gino and Carlo, the bar where my friends and I shot eight-ball at the back pool table for fun while the good players shot nine-ball at the front table for money, and Grant and Green streets, where we used to sit on the sidewalk, drinking bottles of Gallo and listening to the music from inside the bars. We saw the little grocery store where, penniless, I once stole a bag of chips to feed my hunger, and the bakery that set stale loaves of bread in a barrel just inside the back door, free for the taking.

San Francisco in its contemporary incarnation matched delightfully well with my memories, in spite of the many changes that had come since I lived there. AIDS had become a treatable chronic disease. Cell phones had arrived, and the digital age. The dot-com explosion and real estate run-up had been and gone. And the Embarcadero Freeway, damaged in the 1989 Loma Prieta earthquake, had been taken down, opening the eastern part of the City to the sight lines of the Bay that are one of the delights of San Francisco. For all these changes, the City felt like it always did. The streets looked the same, the sound and smell and feel were the same. The same landmark businesses that I remembered were there. I could find my way around without a map.

The next day we walked along O'Farrell Street, continuing the tour of my old haunts. We reached the corner of Larkin and O'Farrell, in the Tenderloin District, where I once lived. Steel gates blocked off the front steps of every building on the block, an innovation since my day, presumably because the Tenderloin is the sort of neighborhood where people use doorways as toilets. Even with the gates, the street stank of urine, as it had when I lived there. The Great American Music Hall was still next door to my old building, and the Mitchell Brothers' Theater ('the Carnegie Hall of American public sex') was still at the end of the block. The area felt scummy, but not dangerous, even with my completely atrophied street sense.

But on our return to the boat I took us north up Polk Street, through an area I didn't remember well. The vibe got worse for a few blocks before it got better. We were presented with examples of several urban archetypes. There was the Statuesque Transsexual. The Strung Out. The Clearly Mad. The Young, Fresh Out of Prison and Soon Headed Back. The Toothless and of Indeterminate Sex. And, to finish the collection, the Runaway Hustler, the abundance of which had made the neighborhood notorious in past decades. Elias, dressed in his natty one-year-old's getup of primary colors and puppy dog prints, took it all in calmly from the vantage of my back. Later, restored to the comforts of *Pelagic*, Alisa said, 'I don't think I need to see any more of your old apartments'.

Before we left Kodiak I had ruled out a visit to San Francisco, thinking that it wouldn't be much fun with Eli. But I was wrong, and this was one little way the actual trip betrayed my best attempts at imagining it beforehand. The next day Elias again happily rode through the city on my back, taking in all the new sights as a matter of course. We walked up Russian Hill and enjoyed the neighborhood feel of the City's quieter, wealthier streets. I leaned forward to shift Elias up the steep sidewalks. We passed side streets that plunged down towards the Bay, lined by buildings that were each their own bit of terraced privacy, the enclaves of remote privilege looking north to the brown hills of Marin, east to the impossibility of Berkeley and Oakland.

San Francisco had been the place where I first pinned maps of Alaska to the wall and dreamed about long journeys on foot across treeless Arctic mountain ranges, clean and vast and innocent of the contemporary world. I was tired of the city then, and wanted something different, something much more different than simple escapes on backpacking trips in the High Sierra. I wanted the capital-A adventures that only Alaska could offer. Eventually I acted on that dream, and I did find myself a new kind of life, with adventures on a fairly grand scale. And after a few years in that new life it was Alisa I was doing ski trips with, travelling self-supported through the crystal perfection and daunting cold of Alaska in winter, the muck and confusion of the city left far behind us. So when we set foot in San Francisco I was completing a circumnavigation of sorts, returning to the City that grew stale for me almost twenty years ago, returning with wife and son and sailboat, in a condition that I only could have dreamed of, and did, all those years before.

19

THE FEW AND THE PROFOUND

I T WAS THE tenth day of our twelve-day stay in Svendsen's boat-yard in Alameda, on the eastern side of San Francisco Bay. The boat was a wreck. Everything was torn up. Nothing was in its place. I had completely ripped up the boat in the service of setting various ills right, and it was clear that I had a couple of very late nights ahead of me to put it all back together again for the scheduled launch.

Covered with the sweat and grime of a full day of hammering away at boat jobs, I sat in the cabin, in a little space I had cleared off on one of the settees, surveying the disorder with a beer in my hand, talking to Alisa on the cell phone.

'Oh, God', I complained. 'There must be a way to go to the boatyard without it ending up like this. But I just can't seem to do it any other way.'

On our way down the West Coast we had been keeping three lists of boat jobs that we wanted to finish before we left the United States. The lists were titled 'Mandatory', 'Good Idea' and 'Would Be Nice', and a substantial portion of each consisted of unfinished jobs we had meant to do before leaving Kodiak. Together, the three lists ran to eighty jobs, many of which would take more than a day to complete. Locating a boat yard in California where owners were allowed to do their own work was surprisingly difficult, but after we had found one, a timely housesit in Berkeley allowed us to move ashore and turn *Pelagic* into a work zone without keeping things baby-proof. Once the boat was in the yard, I threw away the 'Good Idea' and 'Would Be Nice' lists and set to work on the 'Mandatory' items.

Pelagic rested in a cradle on a patch of concrete splattered with old antifouling paint, next to a shed in the yard, looking strangely top-heavy with the hull and rig supported high above keel and rudder. It was an anonymous spot in an old yard where hundreds and hundreds of sailboats had come for maintenance over the years, but I quickly made it mine. I scrounged around the yard for old timbers and sawhorses and a ladder and portable scaffolding and soon had extension cords and lights strung up and paint brushes and rags and gloves and a respirator and tyvek coveralls hanging around the boat, and boxes of paint cans and tools and more brushes huddling beneath the shelter of the hull. Once I was settled in, I went to work. I dropped the rudder out of the boat and pulled our folding propeller off the shaft and sent it away to be serviced. I balanced the rudder on two saw horses and epoxied it fair, so that it wouldn't vibrate any more when we went faster than six knots. I tightened the nuts on the keel bolts that I could reach and took the windvane off the stern and in a borrowed car we drove it to the Monitor factory so that cracked joints in the frame could be re-welded. I greased the through-hulls and scrubbed out the oily residue the last owners left in the bilge. I pulled out the balky transducer for the depth sounder and put in a new one. I epoxied the joint between the keel and hull. I wet-sanded the old bottom paint, kneeling for hours underneath the boat with a compressed air sander bucking in my hands and a slurry of old bottom paint and water pouring over me. I painted the bottom. I replaced the hull zincs. I sanded and touched up the topsides paint. And on and on.

A few days before *Pelagic* was scheduled to be relaunched, Alisa, smartly, decamped for the East Coast to visit family.

'I can't really help since I'm watching Elias all the time anyway', she said when she bought the tickets. 'So I might as well get in a few extra days with my parents.'

'Sure thing', I answered, as I tried to curtail uncharitable thoughts about how that would also put her thousands of miles away when the crunch time hit.

I had been working twelve-hour days, but once Alisa and Elias left the workdays blossomed out of control. I arrived at the yard before sunrise and finished after midnight. Meals devolved into fast-food forays on the way to or from the chandlery. My face was flecked with old bottom paint, my hands were greasy and my knuckles were bruised. My knees ached and my back kinked. Twelve days wasn't such a long time in the yard really, but it was twelve more days stacked on top of the hundreds of hours that I had already spent working on the boat. And it wasn't the actual amount of work that bothered me, it was the idea that whatever I did would not be quite enough, that the boat would never be properly ready for our crossing to Australia.

I had read all the books that tell you how to properly maintain a cruising sailboat, but they tended to be written by people who (God forbid!) had made sailboat maintenance into a profession, and these books dealt in best-case scenarios. They presented line drawings of projects on board idealized boats that were free of the corruption of age and the wear of use. I needed a reference that would show me how good was good enough for our quarter-century-old boat that had already been around the world once, a manual that would show me the golden mean of a reasonable investment of effort in return for a reasonable degree of confidence that nothing would go wrong with the boat far out to sea. But of course, no such manual existed; I was writing it as I went, in the pages and chapters of new skills I learned in the yard. I was serving a self-directed apprenticeship in boat maintenance, teaching myself, by fits and starts, the master's trick of keeping all the balls in the air at once, keeping all of the component parts of *Pelagic* fit. And so, one by one, I came to terms with all the systems: the batteries, and the plumbing; the alternator and its charge regulator and the solar panels and their regulator and the engine; and the standing rig, which we would count on to keep the mast in place through ten thousand gusts of wind, and the running rigging, a hundred bits of metal and line that harnessed the power of the wind; and the sails and the rudder and the keel bolts and the autopilot and the refrigerator and the radios and the radar and the wind instruments and the wiring that made all the electronics work; and the stove and propane lines and solenoid for the propane bottles and the four bilge pumps, and the head and the water pumps and on and on. I was learning to keep them all working even though they were constantly in use in the inimical environment of a salt-saturated little boat. And while I worked on all of it I was thinking, actively or subconsciously, about Elias, and how vulnerable he was, and how important it was that we could trust the boat completely.

The subject of boat maintenance is the bane of sailing writing. Sailors are forever tempted to go on about it, because it occupies so much of their lives, but no one else really cares. All that's important is that you realize that anyone who has managed to go sailing for a few years on a budget has likely put a crushing amount of work into getting their boat ready. People often commented how lucky we were to be able to chuck it all and set off across the Pacific on our own little ship, and certainly we were lucky beyond measure to be able to take on this adventure. But it's not only luck that got us, or any other sailors, to the point of casting off the lines and heading out for a year or three. There is luck involved, and the ability to organize your life around a vision, but also more work than many of our contemporaries can imagine.

We returned from our visit with family and settled back into life aboard *Pelagic,* in a marina in Alameda, with a couple weeks of work still hanging over us before we would feel ready to leave. We found some consolations during that time. Late at night in the marina as we were lying in our bunk forward, with the cityscape all around us gone quiet, there was the conversational sound of train whistles blowing across the estuary in Oakland. And there was the company of our friends Elie and Marie, French sailors we had met when they wintered over in Kodiak years before. They were living at the dock in Alameda, coming to the end of a year-long stay in San Francisco Bay to take care of the business of having a baby, selling their old plywood boat, *Oberon,* saving up money, and getting the new *Oberon* ready to cruise. Elie had a frugal, pragmatic take on cruising that was the product of years spent sailing the world in small boats, and that contrasted wonderfully with the spend-another-grand-at-West-Marine approach to cruising that we often encountered in California. One night, over a wonderful dinner aboard *Oberon* ('*Of course* the food is good', Elie responded when we complimented them on the meal. 'It's *French.*'), I commented that I was so looking forward to being done with our weeks of maintenance and ready for some of the romantic side of cruising. 'Romantic?' he answered. 'Our boats are too complicated, we don't have time for anything romantic.' In his French accent, it sounded great.

Elie also planted an important idea with us when we told him how difficult it had been to stand watch around the clock while taking care of Elias on the week-long passage from Southeast Alaska. 'At sea', he said, 'we set the radar alarm so that it will wake us if there is a ship, and we all go to sleep. Then, when we arrive at port, we are well rested. If I cannot sleep, I *will not* cruise.' Again it sounded great, and somehow more convincing, in his French accent.

Eventually we had crossed off a third of the items on the 'Mandatory' list, nearly killing ourselves in the process, trying to work on the boat in a strange city while we also cared for Elias. When we decided it was time to leave, we were coming to grips with the hardest lesson for novice cruisers: your boat will never be completely ready, and eventually you just have to go.

Thanksgiving Day found us on the Big Sur coastline, sailing past brown hazy mountains coming straight out of the water, with sunlight on the flat sea like beaten copper.

Alisa was in the galley, rising to the occasion. Wisps of her hair escaped from the bun she wore at the back of her head, and I pictured her wearing her hair the same way years in the future, when she would be a doting grandmother cooking for Elias' kids in some land-bound kitchen. At two o'clock all hands gathered for an onboard feast of yams, cranberry chutney, Alisa's famous mashed potatoes and Chilkat River sockeye salmon, gillnetted from the decks of *Pelagic* in Haines and canned aboard by Alisa. We all had double helpings, even Elias, who was all fat cheeks and bulging eyes and soiled bib, unbothered by any notion that this excellent meal was the mark of a special occasion. Alisa and I, observing the custom of the day, inventoried our causes for thankfulness. We concentrated on the few and the profound, rather than the many.

20

OTHER REALITY, THIS REALITY

WHEN WE SET off from Kodiak we had the early parts of our trip broken into two legs: one east–west leg that would get us to Haines, at the top of Southeast Alaska, and a long north–south leg that would take us the length of the US and Canadian coastlines, from Haines all the way to San Diego. A dawn arrival in San Diego, where we were greeted at the harbor entrance by a blanket of smog, saw that second leg finished, and we found ourselves on the cusp of leg three, which would take us the length of Baja California and into the Sea of Cortez.

We tied up to the transient dock at the San Diego Harbor Police office, where we found yet another group of cruising boats making their final preparations before sailing into Mexico. After our maximum stay of ten days at the police dock was over, we moved to a yacht club, and then to an anchorage, as once again we spent much longer than we had expected in port, and the pace of getting things done on the boat while we also took care of Elias was once again frustratingly slow. As we watched the other cruising boats leave for Mexico one by one, morale once again collapsed on board *Pelagic*.

We had two consolations. The first was the way this final stop in the US gave us a chance to reflect on how much living we had packed into the six months since we'd left home. Everything north of San Francisco seemed like it had happened to someone else. Alaska seemed like a different world. Back home we would have been saying how quickly the fall had passed. On *Pelagic* time expanded, and slowed. Our constant exposure to new situations and a lack of a set routine kept us from letting time, and life, pass us by.

Our second consolation was the knowledge that we were still going. Boats without one-year-olds might be getting to Mexico before us, we reassured each other, but we were also going a lot faster than we would have if we had stayed at home. If it was easy, we said to each other during the calm moments when Elias was asleep and I didn't have my head buried in some exasperating boat job, everyone would do it.

We agreed to sail to La Paz and reassess.

Alisa suggested that we skip over Ensenada, the town of 200 000 people just south of the border where most yachts check into Mexico, and instead sail straight to Isla Cedros, off the west coast of the Baja Peninsula about 330 miles south of San Diego. Cedros was listed as a port of entry in our cruising guide. Tired of cities, and land in general, I agreed. Alisa cooked cheeseburgers and fries for our last dinner in the States, and the next morning, December 16th, at nine forty-five in the morning, we finally left San Diego Bay. Just ten miles south of the harbor entrance we passed the Coronados Islands, which are Mexican possessions, and we reveled in the adventurous feeling that being out of the country gave us. We sailed outside of the islands under spinnaker, moving along smartly in only seven or eight knots of wind, with the Mexican courtesy flag snapping under the starboard spreaders.

The spinnaker gave us a beautiful ten-hour sail, the longest time we'd flown that sail on the whole trip from Kodiak. After the weeks of dockside torpor it was great to be moving, to again feel *Pelagic* as a capable traveler under our feet. We were rolling gently back and forth with the swell, myself in the cockpit, keeping an eye on the windvane, which couldn't quite be trusted when we were reaching with the chute, Alisa down below with Elias. One particularly sharp wave gave *Pelagic* a quick lurch, and simultaneous to the motion I heard a sharp thump that I knew, with a parent's intuition, to be a Special Someone's very young skull impacting on the hard hard teak sole of the cabin. This was followed immediately by a long, loud wail. Alisa had taken a minute to do something in the galley, while Elias, who was becoming more agile and mobile every week, had climbed up on the starboard settee, and the wave sent him tumbling.

I went below and took on my astonished air with Alisa, my husband persona that communicates, with the chillingly effective non-verbal communication that exists between married people, my message of, 'What happened? What could have possibly happened when I wasn't looking after things for just a few moments?' Even as I did it, I realized that coming below and blaming Alisa was not a reasonable thing to do. Self-awareness may or may not be a route to true happiness, but it does give you the strange sensation of understanding the stock routines that you fall into in your marriage, even as you're playing them out.

No lasting harm was done to the squirt. We started leaving the lee cloths up to deny him access to the settees while we were underway.

Now a veteran sailor at the age of sixteen months, Elias was getting better at spending time in the cockpit with the on-watch parent, especially in the morning, allowing the other parent to nap. But he still didn't have the motor skills to safely move around as *Pelagic* went through the continual pitching and rolling and yawing and swaying that is a part of life on a small boat at sea, and he needed to be attended every moment he was awake, as we were reminded by his fall from the settee. Since he was the only member of the crew to sleep the whole night, and since he was naturally possessed of a one-year-old's mischief and energy, equivalent to that of a hundred monkeys set free in a nuclear power plant, watching him got to be quite a job. Most of it fell to Alisa, as we continued with the division of labor that left me on deck, sailing the barky. On our second day out from San Diego she watched him down below, where it was easier to keep him safe. Several times during the day I looked down the companionway to see her nodding off with Elias in her lap. In the afternoon I saw her desperately trying to cajole him into taking a nap so that she could sleep for a few minutes without him crawling over her. The motion of the boat down below naturally made us adults groggy, and the sleep-inducing effects were almost impossible for Alisa to fight off when she had been on watch for half the night. Elias meanwhile seemed completely impervious to any suggestion of sleepiness below, but eventually he did get cross with the confinement. Then we in turn both got cross with the lack of any escape at all from the simultaneous demands of sailing and parenthood, and, only thirty hours out of San Diego, Alisa and I lost sight, simultaneously and completely, of why this trip ever seemed like a good idea.

After he finally fell asleep for the night we had a brief *rapprochement* in the cockpit.

'This is hard', I began. 'Sailing to Australia with a one-year-old, and all.'

'This is *so hard*', Alisa said. 'We have to watch him *every minute*.'

'I know. Why didn't some of our family with child-rearing experience warn us?'

'Why didn't they say something?'

'The bastards.'

'*Such* bastards', Alisa agreed. I could feel the marital bond begin to recover as we considered the perfidy of our family members, who, despite their gifts every Christmas and other shows of loving us, failed to step in and save us from ourselves when we first began to talk about quitting our jobs, selling our house, and sailing to Australia.

'It's like we live in an alternate reality to the other cruisers', said Alisa.

'I know,' I answered, warming to her theme. 'Look at them. Working on boat projects whenever they want to. Having drinks in the cockpit. Having *sex* in the cockpit. *Organizing their digital photos.* I hate them.'

'Bastards', said Alisa.

'*Such* bastards.'

We looked up at the perfect roof of stars overhead.

'Still', I said, 'I guess we're kind of committed.'

'I guess so.'

'I always said that having a kid would ruin our lives, so we might as well have ruined lives in the South Pacific.'

'You did.'

'So I guess we'll just have to suck it up until we get to Oz, then re-evaluate.'

'Hold on. I thought we were going to re-evaluate in La Paz.'

On the third day of the passage I kept an eye on our speed and position with the idea that we might make the anchorage on the north end of Cedros. The wind came up, we were making a steady seven knots, and it looked like we had a chance. The allure of setting the hook and sleeping the night through was powerful. But then we ended up falling just short, since dark in December arrived at five in the afternoon, even this far south. We spent the night hove to in the lee of the island. The mountains of Isla Cedros were lit up in front of us by the nearly full moon, the wind came gusting down from their slopes, and the barky sliced towards shore at three-quarters of a knot under heavily reefed main and backed staysail. The waves were big until we were in the lee of the island, and then we had flat water for the rest of the night. At one point I put out some jib and got under way to give room to a passing fishing boat. I was unable to shake the mental picture of the Mexican version of one particular Kodiak acquaintance of ours behind the wheel, a very affable but not-too-competent commercial fisherman. No matter where we happened to encounter a fishing boat at night, I always pictured this same Kodiak fisherman behind the wheel, completely oblivious to our running lights as he bore down on us. Every time the idea gave me a frisson of nerves.

Dawn showed us the island: mountainous, gaunt and unforested, purple, mauve, red and desert-brown in the early sunlight shining across from the mainland, like a wall of the Grand Canyon set in the Pacific Ocean. A fog bank rolled over the summit. We anchored off Pueblo Cedros, a scattered village that from a distance appeared as lines of one-story buildings running down the hillside and along the water, and up close was on fire with the light of the dawn.

Although we were tired from the passage, we rallied to row ashore and handle the paperwork for our arrival. Rowing into the little fishing boat harbor, we came up against signs of poverty that were invisible from the anchored boat: hungry dogs, piles of trash, a rotting dock. The contrast with the wealth and polish of San Diego was glaring. I have read that the US and Mexico have a greater disparity in wealth than any other pair of neighboring nations in the world. Sailing from the Shelter Island Yacht Basin to this isolated village with a depressed fishing economy certainly made that idea plausible.

Although the cruising guide listed Cedros as a Port of Entry, it didn't show any Immigration office on the map of Pueblo Cedros, which left me with a lingering doubt. The Port Captain could check *Pelagic* into the country, but who was going to stamp our passports and check *us* in? We tied up the dinghy and ducked through a hole in a chainlink fence to reach the streets of the village. The man who gave us directions to the Port Captain confirmed that there was no Immigration office on the island.

After finding the Port Captain's office closed, we returned to the barky. Once there, we fell prey to a curse of the traveler – irrational concerns that blossomed in our vacuum of facts, and multiplied as we batted them back and forth.

'If there's no Immigration, doesn't that mean we can't check into the country?' Alisa asked me.

'If we can't check into the country, doesn't that mean we're here illegally?' I asked her back.

'So we're illegal American immigrants in Mexico?'

'Could they fine us?'

'I guess. I mean, if we broke Mexican law, I suppose we could be fined.'

'They wouldn't arrest us? Or take the boat?'

'Maybe we should call the American embassy on the sat phone and ask for advice.'

'I'm not too sure that you would get any meaningful information on the time scale of a sat phone call. Remember those poor people who used to call our office in Kodiak for information about starting new fisheries?'

'Are we even allowed to go ashore without having our passports stamped?'

'Are we even allowed to anchor?'

'Maybe we should just sail down to La Paz without going ashore.'

'I'd hate to miss the whole west coast of Baja.'

There were no other yachts at Cedros who we could ask for information. Sleep that night was fitful. In the morning we rowed ashore, grim-faced, to face the music at the Port Captain's.

We found the Port Captain and his secretary sitting in a pleasant office. He wore a uniform with epaulets, she wore a skirt and hose and lipstick. As soon as they saw Elias padding in through the door holding Alisa's hand, all big diapered bum and bow legs and sun hat, their faces took on expressions of rapt delight.

'No, no problem', the secretary said in response to my questions, in between cooing at Elias and tickling him under the chin.

'You can just check in with immigration at La Paz', the Port Captain added.

I asked if we have to go to the Customs office in Cedros, which was at the salt-loading dock, five miles from the town. There was some disagreement on that, a brief exchange of contrary opinion, before they agreed we could just check in with Customs in La Paz.

At that point I decided to quit asking questions and to just let them make a fuss over Elias.

'Well, that was a huge relief', said the more sanguine member of our team (Alisa), after we dismounted, with freshly stamped ship's papers in hand, from the pickup truck that the Port Captain had provided for our return to the harbor.

'Yeah, we'll see', said the one of us who more habitually looked at the potential downside (me).

'If there's any trouble in La Paz we can just say the Port Captain told us that what we were doing was OK.'

'We'll see how far that gets us. The Port Captain here doesn't care if we get our passports stamped or not. That's not his problem.'

'Well, we'll just have to make sure we take Elias with us to

Immigration in La Paz, and hope that the people there like him as much as the people here did.'

Residual worry over our situation remained with us. But we soon met other cruisers who had done the same thing in previous years, and reported that it was no problem to check the boat in at Cedros, then check in with Immigration weeks later in La Paz.

'Once again', I said to Alisa, 'the things we worry about the most turn out to be the least trouble.'

'So there's no point in worrying.'

'No, I take it to mean that if we could just worry about everything equally, then nothing could go wrong.'

Looking out from the decks of *Pelagic* that afternoon, in the first foreign anchorage of our cruise, the shores of Isla Cedros were a *tabula rasa* of possible adventures looking back at us, with both a fascinating natural history ready for us to explore and a hard-to-reach bit of rural Mexican culture where unknown interactions awaited us. But then we looked down at Elias, drooling on one of his toys in the cockpit, and we quickly recalibrated our expectations for the place. Cedros gave us instant insight into the nature of the alternate realities that exist on cruising boats with and without one-year-old children on board.

Our 'other reality' cruising selves spent a week on Cedros. We found someone who could show us the colony of black-vented shearwaters that nest on the island, and we spent a few hours there one night, listening to the whistling sounds of the nocturnal birds' wings as they came ashore. The next day our 'other reality' selves rowed in early, backpacks bulging with water bottles, and climbed Cerro Cedros, the four thousand-foot peak just north of the pueblo, following the path that confidently began as a full-fledged dirt road, then faded to a track for off-road vehicles as it climbed the steep mountain shoulders, then faded once again to nothing more than a goat trail as we forced our sailors' legs up the final hundred feet to the summit, where we profited by a once-in-a-lifetime view of all of bony Isla Cedros beneath us, rising out of the blue blue Pacific. Later we hauled the anchor and beat back to windward in the lee of the island to reach the north anchorage that we had missed on the way in, where we watched California sea lions from the nearby rookery carving perfect curves through the bioluminescence around our boat. And we sucked it up and beat the thirty miles to windward in the open Pacific to reach Islas San Benito, the spume from the big ocean swell soaking everything on deck from stem to solar panels. On San Benito we went ashore to view the grotesquery of the elephant seal colony, and we spent an evening around a campfire at a fishermen's camp, singing Spanish fishing songs and drinking warm beer.

Our 'this reality' selves actually made just the two trips ashore to visit the Port Captain, before we concluded that Cedros wasn't the place for us and our one-year-old. The few people we talked to in the pueblo were incredibly friendly.

'I'm impressed by your Spanish', Alisa said as we were walking back to the dinghy on our second trip ashore.

'There's a bit of advice I can't wait to pass on to Elias', I answered. '*If you want to have a successful marriage, find a wife who's easily impressed.*'

'Hmm. Elias is either going to be well prepared for life with your fatherly advice or completely in trouble. I can't tell which.'

'Here's another one: *It's up to you, son, but if you want my advice, marry an Arab girl.*' I put my arm around Alisa's shoulder and squeezed.

'But not any Arab girl will do.' She squeezed back.

'Oh, right, more advice about marriage: *Shop carefully.*' I held up a bit of loose chainlink so Alisa could duck through the hole in the fence that gave access to the harbor.

'It is fun to use my Spanish again', I said as I untied the dinghy. 'But for the record, it's right on the bubble between terrible and unintelligible.'

'Other reality' me set aside two forty-five minute spells for practicing every day, one in the morning and one at night. 'This reality' me looked at a vocabulary list for fifteen minutes after Elias went to sleep.

21

EL CLAMPO

THE WEST COAST of Baja is mostly without harbors deep enough for keeled yachts, and the few accessible bays are scattered along the coastline like beads on a string. Our next anchorage was Bahía Tortugas, a short day south from Isla Cedros.

We found *Free Spirit* already at anchor when we arrived in Bahía Tortugas, and this made us happy. On board were Paul and Anne, whom we had met in California. Absolutely chronic travelers ('Everywhere in the world you can buy three things', Paul told us. 'Marlboro, Coca Cola and sex. We were so happy to find a place in western China where you couldn't get Marlboro.'), they had bagged a plan to go backpacking in Central America a few weeks before their departure and instead decided to sail across the Pacific. They flew to San Francisco from their home in Holland and started searching marinas for shabby-looking boats with windvanes on their sterns, reasoning that a windvane signaled the likely presence of other important cruising gear, and a shabby appearance signaled the likelihood of a cheap price when they approached the owner about a possible sale. Three weeks of searching revealed *Free Spirit*, a 39-foot ferrocement boat whose owner had died with his marina bills unpaid. Soon the marina had $7500 of Paul and Anne's money, and they had *Free Spirit*. After three weeks of hard work they were off down the coast, bound for Panama, the Galápagos and New Zealand.

We motored up to *Free Spirit* to say hello before anchoring. 'Anchor close!' Paul said. 'It's not so easy to row far in this wind.'

We dropped the hook a hundred feet from their boat, and then sat there for three days. The wind came up to a steady thirty knots, blowing spray off the tops of the waves. *Pelagic* was fine, we didn't drag an inch, but it was too windy for rowing the dinghy, so we just sat on the boat, staring at the town and waving at Paul and Anne whenever we saw them on deck.

From the boat, the town appeared dusty and crumbling. When the wind finally dropped enough for us to make it ashore, Bahía Tortugas proved to have one paved street and no street signs. The houses showed the improvised construction techniques of poverty, but the streets were full of $30,000 SUVs. Having arrived via the gusting winds and floating kelp balls of Canal de Dewey, between Isla Natividad and mainland Baja, we had only a sailor's context for Bahía Tortugas, with no idea of how far it might be from other towns, or what the people might do for a living. The town was, to our eyes, a stage set that ringed the bay, a tableaux of small-town Baja California that, for us, ceased to exist a few blocks from the beach. Paul had heard that the town was thirty miles of dirt road from the highway, which might have explained all the big four-wheel-drive vehicles on the dusty streets.

People were more than pleasant. They would go out of their way to be nice. A fisherman waded out from the beach to help us land our little dinghy through the waves. Shopping for groceries showed us in absolute terms the difference in standard of living from the US. Alisa wandered the three aisles of a dark little store, lost in the shelves of Spanish-labeled choices. I held a squirming Elias by the door, quickly exhausting my conversational Spanish with the two men behind the counter, their eyes hooded in the leathery skin of their faces, who were politely not staring at Alisa as she wandered up and down the aisles, clearly not finding whatever she was looking for. In the streets the men were mustached, the women either old and heavy, with eyes that stared straight ahead from stoic unreadable faces as they walked, or young, with eyes that stayed resolutely down as we passed, avoiding any contact. Alisa and I imagined the compensations that a life in the little town might have – things like closeness of family and a social warmth that we might lack, without knowing it, in the US. But it was hard to know anything concrete about that, or about the culture at all, since our brief forays into town ended whenever we could sense the approach of Elias' next meltdown. Our time in Mexico had already shown this to be the big difference between travel on a boat and other sorts of travel. Whenever we wanted to, we could retreat back to our own little capsule of the US that we maintained on board, we could tie off the dinghy and go below and literally shut out the foreign world around us. The ability to bring our entire home with us was the key that made months of continuous travel possible with Elias. But it also meant that we missed the central travel experience of being completely immersed, and sometimes lost, in a place where everything was different.

We lived on the anchor in Bahía Tortugas for a week. Each day hundreds of brown pelicans dived for fish in the bay. Massive birds, they began their dives a hundred feet in the air, making adjustments early, steering with one wing and then the other, then tucking both wings and committing into a final streak of feathered piscivore. As many as twenty dived simultaneously on a single school of fish, and they continued to forage well after sunset, up to the point when it was almost completely dark. Rowing back to the barky in the deep dusk, with the explosion of a diving pelican suddenly close by, we wondered how they could possibly see the fish that they were after. Our only guess was that there was some bioluminescence in the water that was tipping them off.

I was on the bow, fixing the running lights, when the man on the ketch anchored next to us waved.

'Hi', he shouted. 'It's good to see you again. Glad you made it!'

'It's good to see you', I shouted back, not quite sure who he was.

'We met in San Diego, at the police dock', he shouted. He then held up a radio and shouted, 'What channel?'

We talked on the radio, everyone else in the anchorage doubtless listening in.

'I had a bad storm when I was anchored off Cedros', he said. 'Thirty-five knots, bent my anchor tray. Had to pull into the little harbor there, I was tied up along a lobster boat and oh! the smell. Anyway, it'll only take me fifteen minutes to get the anchor tray off. I'm going to go in and see if I can find a little machine shop that can help me out.'

He stopped by an hour later in his little gray inflatable. I was pretty sure that we hadn't met in San Diego.

'Have you been into town?' he asked. 'Any idea where I might find a machine shop? I just need a big vice to straighten that three-six-teenths stainless.'

I thought about the dusty town and failed to picture a machine shop that had ever seen a piece of shiny stainless steel. He was in his fifties or early sixties, with a trim little bottle-brush mustache and a neatness around him that made me think of the epicene.

'No. I didn't see anything like that', I said.

He buzzed off in his inflatable and then I was surprised to see him buzzing back ten minutes later.

'Any luck?' I asked.

'No. Those guys at the fuel dock just wanted to know how much diesel I needed, that's all they were interested in.'

'Maybe they just didn't understand you', I said. 'People seem to be really helpful here. How's your Spanish, do you know the word for vice?'

'No Spanish', he said. 'But I said *el clampo* three or four times and they didn't get it. I think they were just embarrassed that they don't speak English.'

The delicious possibility that *clampo* might be the Spanish word for some gynecological instrument came to mind. I pictured the poorly disguised alarm of the men on the dock at his inscrutable, two-word request, repeated several times, for a speculum that was urgently needed on his boat. God, I thought, I hope that's what it means. He buzzed back to his boat and I went downstairs for the Spanish-English dictionary. A vice, I found out, is a *tornillo de banco*. And *el clampo*, to my disappointment, was not there.

22

UN REMO

ON OUR LAST night in Bahía Tortugas the full moon rose above the low mountains to starboard while the sun set over the open Pacific to port. The eastern sky glowed purple. The last rays of sunlight splashed across Eli's head, firing his fine hair into a halo as he sat on my lap in the cockpit, pointing at the moon and saying, 'Muh!' In the morning we pulled the anchor at the same time as *Free Spirit* and sailed down the coast in the company of Paul and Anne, their tanbark sails that had once fueled the dreams of a man now dead complementing the deep blue Pacific on one side of us and the desert mountains forever brown on the other.

Our two boats pulled into Bahía Asunción together where the water was clearer than that in Bahía Tortugas, so that we could see the bottom as we anchored in 23 feet of water. It felt disconcerting in a way, as we could never see the bottom when we were anchored back home in Alaska. Two sheer mountains rose far away across the plain on the south side of the bay, promising spectacular scenery to come.

Paul and Anne left at noon the next day, planning on sailing the two hundred miles to Bahía Magdalena in a single jump. After pulling the hook they motored close by us to say goodbye. We waved as they motored off, knowing it was unlikely we'd see them again in Mexico. They were going all the way to Panama before setting out to cross the Pacific, and had a lot of ground to cover, while we were only planning on going to La Paz, at the tip of the Baja, before crossing.

After they left we rowed ashore to explore the town. With a stiff breeze blowing out to the open Pacific, I wondered for a minute if I should give the dinghy a try before the three of us loaded up for the long row into the beach. One of our oars had somehow contrived to fall out of the dinghy while we were anchored in Bahía Tortugas, and our replacement was a little aluminum oar that was a full two feet shorter than the one it replaced. The three of us piled in and I had the briefest moment of fear when we cast off and I could not quite keep pace with the wind blowing us away from *Pelagic,* towards the mouth of the bay and the open Pacific beyond. I gained momentum, though, and while it was much more difficult to row with the mismatched oars, I could make progress. A new oar was clearly a priority.

A man and his son took a break from unloading their *panga* on the beach to help us in through the gentle surf, keeping Alisa and Elias from getting wet, and then the boy helped me pull the dinghy up the beach. I was armed with the word for oar, *remo*, that I had gotten from the dictionary, which also informed that *remo* could mean a hard job or the leg of a horse. No, the man and son informed me, no store in town that sells *remos*.

Bahía Asunción proved to be much more of a town than Bahía Tortugas. Paved roads, street signs, and none of the contrast between flash motor vehicles and houses that were halfway to being shanties that made Bahía Tortugas so startling to visitors. I bought a can of coffee at a local store and enquired of the girl behind the counter if she could change one hundred dollars into pesos. When I tried to negotiate the rate, though, my Spanish took a sudden holiday and she thought that I was just having trouble understanding the numbers involved in the transaction. Which I kind of was. Amid her blushes and giggles, we struck a deal right at the first number she had suggested. I was a bit chagrined at my inability to bargain, but it was also a classic travel situation where I was making an effort for a slightly better rate to save a buck fifty, while another day might see us blowing forty dollars on an unplanned dinner out. The great consolation, though, aside from the friendly laughter over my bad Spanish, was having the girl tell me that she was learning English, even though she didn't venture to try any on me. I always imagined a bit of a contest when talking with a Mexican with rudimentary English, as we quickly determined which language was easier to communicate in, and thus whose grasp of the other's language was more sure.

Alisa, meanwhile, had been looking for a store that might sell us a *remo*. She had met a couple who didn't sell oars in their fishing supply store, but who produced two oars that had been doing duty as yard décor outside their house. One was ancient, painted blue and worn down in the middle where ten thousand strokes had ground it against an oarlock, and the other was truly ancient, all paint gone from it, something that might have been in use when John Steinbeck visited Baja California in 1940. Refusing all payment, they insisted she take both.

'That was so *nice*', Alisa said when we met up. 'They were *so nice*. I wish we were staying here another day so I could bring them some fresh bread.' Alisa had been feeling the loss of the oar keenly, since she had been the one to tie it in place. We had also lost a floating cushion in Bahía Tortugas, and she was hard on herself about the two items in the way that you can be hard on yourself about mistakes on a boat. When we got back to the dinghy, which the man with the oars had called our *lanchita*, it turned out that the blue oar was exactly the same length as our remaining wooden oar, a perfect match.

We left Asunción at dawn to make the forty-something mile trip down to Punta Abreojos in daylight, followed by three yachts that had anchored up late the previous evening. A few miles from Abreojos I saw a small shape, taking off from the water. At first my mind resolved it as a seabird. Then pectoral and pelvic fins fanned out from the cigar-shaped body, and the shape became a flying fish, flying itself away from *Pelagic*. Along with the sunshine, the blue water and the desert mountains of the coast, the flying fish was a material reminder of the fact that we were in a very different ecosystem from the one we had left behind in the Gulf of Alaska.

Abreojos means 'open your eyes', and the chart showed a couple of reefs that looked like they would be hard to see from the deck of the barky. Pulling in at the head of our little four-boat parade, we found ourselves a nice little anchorage away from the reefs. The next day was New Year's Eve, and Alisa made a great holiday meal – pan-fried canned salmon, holiday rice (with cranberries and pine nuts), artichoke hearts and chocolate pudding. She used the last of our home-canned salmon, possession of which we count as one of the great benefits of being Alaskan, and also the last of our pine nuts, which I consider one of the great benefits of being married to an Arab cook. Just as Alisa was putting Elias to sleep, the wind shifted abruptly and sent steep little waves into our anchorage, so much so that *Pelagic* was pitching up and down and we had to hold on with one hand when walking around the cabin. I forewent my holiday gin and tonic for fear that we might have to pull the anchor in the middle of the night to find a more sheltered spot. Alisa lay down on one settee to write in her journal, and I lay down on the other to read, and by ten thirty we were both asleep, the first moments of 2008 be damned. Luckily the banging of our anchor chain woke me up at eleven thirty, so I was awake for the advent of the new year, even if the stroke of midnight found me hanging head down over the bow pulpit, checking the snubbing line on the anchor chain.

A day later we started the overnight trip down the coast to Bahía Magdalena, hoping to make good on a light land breeze in the face of a forecast for no winds. The wind died two miles off the coast. We motored all the night on flat water.

23

TROUGH TO CREST

THE UNLIT WESTERN shore of Baja spooled by and two-thirds of our little family slept below. Alisa and I each took five hours of being the one who was awake, alone with the boat and our thoughts and a good book. Dawn found us near Bahía Santa Maria, just outside Bahía Magdalena, though a fitful breeze delayed our arrival to the early afternoon. Two whales jumped almost clear of the water in the distance, a mola mola floated by on its side and our two lures trailed behind us, the lines gone limp and lazy with our low speed. We heard another boat hailing *Free Spirit* on the VHF, and I tried hailing them as well but got no response. We agreed they must have been too far south to hear us, the call of Central America keeping them on the move.

We pulled into Bahía Santa Maria, a vast plain of water surrounded on three sides by the bare rock and scrubby hills of Baja California. Frigate birds soared overhead, surf zippered in all along the shore, and a tumble-down fishing camp occupied the head of the bay. Alisa and I were both tired from being up half the night, but Elias was full of energy, and the beach beckoned, so we roused ourselves to the job of unlashing the dinghy from deck. And that was our undoing. Both irritable from lack of sleep, our patience paper-thin and our unreasonable alter egos lurking just below the surface, we embarked on the job of putting the two dinghy pieces together and getting the whole thing in the water, the task on *Pelagic* that demanded more patience and cooperation than any other. Before long we embarked on the downward spiral of group morale, where one person's bad mood infects the other. For the third or fourth time on the trip, we got incredibly mad at each other, for no other reason than being so tired and irritable that it was easier to be awful than to be restrained and polite. Elias, who had been running around the cabin happily when we were below, of course began screaming and crying when we went on deck to launch the dinghy. An hour of slow marital boil passed as we prepared the awkward little boat. By the time we had the oars in place and everything else ready, the wind had come up too hard for us to feel safe with Elias in the dinghy. Alisa put him down for a nap and then, finding herself at the bottom of the downward spiral in morale, came up to the cockpit with a cigarette from the carton we had bought to use for barter in out-of-the-way places we would visit. Her eyes hidden behind her sunglasses, she smoked in the cockpit, not looking at me. I rowed in alone.

I pulled the dinghy above the high tide line and found myself alone on the broad beach, which curved around the bay for miles. Wind blew sand off the dunes behind the beach and out over the water. Ospreys cruised low over lagoons behind the dunes, scouting for their next meal. I took a walk and found two shells to bring back to Alisa. I returned to *Pelagic*, and found that we were still barely speaking to each other.

The next day the wind was still too strong for rowing Elias into the beach, so we pulled the anchor and sailed under jib alone down the ten miles of coast to the entrance to Bahía Magdalena. A northbound yacht passing close by hailed us on the VHF, complaining about the stiff breeze and steep waves that had their bow occasionally under water and spray flying into their cockpit, while we, southbound, enjoyed the delights of having the wind behind us. Getting from the southern tip of Baja back to San Diego involves 750 miles of travel into the prevailing northwesterly winds, a proposition that is widely considered to be no fun whatsoever. Seeing that boat heading north, working so hard to reach a destination of such dubious merit, I was quietly smug with the knowledge that we wouldn't be going back, at least not that way.

After we finished talking with the northbound boat on the radio we got a great surprise – a hail from *Free Spirit*. It turned out Paul and Anne, who we hadn't seen since Bahía Asunción, were anchored in Bahía Magdalena, just a few miles away from us. We anchored next to them, off the tiny hamlet of Puerto Magdalena, and had a great time catching up. Two days later when they pulled the hook again we sent them off with the loan of our charts of the Galápagos. 'With Elias on board, we're not going to put in the extra passages to reach the Galápagos', Alisa explained. 'And we figure that if we lend you the charts that makes it more likely that we'll see you again down the line.'

The two days with Paul and Anne had given us the gift of a social life outside of our marriage, just when we needed it. Alisa and I stood arm in arm in the cockpit, waving goodbye to *Free Spirit*, and we couldn't have told you why we had been so out of sorts a couple days earlier, except that it had to do with the pressure of living on top of each other, with Elias in the mix, and nowhere to blow steam but at each other. When Paul and Anne showed up we had to put on smiles and pretend that we were having fun, and soon we weren't pretending at all. So this time, Paul and Anne had been the impetus to distract us from being unhappy. But we were also starting to see the larger cyclical pattern of our collective joy and misery. In our old life, based in a house, with jobs and friends and outside interests to distract us, we roamed the flat plains of happiness. When we left

Kodiak, we thought we were just setting out on a very long sailboat trip. But it turned out we were also embarking on an interior journey, from that old life of stability to something more suited to two people who had cast their marriage out on the ever-shifting waters of the sea. Now our life together carried the two of us from trough to crest, trough to crest – our joy, our marriage, forever cycling, never still. In the future, we needed to always remember the crest ahead. That, and the fact we weren't still sitting behind our desks in Kodiak, living life on a flat line.

Bahía Magdalena had attracted my attention when I first started looking at Baja charts before our trip. It's a huge embayment, blessed with a deep-water entrance, fringed with biologically productive shoals and mangrove swamps. Magdalena is also one of the bays where gray whales famously come to calve every winter. Once we arrived, I was ready to slow down and spend as much time as we wanted to. 'Where are we going that's so much better than this?' I asked Alisa. So we whiled the days away. We each took a turn catching a ride with other cruisers in a local *panga* to visit San Carlos, the big port on the north end of Bahía Magdalena. And we took great walks in the mountains and coastal plains around Bahía Magdalena. Other cruisers came and went, but we were happy to just stay anchored, taking care of Eli and getting ashore for a little while each day.

But independence and languor last only so long and, on a sailboat, these things are inevitably the casualty of some mundane detail. In Bahía Magdalena it was our diminishing supply of propane for cooking that set us moving again. One of our two bottles was empty, and we couldn't remember when we had switched over to the second, and so didn't know how long it would last. Suddenly, we had a reason to get going, and we did, pulling the hook at noon one day and setting off on the 220-mile trip around the tip of the Baja peninsula to La Paz.

A few weeks later, our friend Jamie asked us if we had seen scads of little gray whale calves in Bahía Magdalena. The truth was, we hadn't seen one gray whale. We had heard that it was still too early in the year for the whales to be arriving, but we never checked it out for ourselves, had never left Puerto Magdalena to explore the shallower parts of the bay where the whales congregate. We had a fine visit, and as always were restricted in how much we could do by the fact that we were involved in intensive parenting every day of the trip. But talking to Jamie, I thought of all the great-looking country on the chart of Magdalena Bay that we had never explored, and how we had managed to spend more than a week sitting in one of the two anchorages recommended by our cruising guide without seeing anything else. It was a good lesson, early on, about the hazards of staying on the defined cruising routes, anchoring in the prescribed anchorages, and not taking the time to explore the world for ourselves.

24

THE WORLD AS IT SHOULD BE

ON OUR FIRST night out of Bahía Magdalena I handed the watch to Alisa at one am, and then took over again at six, before sunrise. I went through my normal routine of waking up at sea – plotting our position and course, taking stock of the sails. When I settled into the cockpit with a cup of coffee it was still dark, and I looked up, with no idea of finding the Southern Cross at all, and there it was, low over the southern horizon, looking just like it does on the Australian flag, our first sighting of the celestial emblem of the still-distant southern hemisphere.

The black night was swallowed by a purple dawn and then replaced by the deepest blue of early morning. A masked booby flapped heavy-winged by the boat, our first booby of the trip, and, since boobies are strangers to temperate seas, a good sign that things were getting firmly tropical. Shortly after dawn this became literally true, as *Pelagic* crossed over latitude 23° 26.37' N, the Tropic of Cancer. We had now officially, improbably, sailed all the way from 60° N to the tropics.

Pelagic, unconcerned with the abstractions of geography, made good time on twelve knots of wind and a flat sea, the sails pulling us insistently further south. Just seven hours earlier I had been huddled under the cockpit light, writing in my journal about how acting on a dream is a step towards acceptance, since even when you live a dream you continue to live under the constraints of the demanding everyday. But after seeing the Southern Cross, and the booby, and the everyday miracle of dawn at sea, I wasn't thinking of constraints any more. With the brown mountains of Baja backlit by the rising sun to port, water all around us that was the essence of blue, and my wife and son sleeping peacefully in the bunk below, I went forward to the bow to adjust some piece of rigging. I finished the job, then looked up at our bow wave cleaving across the ocean and the frigate birds wheeling overhead. I found myself pumping one fist in the air for no reason, except the momentary enlightenment of finding the world as it should be.

25

WE HAVE NO IDEA

'HAVEN'T YOU GONE yet?'

It was a man I recognized from the marina, who I had said hello to but had never talked with, someone who had picked up on our business from the swirl of boat gossip in the La Paz harbor.

'We're going *right now*.' I tried to keep my voice flat but the excitement of the moment came through. The lines where the man's face had fallen onto itself through the years suddenly lifted and he grinned a radiant smile. 'That's *great*', he said.

I hurried back to the boat and hooked up the water hose. We had paid for an hour of dock time at the marina so that we could top up the water tanks. I pushed the trapped air out of our flexible tanks so that we could take on every possible ounce of water. Then I filled the four jerry jugs lashed on deck, and the solar shower, and the water bottles we drank from during the day. I even filled Elias' sippy cup. We were leaving the desert of Baja for the much larger desert of the Pacific Ocean.

It was the end of March, and we had spent the better part of three months using La Paz as a base for visits from both our families and from Alaska friends, and as a place to get more work done on the boat (!), with occasional forays out to enjoy the Sea of Cortez. The La Paz that we had found was still recognizable as the old colonial city of the Baja peninsula. On cool nights we walked along the seaside promenade, the *malecón*, to the café district where we treated ourselves to gelato. Days saw us navigating the dusty streets to search out hardware stores and supermarkets in our endless rounds of keeping boat and crew well-supplied in a foreign port. We spoke some Spanish every day, and rubbed shoulders with the resident yachties who huddled in the marinas, which were little American outposts. And when we tired of it all we could, as always, retreat to our cocoon aboard *Pelagic*.

And now we were leaving. The water I had spilled on deck reflected the sun just coming up over the mountains behind La Paz. The day was fresh, full of promise. Our preparations were done, we were satisfied that we were ready. The adventure lay ahead.

We cast off the lines and buried them deep in a locker. No more docks for us for months to come. *Pelagic* motored away from the marina. Alisa and I were solemn with the moment, excited, eager to be gone. Elias sat in his car seat in the cockpit and fussed.

'Hey, eint you guyz left yet?'

'Oh God', I said to Alisa. 'It's Bernard.'

Bernard was a German who had been living in America all his adult life. Alisa had met his wife, Sally, at a laundromat the day before we left Port Townsend, way back in Washington State, when they were also about to leave on an open-ended trip to Mexico and the South Pacific. But a few days later Sally had left a garbled message on our cell phone, saying they'd gotten beaten up coming around Cape Flattery and were rethinking the trip. We had completely forgotten them, and so were surprised to see *Rhoda*, their little wooden boat with the big windows that made it look especially vulnerable, anchored happily in a cove outside of La Paz, at the southern end of the Sea of Cortez. We caught up with them, of course, and ended up seeing them a lot when we stayed in the same marina for a while. But there was something in the connection that didn't quite click.

'Is Elias toilet trained yet?' Sally had asked Alisa one day.

'No', said Alisa. 'But he's only eighteen months old.'

'Oh, I've got a friend who had her son completely toilet trained at a year', answered Sally. 'But she was a really exceptional mom. You could tell how much she loved her son, and I think he responded to such strong love by moving away from baby behavior early.'

Now Bernard was leaning off the stern of his boat, anchored in the little bay next to the marina, waving at us.

'Right now', I called out. 'We're leaving *now!*'

'You're leefing now!? Not *now*, there is no wind forecast, it will take you *forever!*'

We puttered through the narrow channel past the marinas and resorts and the bay where the proper ships tied up. We felt the confusion of the genteel old city draw away, felt it fade into the distance over the stern as the peace of the sea drew around us.

Once we were out of the La Paz harbor, the Sea of Cortez spread before us, intimate and vast, waiting. The wind was elsewhere, leaving the ink-blue water unworried and unruffled. We motored past islands and headlands that calmly showed us their history, a great geological peep show of naked rock strata – purple, and mauve, and red and gold, all of it without enough vegetation for a decent veil, the layers telling stories of geological time.

We motored over the still sea, following the turns that took us to the south, familiar territory from our previous side trips from La Paz. We motored towards the tip of the Baja. We motored all the day long, *Pelagic* as still as a house, unbothered by the slightest shrug of the sea, a perfect V of waves from our wake spreading out behind us. We motored until we came to Bahía de los Muertos, a gorgeous bay where we anchored for the night, then to Los Frailes, where we hadn't been since we were running low on propane on the way into La Paz. The ham radio net that served English-speaking sailors on the Baja carried forecasts of a northwest blow coming in a few days to the outside coast, just the conditions to get us well started into the vastness of the offshore Pacific, where we would find the northeast tradewinds. The tradewinds! The idea of tradewind sailing fired our imaginations. We told each other there was nothing more romantic than a tradewind passage. Sailing the trades meant sailing that was easy and fast; but also languorous and sensual and untroubled. The northwest winds would get us to the tradewind belt, but those winds hadn't arrived yet. So we sat at anchor in Los Frailes for two days, without impatience now that we had left La Paz, untempted by the idea of unlashing the dinghy for a trip to the beach, waiting for the wind so that we could begin our crossing. We looked ashore at the brown mountains and the rich foreigners' houses along the beach and we were already long gone in our minds, looking at a place we had visited in the past.

We knew our wind would come.

While we waited in Los Frailes, Alisa worked out the process of washing cloth diapers on board. Reasoning that proper landfalls for disposing of plastic diapers would be hard to come by on the coral atolls of the South Pacific, we had switched to cloth for the duration of the trip to Australia. *Pelagic*, already squatting low in the water with full tanks and every spare part we could carry, now sprouted rows of drying cotton diapers hanging from jib sheets and staysail sheets and lifelines and clotheslines. We looked like a tenement afloat on wash day. After she finished with the diapers Alisa took Elias to the bow, foreign territory for him, and he toddled back and forth on the little triangle of deck, all bum and stumpy legs and sun hat, a little Nelson in his baby sailor's harness, pacing the deck beneath the bunting of drying diapers. I oiled the steering gear, I worried away at inconsequential jobs. On the second evening in Los Frailes the ham radio predicted the imminent arrival of the northwesterlies. The next day would be ours.

Just as we left the Sea of Cortez, while we motored around the very tip of the Baja Peninsula, our two fishing reels suddenly sang out. Reeling them in, we discovered two golden-green fish side by side – long and lithe and covered with blue spots – *mahi mahi* in Polynesian, *dorado* in Spanish, or dolphinfish in English. One got away from my gaff, but the other came aboard where we looked, in disbelief, at this famous fish of the open Pacific that we had never seen before. It was, we agreed, a fine omen for the beginning of a Pacific crossing. The *mahi mahi* provided a succulent white meat that was perfectly complemented by a can of coconut milk that Alisa fished out from the stores beneath the port settee. After the meal all three of us sat back in a daze. Elias' mouth was still smeared with bits of fish.

'I think I have a new favorite meal', said Alisa.

After Elias was asleep we sat together in the cockpit and watched the lights of Cabo San Lucas pass far to starboard. *Pelagic* followed a course that slowly took us away from the desert shores of the Baja, and launched us onto a passage that would see 2700 nautical miles pass before we made landfall at the easternmost archipelago in French Polynesia, the Marquesas Islands. That vast landless expanse of the eastern tropical Pacific is the great guardian of Polynesia, a master test that must be passed by any sailor who wants to follow the tradewind passage from the Americas to the palm-fringed islands of the South Pacific. Our route would take us across one of the largest pieces of wilderness on our ocean planet. As we sat companionably in the cockpit, feeling the ocean swell bring *Pelagic* to life beneath us, the lights of Cabo San Lucas dancing to starboard, the warm night breeze washing against our cheeks, Alisa and I agreed that crossing this particular piece of ocean would be one of the great adventures that we might tackle during this life.

'Remember when we were going to get as far as La Paz and then reassess the trip?' I felt the risk of ruining this hopeful moment with an unhappy memory.

'That seems like an agreement that was made by two other people', said Alisa. I could sense her smile in the black night.

We watched a booby that was lit up by our masthead navigational lights as it tried to land on the gyrating top of the mast. Tantalized by the possibility of firm footing in the midst of the ever-moving sea, it came back again and again, but could never quite hold on.

'So, recap', I said. 'We're leaving on a three-week or month-long trip. With a one-year-old for crew. And we have no idea what will happen on the way.'

Alisa leaned against me. 'That's right', she said. 'We have no idea.'

Solomon Islands

Vanuatu

I turn forty

Sa

Fiji

New Caledonia

Suva

Noumea · Lifou Island

To

An inconvenient
place to run out
of propane

Bundaberg

Welcomed to
Australia by
a shark

N

W E

S

Australia

310 nm
0 ——————
500 km

New
Zealan

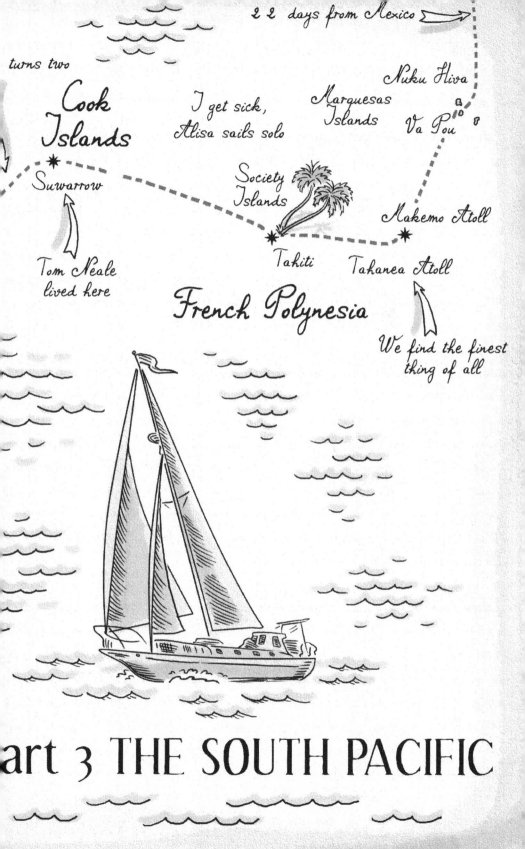

2 2 days from Mexico

turns two

Cook
Islands

I get sick,
Alisa sails solo

Marquesas
Islands

Nuku Hiva

Ua Pou

Suwarrow

Society
Islands

Makemo Atoll

Tahiti

Takanea Atoll

Tom Neale
lived here

French Polynesia

We find the finest
thing of all

Part 3 THE SOUTH PACIFIC

26

THIS OCEAN, MILE FOR MILE

TIME BLENDED INTO itself and flowed away unbidden. I tried to get in the habit of entering our location, course and speed in the log every four hours. But in this lazy era of constant updates from the GPS, entire afternoons melted away, unchronicled.

Mixed sea salt, dried sweat and old sunscreen covered us all. The settees were sticky with it. My deck harness bore a big grease stain from rubbing on the back of my neck. My shirt was inexplicably falling to pieces, giant rents opening in the back.

We were as alone on the face of the planet as we could be, barring a trip to the Southern Ocean, or the heart of Antarctica, or something silly like that. It had been a week since we laid eyes on a ship, and of the twenty-five or so Marquesas-bound yachts that we were keeping in touch with via ham radio, the nearest were more than 150 miles away.

Every day we were surrounded by a heaving expanse of ocean. The water was a mythical blue, the color of the earth as seen from space. We were intimate with the three or four waves that were always right behind us, always just about to sweep under our stern and make us grab onto something as the barky rolled under our feet.

The other waves and whitecaps that reached to the horizon all around were abstractions, they had nothing to do with us. I stood up on the bow and watched them for half an hour at a time, mesmerized.

At night, if the wind and waves were low, the three of us in our little boat cabin could be anywhere. The motion was gentle. I had to remind myself of the indifferent vastness outside. While we ate our dinner and got Elias ready for bed, *Pelagic* did the work of hurrying us along to Australia. That's one of the great qualities of any capable cruising boat: the ability to cover miles efficiently without constant attention from the crew. For twenty-four hours after we left the lights of Cabo San Lucas behind, I had been sick – not really seasick, but for some reason barely able to get up from my bunk. That left Alisa looking after both Elias and the boat. She was able to do it, going on deck now and again to reef the main or shake a reef out. Otherwise the windvane steered and the boat sailed and everything was fine.

As soon as we rounded the tip of the Baja peninsula we picked up the stiff northwest breeze that lasted for days and carried us far out into the open ocean. This was the perfect start, since our greatest chance for a slow crossing was right at the beginning, in the often windless hundreds of miles between Mexico and the start of the northeast trades. In spite of the forecast for fresh northwesterlies, it was a surprise that first night out of Cabo to find ourselves rolling gunwale to gunwale in a beam sea and putting a second reef in the main. The day that followed, the first day of weeks that we would spend out of sight of land, was blue and clear with occasional ships.

After a few days the wind switched from northwest to northeast, and we realized that we had reached the trades. (The tradewinds blow from the northeast in the northern tropics, and from the southeast in the southern tropics.) The reality of this first taste of tradewind sailing was, as always, a little different from our expectations. We fought a contrary current for much of the time we remained in the northeast trades, which slowed us down, and the action of wind against current produced a steep swell that had the boat constantly swinging back and forth and occasionally tripping down the face of a particularly big wave, to land in a roar of whitewater in the trough. The effortless sailing of our dreams was elsewhere, keeping some other crew content.

During every previous passage on *Pelagic* we had kept a constant lookout, but the trip from Alaska to Washington had proved that a week was the limit of our endurance for trading off watches during the night and then keeping up with a one-year-old during the day. After that the fatigue would become too much, since standing constant watch meant we could only sleep when Eli slept, with Alisa and I splitting eight or nine hours of sleep at night and an hour or so during his nap time. We knew we couldn't maintain that schedule for the entire three or four weeks of a passage to the Marquesas. The solution, both of us going to sleep and trusting the radar alarm to wake us if a ship were nearby, had been suggested by our friend Elie back in San Francisco.

There is a strong taboo in the American cruising community, or at least that part of it that expresses itself in sailing magazines, against not keeping a 24-hour lookout at sea. And there is no doubt that keeping a constant lookout is the proper thing to do. But what I liked about Elie's approach to sailing the expanses of the world was that he was not afraid to find his own solutions to the various problems that came up. Talking it over, Alisa and I came to the conclusion that sailing with Elias in a sense made us quasi-singlehanders, since his demands occupied one of us full time, leaving only one person to mind the ship. Singlehanders of course cannot keep a constant watch, yet most of them seem to make it where they're going. And so, although we had stayed up during that first rolly night looking out for coastal traffic as the lights of Cabo faded from view over the stern, every night after we turned the radar alarm on and both went to bed.

We woke often during the night in response to changes in the barky's motion or flapping of the sails, and sometimes I spent half the night in the cockpit, adjusting sails and the windvane or keeping an eye on passing squalls or ships. Those might have been the most impressive moments of the trip. I would jump out of my snug sea-berth and clamber up the companionway steps, half asleep and wondering what had woken me up. Out in the cockpit I would see only the faint glow from the compass at the binnacle, the wind and speed instruments over the companionway and the masthead light waving its constant arc beneath the black sky. Everything above would be stars and the negative space of clouds. On both sides of the boat invisible water would rush by with a hiss. One of the really neat things about the low freeboard and narrow stern of *Pelagic* was how immediate the ocean felt at times like that, how intimate. But I also experienced a brief shudder of realization whenever I stepped sleepy-headed into the cockpit at night, especially if we were heeled over so that the black water was below me. That water was death, pure and simple. If I fell in I'd never be found, and looking down into the water as I stood in the sloping cockpit, one hand on the dodger and the other on the steering pedestal, gave me the same sort of feeling that you get from looking down from some ghastly height. I would make sure that my grip on the steering pedestal was extra firm as I walked along the cockpit seat to reach the helm.

On these starry, moonless nights, when I had awoken for no reason, I would sit behind the wheel, keeping an eye on the compass and occasionally tweaking the windvane, the wake behind me the color of starlight and stretching unbroken all the way to Mexico. I began to feel the scale of this ocean, and of our trip. The world may be shrinking culturally – we might find Michael Jordan t-shirts in the Marquesas, and our ham net was updating our position on the web every night for people back home to track. But there is also an irreducible mass to the earth's geography. This ocean, mile for mile, was as big for us as it was for Magellan, or Cook, or the Polynesian navigators.

Another thing that we had in common with the Polynesian seafarers, but that Magellan and Cook never thought of during their voyages of discovery, was toilet training. The switch from disposable to cloth diapers meant we were suddenly unable to throw away diaper bombs and forget about them. Our interest in toilet training blossomed. The book on child rearing that we carried in the *Pelagic* library suggested that the first step in toilet training is to build your child's awareness of bodily functions, with an eye towards reaching the point when he can tell you that he's gotta go. So 'pee' and 'poop' were suddenly leading members of our lexicon. Sometimes, as we undertook this bold crossing of one of the great expanses of open water on our planet, as we followed the tradewind paths that sailors have used ever since the dawn of navigation on the Pacific, as we aimed for the tiny isolated gems of islands that have stood in for our culture's notion of an earthly paradise ever since the eighteenth century, it seemed that all we talked about was pee and poop.

The equator, at sea.

These four words bring to mind a picture of a painted ship on a painted sea. Blinding light, merciless heat, a stifling atmosphere forever devoid of profitable wind. Our experience, as ever, diverged from expectation.

Crossing the equator, as we were, to get from the northeast trades to the southeast trades, involves crossing the intertropical convergence zone, or, in our era that is so short on poetry and so long on acronyms, the ITCZ. The ITCZ is the belt around the equator where north and south tradewinds meet and rise into the upper atmosphere before they drift back to higher latitudes, fall again to the surface, and refresh the tradewind flow. The rising air around the equator means that there is little wind along the surface (thus the other name for this area, the doldrums), interspersed with violent squalls and thunderstorms that are created by the energy of warm air continually rising into the atmosphere. The ITCZ is therefore something of a sailor's non-delight: flat calms, interspersed with really rotten localized weather. We were following the conventional wisdom for dealing with the ITCZ, which was to spend as little time in it as possible. We had sailed a southwesterly course from Baja, keeping in the northeast trades, until we reached 5° N, 130° W, which put us just north of the narrowest section of the ITCZ. Once there, we changed course to due south in order to cross the ITCZ at right angles and spend as little time as possible in the area of disturbed weather. The convection cells that create disturbed weather in the ITCZ form and dissipate too rapidly for a slow-moving vessel such as *Pelagic* to steer a planned course through them. So at 5° N, 130° W we simply turned south and touched wood for a good crossing, knowing that we would have to take whatever weather we found. Alisa called a West Coast sailing weather guru named Don Anderson on the ham radio the morning that we changed course south, asking for current information about the extent of the ITCZ. He told her that boats crossing in our longitude in recent days had experienced 35-knot winds, torrential rain and zero visibility in a 200-mile diameter convection cell. These are conditions that rate as 'Like Fun, But Different' on the *Pelagic* weather scale. He figured our chances were fifty-fifty for finding the same.

What we found as we sailed and motored south was a zone of flux and disturbance, random seas and towering clouds. We were sailing at the heart of the world, the center of things. Long lazy swells rolled in from both hemispheres and met in a sea that undulated like the breathing of the world. We were also in the earth's furnace, the place where huge volumes of hot air went rising up before spreading north and south at incredible altitudes to drive the weather over a vast swath of the planet. So it was a furnace we found ourselves in, but not a basement furnace; rather an airy, ethereal furnace as befits this planet of ocean and atmosphere. Enormous stacks of cloud rested on the horizon all around us.

On our first night in the ITCZ we sailed through the first squalls of the trip. The radar alarm woke me up and when I looked at the screen I saw tight little weather targets clustered in front of us, soft on the edges unlike ship targets, but black and impenetrable in the center. I sat at the chart table for twenty minutes, stupid with sleep, wondering if we would get past them or not. Then I stirred and put a second reef in the main, insurance against any sudden increase in wind strength.

Shortly after I reefed, at two in the morning, it started pouring rain – the first rain that we'd had on deck since San Diego, in December. I huddled in the companionway in a jacket, the hatch boards up to keep the rain out of the cabin. It was suddenly cold, only a couple of hundred miles north of the equator. I looked at the compass and tried, with my sleepy brain, to understand a fifty-degree windshift. The windvane steers a course relative to the direction of the wind, so when the wind changed direction, so did we. I began an endless round of adjusting sails, reefing, easing, sheeting, shaking out, as the wind blew from five knots to twenty, and halfway around the compass. I worked the sails and tweaked the windvane, trying to bring the boat's disparate parts together to channel this incoherent wind into a steady course south. Finally, the wind settled into fifteen to twenty knots on the beam, the ingredients for a heroic sail. The rain eased to a drizzle and I stood at the helm in my jacket, watching the illuminated compass for evidence of the windvane's ability to keep us going where we want to go.

With the increased speed of the boat, and my eyes' habituation to the dark, the world became froth and low light. Our wake shook the bioluminescent plankton to life so that each wave crest glowed back at me in the exact same ghostly green as the compass light. The motion was exquisite. I, who was forever resisting metaphors of sailboats as living things, found myself enmeshed in the dance that *Pelagic* danced, picking us from trough to crest as waves came at us from three or four different directions at once, legacy of both the recent wind shifts and the opposing prevailing winds in the two hemispheres of the globe. Sometimes our motion was gentle, the boat rising buoyant at just the moment to let a whitecap slide through. Other times we put our shoulder down and pushed through ten tons of water. Spray leapt into the cockpit and was washed clean by the rain. I held onto the pedestal and let myself swing back and forth with each roll, now standing straight in a level cockpit, now suspended out over the rushing ocean. Jellyfish came sliding by, their big saucer-shape bioluminescent signatures as monuments in the green lawn of the plankton's background glow. The clouds overhead thinned. Stars shone through. A flying fish hit me in the back of the leg and rattled around in the well of the cockpit, scaly and crisp from the ocean. I was no longer needed, the wind had steadied and *Pelagic* was well on course. But I stayed at the helm, watching this display of the world as it truly was, this verity that I had not once seen before.

Finally I put a reef in the main to give myself even odds of sleeping the rest of the night through and retired, reluctantly, to my damp bunk. I woke a few hours later to hear Alisa saying, 'Shhh, Daddy's sleeping'. The cabin was alive with a thousand suns' light. Our motion was gentle, the wind almost gone. Elias was peering over the lee cloth to my bunk, finger to his lips, saying 'Thhhhh!' in his one-year-old's imitation of a shush.

Eli was, not incidentally, doing very well with the passage. He was covered by sweat night and day, leaving great salty puddles on his pillow at night, his hair plastered to his skull all day. Poor little Alaskan boy in the tropics. But he was also suddenly starting to imagine, and to act out his imaginations. He pretended to catch fish with a short line dangled from the settee to the cabin floor: 'Boom, fish!' he yelled over and over. He pretended that his toy puppy ate the birds off the page of our field guide to the birds of the tropical Pacific. When we heeled over with the spinnaker, making the most of a light breeze before the beam, he leaned forward to walk up to the high side of the saloon, like a man walking into a gale, then jumped in the air and went running downhill into his mom's lap.

And he suddenly picked words out of our sentences to repeat. 'Reef!' he said. 'Grease!'

It was one in the morning local time. We were nineteen miles north of the equator, on our sixteenth day at sea. The line would pass beneath our keel some time before dawn, after Alisa had taken over the watch. Once again we were following the conventional strategy for crossing the equator, in this case by using the motor to burn through the shifting winds and flat calms of the doldrums and ITCZ, and to carry us on to the tradewinds on the other side. We had been motoring for long stretches, thirteen hours and more at a whack, and, more predictably than I would care to admit, the autopilot was not working. As near as I could figure, the problem was a spike in voltage from the alternator through the full batteries. The solution was certainly beyond us there in the middle of the watery world, so, without much sense of surprise, we had resigned ourselves to an autopilot-less passage. The windvane still worked great when we sailed, so once we reached the southeast trades everything would be fine. In the meantime, though, we were back to standing watch all through the night and hand steering, just as we had on our endurance fest of a seven-day passage from Alaska to Washington, when the autopilot was not working and we motored for days against very light headwinds, bleary-eyed and semi-rational behind the wheel.

That passage, the nadir of the entire trip so far, was seven months earlier – before Elias could walk, and while we were still in the very difficult transition from land life to life afloat. Seven months, but enough had happened since then to fill a decade or so, it seemed, of our old life.

The steering wasn't very demanding. During my last watch in the northern hemisphere I looked at the compass every couple of minutes and made a little correction if it was needed, and I read, and wrote in my journal, as I sat beside the wheel. But I couldn't leave the wheel for more than a few seconds unless I woke Alisa, and one of us would be chained there, in the cockpit, through the day and through the night, until the wind returned.

I went to bed, and at ten minutes to five in the morning, with Alisa at the wheel, *Pelagic* crossed the equator. She tried to get a picture of the GPS reading precisely zero degrees, zero minutes latitude, but found that after our days of anticipation the actual event moved surprisingly quickly. She ended up with one photo showing us at zero degrees, 0.032 minutes north, and another showing zero degrees, 0.030 minutes south.

'I wonder when we'll be in the northern hemisphere again', said Alisa at breakfast. We had left Alaska with the vague plan of spending a year in Australia and seeing how we liked it. Now that we were in the South Pacific, our impending stay in Australia was real, and immediate, although still months away. While we had been sailing the 2000 miles that it took us to get from Kodiak to Egg Harbor, our last anchorage in Alaska, one of our favorite topics to discuss had been which Alaskan town we would likely settle in once we returned, as we were confident we eventually would. We hadn't talked about that for months, though. Now that we were so far away, returning to Alaska was too abstract an event to worry about. At our first breakfast south of the equator the GPS showed Brisbane, our likely landfall in Oz, as 4140 nautical miles away.

When ships and boats cross the equator at sea, King Neptune comes aboard to initiate first-time crossers. Normally someone who has crossed the line before, a shellback, plays the role of Neptune. We lacked a shellback, so Elias stood in, making his appearance in the cockpit after breakfast, wearing a tinfoil crown and carrying a tinfoil trident, the universally recognized emblem of his office. King Neptune decreed that the two initiates on board should each swim one lap around the boat. Alisa went first, and found that the endless blue depths beneath *Pelagic* made for a nervous swim – the careful psychology of ignoring the void beneath the keel was suddenly violated. I followed, and was amazed at the long gooseneck barnacles that had grown on the stern, in a spot kept perpetually wet by the wave created by our motion. After I scraped off the barnacles, I came aboard and found that Neptune had further plans for the captain, as befits a long-recognized moment when the hierarchies of life afloat may be reversed. He decreed a shaving of my beard and a close trim to the locks. I had been preparing for this moment for months, refraining from trimming my beard to the point where I had a satisfyingly bushy growth that, once shaved, allowed a clean contrast between my hirsute northern hemisphere and clean-cut southern hemisphere selves. After the shave, tots of seven-year old Cuban rum were drunk, and King Neptune's dram was poured overboard for his enjoyment. And then we sailed on, all three of us now confirmed shellbacks, Elias reaching this status at an astonishingly tender age.

The southeast trades turned out to be what we had in mind when we thought of tradewind sailing before this passage. The swell was gentle, the wind was behind us, sea and sky were flawless blue. Sapphire blue. We moved along effortlessly, flying the spinnaker when the wind was light and jib and staysail when it came up to fifteen knots. We finally had current with us, and started to record ridiculously good 24-hour runs: 140, 150, even 160 miles. The only flaw was the temperature. It was brutally, blisteringly, despotically hot. We huddled in the shade of the dodger when we ventured out into the cockpit, and kept Elias down below for days at a time because the sun was just too much. When the wind came forward of the beam we closed all of the hatches and portlights against spray. Deprived of ventilation, we actually began to suffer from the heat. We were always covered by a film of sweat, whether awake or asleep.

The child-rearing book encouraged us to let Elias run around without a diaper as a step towards that dreamed-of state, toilet-trained-ness. Two days after he became a shellback I looked down from the cockpit to see him starkers in the cabin, running circles in complete glee. A half-hour later Alisa called up, 'Uh, Mike, I need your help'. She spoke the sentence slowly, as if willing herself to put together the words for effective communication at the same time that her brain was struggling to make sense of the sight before her. When I came downstairs she was leaning into the head and holding Elias by both arms. I peeked through the head door and saw that he was surrounded by the wreckage of a bowel movement that, in its scale and narrative complexity, could only be called Homeric.

'I can't believe that just happened', said Alisa.

'I know what we're doing for the next hour', I said.

'Poop!' said Elias.

27

THE OTHER SIDE
OF SOMETHING

THE PASSAGE TO the Marquesas was over, and I immediately began to forget what it was.

I remember that for days the GPS in the cockpit was counting down the miles to Nuku Hiva. The favorable current kicked in behind us and we could suddenly calculate how many more days the passage might last. During the day the sun was white and its light fell like knives on the sea.

The moon was growing full. After Elias was asleep we sat in the cockpit with gin and tonics. The stars were everywhere, the sails and waves illuminated by the moon. The cockpit heeled out over the water and we braced ourselves on the high side.

I remember Alisa saying that she didn't want the passage to end, I remember that for days she looked surprised every time she told me how much she was enjoying the trip.

I remember that after weeks of leaving our wake across the sea, the constant motion was part of us. We pulled tuna out of the water and ate them an hour later. Elias watched me fillet and learned to say 'meat'. The boat travelled and travelled while the three of us stood still, sleeping in the same bunks every night and walking the same decks every day.

I remember that we had a strong sense of reaching the other side of something. I know that feeling was related to all the years we saved for the trip, the years we worked on the boat, and the months we travelled down the West Coast, trying to shoehorn our familiar lives into the new constriction of a space 37 feet long and ten feet, ten inches wide. The feeling had something to do with the dreaming and preparing, and then the doing, we finding ourselves competent in a new way of doing things and liking it, and suddenly feeling unbounded in the possibility of where we might go.

The feeling of the passage had something to do with all that, but there was something else as well. It might have just been something about how each day was built around the same schedule of meals and diaper changes and on-deck chores and ham radio nets, and therefore each so similar from one to another, but also how different each was in the details of fish caught and winds encountered and moods that suddenly swept through the little ship for no reason.

We did get to the other side of something in ourselves. But I knew that we'd have to go to sea again to remember exactly what it was.

Twenty-two days out of Cabo San Lucas, we sighted the island of Ua Huka, its glorious tropical repose mostly obscured by a shroud of towering squall clouds. On the last night of the passage we ate fresh tuna as Ua Huka and its neighboring island, Nuku Hiva, drew slowly closer. The sunset turned the islands, and the clouds, blood-red and amber. The village of Taiohae on Nuka Hiva was about ten miles distant at nightfall, and rather than enter the unfamiliar port in the dark we decided we would heave to for the night. Alisa made her nightly call to the Pacific Seafarers' net on the ham radio. We observed the ritual of putting Eli to bed, going through the commonplace steps of brushing teeth and reading books and giving goodnight kisses, all in the exotic setting of a tiny ship pitching and rolling her way down the southern hemisphere tradewinds. Alisa went to sleep and I took the first watch, slowing *Pelagic* down and conning a route between the young volcanic islands that reared up into the sky on either side of us, blocking out the stars with elementally black silhouettes unmarred by any electric lights. When the squall clouds caught up with us and it started to rain I took off my clothes and, naked beneath my deck harness, made the adjustments to heave to. For Alaskan sailors, nothing says 'somewhere far far away' like naked sailing.

After midnight the squalls intensified. Rain poured out of the skies, worthy to the task of filling a new ocean. Lightning surrounded us. Thirty bolts fell in an hour. The squalls never blew past, and we spent a raucous night hove to off of Nuku Hiva, enduring the most difficult weather of the entire passage. Whichever one of us was on watch stood in the shelter of the companionway, wondering if each lightning flash would be the one to seek out our mast as the highest object on the sea. When the pre-dawn light finally arrived it showed us a sulfurous yellow sky, crowded with clouds that sagged low towards the water. The rising sun turned that evil-looking sky into the normal leaden gray of a rainy day in the tropics. Two hours later we sailed into Baie Taiohae, tradewind swells smashing them-selves to a heaving nothing on the lava islands on either side of the entrance. In that single moment we transitioned from one world into another.

A landscape (seascape, skyscape) that looked like nothing that should have actually contained us and the shabby little fiberglass yacht.

Elias pointed at the swirl of fish and looked up at us, breathless in laughter, to make sure we saw them.

The canoes cleaved the water with purpose and efficiency.

We saw neither eggs nor chicks, and had to be content
with the sight of two adults, each flapping their wings
to hold their place on the wobbling perch.

This ocean, mile for mile, was as big for us as it was for
Magellan, or Cook, or the Polynesian navigators.

The hands of the nobles.

The title of *matapule* is hereditary, with a son assuming
the office only after his father has died.

The king looked right at her, smiled, and waved.

Exactly what we had come for - a deserted tropical island.

Alisa found one of the women she had been interacting with and completely bowled her over with the picture she had taken.

I looked at the huge space surrounding the decks of
our little ship, and I felt the ineffable peace that comes
to people who sail oceans in small boats.

We festooned all the rigging and lifelines with
clothes and cushions to dry in the sun.

After all these places we had visited, our last new country for a while.

28

DAD WENT OUT FOR WATER

P ELAGIC SWUNG TO her anchor among the thirty-odd yachts
in Baie Taiohae. I threw the last of the jerry cans into the dinghy
and started rowing in towards land. Alisa held a tear-stained Eli in the
cockpit and watched me row away. As the distance between dinghy
and sailboat grew I called back to her.

'Dad went out for twenty gallons of water', I said, 'and we never
saw him again'.

'Don't make that joke too many times', said Alisa.

Ever since leaving Alaska we had been prone to let-downs after completing passages. When places like San Diego were our landfalls,
indifferent harbors that we were visiting just because they were on
the way to somewhere better, it was easy to blame the destination.
But there is also an effect of stepping away from the simplicity and
purity of life at sea, and back into the complications of life ashore,
however briefly, that tends to bring the group vibe crashing down
no matter how wonderful the destination.

As many landfalls as we may ever make as a family, I trust that
there will be nothing quite like that end to our first long passage.

Making landfall in the Marquesas is such an evocative moment for aspiring world sailors, since it means that you are no longer a neophyte, but a bona fide ocean sailor able to safely navigate across thousands of miles of open ocean on a small boat. The Marquesas are also the first Polynesian islands that a sailor making the tradewind passage across the Pacific reaches, so getting there means that your dream has suddenly become real – *you* are about to spend months sailing downwind through the most beautiful islands on earth, not someone whose exploits you read about in a sailing magazine. And it's happening *right now*, not in some dreamed-of future.

So, sailing off those volcanic islands at night with blood-warm tropical rain running down my bare skin, my little family slumbering contentedly beneath the decks of our own little ocean-going yacht, I had the delightful and rare feeling that everything in life was working out just about perfectly, thank you very much.

But moments of transcendence are brief, even for people who have managed to chuck it all to follow a dream. As I conned *Pelagic* through the dark night between the two islands, I was conscious that this peak moment wouldn't last.

What I didn't know was how steep the drop-off might be.

Yachts clustered at anchor at the far end of the bay, all recently arrived after three or four weeks at sea. Waves crashed on the beach and pickup trucks drove along the beachfront road. Heavy green trees spread protective arms over tin-roofed buildings. Houses and gardens clung to the incredibly steep hills over the bay. The town and bay were ringed by the walls of an old caldera, a vertical wall of lava that made the little town below look like a stage setting.

Three hundred years ago raiding parties paused on the caldera rim to whoop victoriously as they carried away the body of an unfortunate local to serve at a chief's funeral feast in the next valley.

After our three weeks of blue skies and blue seas and the constant, illimitable horizon, we found ourselves in a place that was close and green. The water near shore was brown with soil washed off the mountainside by the squalls. We could smell the earth, our natural home that we were returning to after our journey through the vastness of the eastern tropical Pacific, a place that we could transit but where we could never come to rest. We smelled the earth, and its familiarity, but the specifics were all new – smells of the vibrating growth and quick rot of the tropics. It was like we were coming home to a place where the language was universal but spoken in a strong accent that we couldn't place. This, I imagine, is the dissonance that seafarers have always experienced when making landfall on distant coasts. Everything before us promised a new world – new culture, new foods, new languages, a new adventure. Alisa and I grinned at each other with excitement, brimming with the accomplishment of having reached this little corner of the oceanic world.

That first look was very nearly the peak of our experience in Taiohae. And, as is usual in these situations, we brought the seeds of our own discontent with us. After we had set the anchor and shut down the engine, we looked over the side and saw the water around us covered by an oil slick. After a moment of trying to think of some other source for the oil, we realized it must be coming from *Pelagic*. Which in turn meant that something Bad and Unexpected was happening on our boat.

When things electrical or mechanical go wrong afloat, our first recourse is to reach for Nigel Calder. His *Boatowner's Mechanical and Electrical Manual* has steered us through many a dark and tortuous crisis of boat maintenance. For the current situation, though, the big guns were called for, and I reached for the same author's *Marine Diesel Engines*. A quick read identified the oil cooler as the likely cause. I hadn't even known we had an oil cooler. But we did, and it had corroded through, so that engine oil was escaping into the cooling water and exiting the boat in the exhaust. Even worse, Nigel advised that there was also the possibility that water could siphon back into the engine through the corroded cooler.

'Water in the engine' is one of those phrases of boat ownership that I do everything in my power to avoid using.

Especially in a place like Nuku Hiva, so remote that it makes Dutch Harbor, Alaska, look like the fifth *arrondissement*.

Especially when my wife and one-year-old son and I were living on our boat with all of our household goods, completely dependent on that boat to get us the next four thousand miles to Australia.

Nigel offered me a ray of hope, noting that the engine could be run until we could locate a replacement cooler, as long as fittings could be found to bypass the failed cooler. And so our first stop in 'paradise' was devoted to the quest for suitable fittings.

I made the rounds of the local hardware store and other cruising boats, looking for the raw ingredients for a skookum jury rig. Alisa, meanwhile, was stuck watching Elias in a boat that was half torn up to provide engine access. The little fellow was in a terrible mood half the time, banging his forehead against the bulkhead in anger and frustration and screaming his fierce little animal screams that made our teeth vibrate in our skulls. I was spending most of my time crammed into our tiny engine room, sweat pouring off me as I struggled to pry various pieces free from the engine. Once again, spirits on board plummeted.

There were, of course, bright moments mixed in with all this. We went ashore that first day after the passage and found a group of Marquesans taking shelter from the rain under a covered section of the wharf. They had an instantly recognizable look, something very Polynesian with a hint of eighteenth-century English sailor mixed in: broad hips, flowered shorts, flip flops, tattoos and top knots. We made our number at the gendarmerie, and the gendarme who checked us in was friendly. Ethereal *Gygis alba* (wonderfully called 'common fairy terns' in our one field guide, more prosaically 'white terns' in the other) fluttered in the trees lining the sodden main street. Young men with striking facial tattoos galloped by on horses, riding bareback. Out on the water, brown boobies and frigate birds made a steady commerce preying on the little fish that aggregated around the anchored yachts. From *Pelagic* we looked down on black-tipped reef sharks cruising around us in their endless motion. One memorable dawn we all sat on the side decks and watched three manta rays, each of them more than three feet across, filter feeding in graceful arcs around the boat.

But the village of Taiohae offered an indifferent welcome. Alisa bought a watermelon at the store for 1000 Cour de Franc Pacifique, or CFP, the currency of French Polynesia. She did the conversion as we were walking back to the boat and announced, 'That's a fourteen dollar melon!' And then there was the remoteness we felt from the locals. We found evasive eye contact and restrained smiles to be the rule. And, greatest insult of all, Hinano, the local beer, was too expensive for our budget.

Meanwhile we were meeting some of the boats we had heard on the ham radio on the crossing from Mexico, and hearing rhapsodical stories about the smaller villages they had visited on other islands where the Polynesian warmth was almost overwhelming and the superabundance of fruit was enough to keep Marquesans and yachties satiated. But we were still stuck in Taiohae, trying to figure out the engine. Cloudy skies and high temperatures were keeping our solar panels just barely ticking over, and we couldn't charge the batteries with the engine. We cut down the fridge-running time to two hours a day, and our cartoned milk started going off.

It must sound a bit self-pitying to carry on so about a simple engine problem. But, just as with the leaking caprail on the sail from Alaska to Washington, this boat problem that made a chaos of our cabin while it refused to be fixed robbed us of the central illusion that we strove to maintain: the illusion that no matter what conditions we might find outside, retreating inside *Pelagic* would give us access to a comfortable little home afloat that was suitable for raising our son while we crossed the Pacific. Sailing huge distances with a completely dependent one-year-old kept us working with a small enough margin that the typical ups and downs of travelling became ups and disasters. And then, in the development that shouldn't have surprised us any more, but did, Alisa and I reacted to our momentary hardship by lashing out at each other, something that never happened back home in Kodiak.

The vibe on board *Pelagic* reached such a low that when Alisa fell off our anchored boat one dark night ('someone' had left the gate in the lifelines partly open), her first words on being fished out were, 'I'm glad you weren't so mad at me that you just left me in the water!'

She was joking. I think.

Every attempt to come up with suitable fittings to bypass the oil cooler had failed. Finally another sailor helped me to hacksaw the ends of the oil pipes off and link them together with a piece of fuel hose, thus bypassing the failed cooler. I spent another few hours getting the patched-together pipes back onto the engine, and then had massive second thoughts. What if the patch didn't hold? If the jury rig failed it would mean the instant loss of our engine, something that I reasonably feared given that we were about to transit through the highly tidal atoll passes of the Tuamotu Archipelago, where losing our engine at the wrong time could mean losing the boat.

I finally fired up the engine, and the patch held. Touch wood. When I changed the oil in the engine, two-thirds of a quart of seawater came out of the crankcase in addition to some heavily emulsified oil. At this point the real problem was fixed – the water was out, the engine would run fine temporarily without the cooler. But I was still left with the psychological challenge. It's hard to overstate how much I felt the responsibility of caring for this twenty-five year old boat that was meant to take my wife and son across the inky blue depths of the Pacific Ocean. A boat like *Pelagic* is nothing more than a collection of ten thousand pieces, each of which will sooner or later corrode or wear out or freeze up. I always tended to worry that some very important piece that I had ignored would announce itself by going catastrophically wrong. In a crisis, I do fine, I can keep my head and work quickly. It was the non-crisis, regular sort of boat problem that set me to worrying over my abilities to keep my little family safe as we crossed the Pacific. If it had only been Alisa and me, the pressure wouldn't have been so great. But looking at Elias' drooling little face and dimpled hands was enough to make me imagine all sorts of horrific outcomes of any possible shortcoming in the way I took care of the boat.

So now, with the oil cooler successfully bypassed, I began fixating on the oil pressure. It had always read low, and we had been reassured by the mechanic who surveyed the engine before we bought *Pelagic* that this was typical of our model, and not a problem. But after the recent engine drama I was less willing to take low oil-pressure readings in stride. And when we ran the engine at idle and saw the gauge plummet to an astonishingly low pressure, I was completely spooked.

We were finally in the Marquesas, and sweaty bouts of engine maintenance dominated each day. Alisa and I fell, one after the other, into the funk that often visited us when we reached port. Elias followed the adults around him, and the little sailor angel who had accompanied us on the passage became a snarling, pre-verbal beast of a one-year-old. I gravitated towards the worst possible interpretation of our low oil pressure and bad oil cooler, and the drawbacks of a twenty thousand dollar engine replacement were freely discussed. When we looked on the bright side we reminded each other that we could just *sail* to Tahiti or all the way to Oz if the engine conked out. But with the engine problems, and the difficulties of getting anything done while sharing the boat with Eli and his hourly temper tantrums, the wheels of our collective vibe really started coming off. Alisa and I took turns descending into Neolithic rages at the heat and the confinement and the constant baby care and Eli's high-pitched screams. And well. You really don't want to hear any more.

After nine days in Taiohae we seemed to have the engine worked out. Heavier viscosity oil overcame the tropical heat and brought the pressure back up. We stayed in Taiohae for one more day to visit with the crews of three boats that were, improbably enough, about to head to Alaska. We had dinner with these sailors on board *Compay*, the boat of a Swiss singlehander named Eric who was planning on leaving the Marquesas in mid-May for a non-stop passage to Kodiak, of all places. Alisa and I dropped our jaws to think of a boat simply sailing straight back to our home port after we had just taken ten months on the roundabout route. The dinner was a blast – the five others who made up the party were French sailors in their fifties or sixties who had an openness about them, especially the men, a quick willingness to smile that really contrasted with the cynicism and bitterness and just plain tiredness that we found in so many US and Canadian cruisers of the same age. Not to judge a nation based on five individuals, but Alisa and I came away from the meal with our Francophilia confirmed.

Elias had been acting up so badly before that dinner that we thought that one of us would have to just stay home on *Pelagic* to watch him. But we rallied, and he sat on our laps for most of the dinner with a stunned look on his face. He was so verbal at that point, and so quick to assimilate language, that all the strange noises of French being spoken seemed to leave his head spinning.

We made our excuses early to get him back to *Pelagic*, and we heard the laughter and vigorous conversation floating over the anchorage from *Compay* far into the night.

Finally, *finally*, we were ready to leave Taiohae the next day. We were only sailing about ten miles to our next stop, so we got a late start after packing up the boat all morning. Elias wouldn't stop screaming as we worked, and that noise and the feeling that we were joined at the hip on a yacht that suddenly seemed to be nothing but an endless maintenance project had adult tempers at an all-time low. Anything good that might come out of the trip just didn't seem worth the constant headaches. More than once in the previous days each of us had wondered aloud if we would make it. We kept up our smiles for strangers on other boats and then in the privacy of *Pelagic* wondered aloud if our old happiness was gone forever.

We pulled the hook and motored slowly out of the bay, pampering our patched-up engine. At the mouth of the bay we found wind. I made sail while Alisa steered. Elias started fussing in his baby car seat strapped into the cockpit. After everything else it was too much for me. Sailing with a toddler was clearly madness. I found myself screaming at him to pipe it down. 'This isn't working', I said to Alisa as *Pelagic* started feeling the tradewind swell. 'Let's just sail straight to Australia and get this kid into daycare.'

29

CROSSING THE BEACH

THE COAST THAT we sailed along was uninhabited. Vast green-clad cliffs plunged into the sea. Spires of rock stood in impossible positions where they had been left by volcanic eruptions and subsequent erosion. Clean Pacific air let the afternoon light pass nearly unobstructed, giving the whole scene a lambent overtone. Rays of sunlight defined the distance between volcanic summits and the tradewind clouds above. *Pelagic,* an animal of the sea, sailed along the north shore of Nuku Hiva.

Alisa conned us into Anaho Bay at dusk, wearing her safety harness and bikini top and shorts and a hair band over her forehead with her hair hanging loose behind. Elias sat in his car seat in the cockpit, reading a picture book. The tuna we'd caught was now steaks in the fridge, we'd had a great sail, and we had the promise of a secure anchorage for the night. Everyone was happy.

We woke to find that the anchorage was at the head of a volcanic bowl, with huge green cliffs above us. There was a channel blasted through the fringing coral reef to give access to the beach, where a few houses sat under palm trees. That day we hiked over the ridge surrounding Anaho Bay to the village of Hatehau in the bay to the west. It was May Day. Tattooed men celebrated the holiday by playing *petanque* in the muddy main street, tossing metal balls in graceful arcs. Women wearing flowers behind their ears ate vast meals at a pavilion that had been erected at the school. Children swam in the surf that broke all along the beach that fronted the village. When they spotted a shark in the waves they warned each other with the same sign we had taught Elias, a hand held over the head to mimic a dorsal fin. Back in Anaho at the end of the day, we found the people friendly. But we also felt a reserve created by the number of yachties coming through the anchorage. Fewer than ten people live in Anaho Bay. There were twelve yachts at anchor while we were there, most with two or more people on board, meaning that visitors outnumbered locals by more than two to one, and the progression of visiting yachts would continue all through the cyclone-free cruising season. In any place where the local population is outnumbered by tourists, locals inevitably stop seeing the visitors as individual people. Visitors are common enough to be unremarkable, are similar enough to each other to be classed as a homogeneous group, and are different enough from locals to be too much trouble to try to get to know.

The clichéd metaphor for cross-cultural contact in histories of the South Pacific is 'crossing the beach' – the beach as the boundary between European seagoing cultures and local island cultures. After watching our yachtie friends travelling in a scrum through the village of Hatehau, herding together to buy ice-cream and shop for souvenirs and visit the *tikis*, I became determined to cross the beach in Anaho and break through the more normal yachtie–local interaction.

The language barrier was certainly going to be a problem, since I only had the fifty-word French vocabulary that I had managed to learn on the passage from Mexico. I saw my chance when I rowed ashore to fill our jerry jugs with drinking water. An outrigger canoe powered by an outboard had arrived with a local family, back from a shopping expedition to Taiohae. The water became too shallow for the canoe a hundred yards from the beach, so the boatload of supplies had to be carried ashore piece by piece. Shared labor is a wonderfully universal sign of friendship, so I pitched in with the half dozen other people who were ferrying loads across the calf-deep water.

No one would make eye contact with me. Afterwards, a big bearded biker-looking fellow named Ta'aroa helped me carry jerry jugs of water back to our dinghy. It seemed like we had made a friend, but the next day when Alisa took Ta'aroa a loaf of bread she had baked, he said he wasn't hungry.

So Alisa stood there on the beach in front of Ta'aroa and two other men, with a fresh-baked loaf of bread in her hand, not sure how to retreat gracefully with her spurned gift in this place where the habit of giving seemed so deeply infused through the culture.

'Maybe Ta'aroa just wasn't hungry?' I suggested afterwards.

'I know, I thought of that. But then I just felt so stupid, standing on the beach in front of this group of men with a loaf of bread in my hand.'

'Maybe he didn't want to have to reciprocate?'

'I thought of that, too. It's just so hard to know what's going on.'

'Maybe we should leave tomorrow.'

'I was thinking the same thing.'

And so we availed ourselves of the great right of yachties: our dispensation, if the locals didn't feel like getting down with us, or if we felt like seeing something different, or just for no reason at all, of moving on. Every bay we visited was at first full of the promise of a place we'd never been to before, and then, a few days later, became a place that we would likely never see again.

That night I rowed in for more water. A group of teachers and students was visiting from Tahiti, sleeping in tents on the beach and getting down with their Marquesan brethren. People were eating under the tin-roofed pavilion just behind the beach, and a local man named Michel, hugely obese with a thick black mustache and shaved head, sent me home with a dozen bananas and a kilo of barbecued goat meat. I rowed back through the gap in the reef in the gathering dark, listening to Ta'aroa and two other men and a woman playing music under a palm tree. They played two guitars and a ukulele and the spoons and they sat straight-backed on the beach, looking out to their bay where boats from all over the world arrived for no reason and then went, in the way that sailing vessels have visited this bay and these islands and these people for hundreds of years. They sat straight-backed, their strumming hands moving in unison, and sang out to the bay with their heads tilted back so that they might have been looking at the mountains on the other side of the bay or at the stars that were beginning to dominate the sky.

Alisa and Elias and I ate the bananas and goat meat for dinner and we puzzled over the kindness of this parting gift from a place where our various attempts at friendship had fallen flat. Getting to know a place like Anaho Bay, we agreed, was the project of a year and not something that would bear fruit over our four-day stay. As we went to sleep under the open forward hatch, we could hear the reedy, vowel-rich Marquesan singing that reached us over the dark still water from the beach. It was beautiful, plaintive music, a music of endurance, music that said, 'we're still here'.

30

GETTING DOWN
WITH THE PEOPLE

IF YOU TRAVEL you tell yourself stories about the people you meet. There are so many people and they all sweep by so quickly. The traveler needs to make sense of this parade of people, needs to differentiate them if there is to be any point in travelling at all. So a story assembled from a few observations turns a chance acquaintance into a person of depth, a person who stands on the platform of their unique history and bears the uncertainty of their own future. In a way these stories are all that a person has to show from travelling – the views of so many famous sights fall into dust when he tries to recount them back home. So the traveler maintains confidence in his stories, but he also knows that the stories he builds for himself are like newspaper stories, written to seem complete no matter where the editor decides to cut them. When the traveler's story ends it always seems final, even if another sentence would have changed it into something different completely.

The five spires that towered over the island of Ua Pou ('WA-poo') as we sailed in turned out to be the backdrop for the village of

Hakahetau. With the gray stone rising vertically into the tradewind clouds that forever sat over the island, with the steep beach continually worried by breakers, with the dense green foliage that hid everything from view except a few waterfront buildings, Hakahetau as seen from the water was the tropical paradise that westerners have been idealizing ever since the days of Captain Cook.

The anchorage was rolly, and the beach was a steep, wave-punished affair that would be too dramatic for our little rowing dinghy. Luckily, there was a modern concrete wharf that provided a protected space for dinghies. We rowed inside the wharf and found steps leading from the water to the wharf top. But it was low tide, and the lowest step was separated from the water by six feet of vertical concrete. Someone had hung a homemade rope ladder off the steps to bridge the gap: a very slippery, unstable rope ladder. I rowed up to the bottom of the ladder. It swayed back and forth with the waves, the bottom steps coated with green algae. I looked at little Elias sitting in Alisa's lap, his trusting one-year-old face squeezed between oversized lifejacket and sunhat, and then I looked back at the ladder.

A voice called down from the wharf, 'You want me to take the boy?'

I looked up to see a youngish man, his face almost entirely hidden by a pair of huge square sunglasses, a New York Yankees cap worn backwards over his long black hair. He wore a tank top that revealed one arm covered in traditional tattoos and the other tattooed with designs that looked like they came from a French heavy metal magazine.

If you travel with a very young child, you will be faced with situations when you find yourself willfully ignoring the little voice in your head that warns you against things like handing your one-year-old from a tippy dinghy to a stranger leaning down from a slick wharf step. And so, as surprised to hear English from the first person we met as we were glad for the help, I stood up, hefted Elias up over my head, and handed him to the stranger, who grabbed him just as the dinghy was lifted to the top of a passing wave.

Alisa and I scrambled up the ladder and met our helper, Holer Hokaupoko. Elias was standing a few paces behind Holer, the blank look on his face announcing that he was waiting for the adults on the scene to make the next move. Holer asked us where we were from and, almost before we could answer, invited us for lunch at his father's house the next day. We were touched by this evidence of the traditional Polynesian hospitality, the demise of which Westerners have been lamenting ever since the death of Captain Cook. We were no less touched, though a little puzzled, when Holer added, 'I invite you, so you do not pay.'

The next day was Sunday, and attendance at either of the two churches in the village was nearly universal. On the way from the wharf to Holer's father's house we lingered outside the Protestant church where people were mingling in the street and waiting for the service to begin. The men wore slacks and floral print shirts and had single flowers tucked behind their ears. The women wore crowns of flowers and floral print dresses. Half of the fifty people gathered wore clothes made from the same fabric – yellow and red and white flowers against a blue background, repeated over and over in the men's shirts and women's dresses. Two other fabrics clothed the other half of the group: one green with white flowers, the other red with white flowers. The effect was of three species of birds flocking together. The birds all filed into the church and began singing hymns in Marquesan, a sound warm and solid like a great piece of mahogany.

At Holer's father's house the kitchen was a separate building in the back yard, with no walls and a dirt floor. There was a stereo, a water tap, a cookstove, a table and chairs, and a daybed. At the table was Etienne, Holer's father who was mentioned in our cruising guide as being eager to meet visiting sailors. People in Ua Pou use both French and Marquesan names, and you usually get only one when you meet someone: thus Etienne, father of Holer and A'tai. Etienne was fleshy and subdued and wore glasses and big sideburns that gave him the look of an intellectual from the 1970s. On the other side of the table were the Americans Rick and Dianne, who had a 60-foot schooner anchored next to us in the bay. Etienne was holding CFP notes that were folded together, a 1000 franc note on the outside, but neither he nor anyone else looked at the money.

We had been invited for one o'clock but the others for twelve so Alisa and I ate while the others watched. We ate *poisson cru,* which was delicious, and we ate fish fried whole. In order not to waste the fish like a spoiled Westerner I sucked at the bones and paid special attention to the meat on the head. We ate tender bits of beef that we later realized were likely horse, marinated and grilled on a stick. We ate breadfruit and drank instant coffee. When the meal was over Holer took my plate. I could tell from his face that I hadn't been thorough enough with the fried fish.

Etienne told us he had been born in Anaho Bay on Nuku Hiva and adopted immediately, taken on his first horseback ride when he was two hours old, over the ridge to Hatiheu and his new home. At ten he was adopted again, by a man from Liverpool, and learned English. Rick and Dianne told us their schooner had previously been a floating casino somewhere in the US, with black shag carpet on the bulkheads and a roulette table in the center of the cabin. After doing service as a casino the schooner had been used to smuggle drugs and after that it sank. Rick and Dianne bought the schooner at a Drug Enforcement Agency auction and fixed everything, beginning by tearing up the sodden carpet.

After the difficulties in crossing the beach in Anaho Bay we were delighted to fall in with English-speaking Marquesans. Holer said something about fixing coconut chicken for us another time and we said we would be very glad for that. That evening when we were back on *Pelagic* Elias kindly took a nap before dinner so Alisa and I were able to sit in the cockpit with gin and tonics in our hands like proper cruising sailors, watching the racing canoes that came out in the evening. They were one – and two – and six-person canoes, made of fiberglass but loyal to the lines of their Polynesian descent, each with a narrow hull stabilized by a single short outrigger mounted on two elegantly curved wooden crosspieces. The men in the canoes returned our waves even if it meant losing their stroke. They paddled hard, and the canoes cleaved the water with purpose and efficiency.

The racing canoes sizzling by our anchored sailboat rounded off the scene in a very satisfying way. Out to sea was the sun, getting ready to end the day with its swift and mercilessly beautiful setting. Behind us were the giant rock spires of Ua Pou turning blood-red in the failing light, below them the little village of Hakahetau that was already in the shadow of dusk. And out here on the water with us were Polynesians, paddling the descendants of swift war-making canoes. The scene strengthened my impression of the Marquesas as a version of Hawai'i from an alternate universe. Like the Hawai'ian archipelago, they are geologically young islands of Oceania, high and volcanic, clustered together and separated from all other land by extremely great distances. But unlike Hawai'i, there is no urbanization, the population is overwhelmingly Polynesian, and you hear the indigenous language everywhere.

Holer's brother, A'tai Hokaupoko, paddled his canoe up to *Pelagic*. I had seen him an hour earlier as we were getting into the dinghy at the wharf: a slender man in his mid-thirties, his black hair in a single braid down a back that was v-shaped from paddling, holding his canoe with the hull on one side of him and the outrigger on the other, waiting for a pause in the breakers that swept the steep gravel beach. When he paddled up to *Pelagic* he went through very little in the way of small talk. He just asked if I spoke French, learned to his disappointment that I did not, struggled on nonetheless in English, and invited me to go goat hunting the next day. Equally surprised by the invitation and its abrupt delivery, I accepted.

The whole point of travel, after all, is Getting Down With the People – sharing genuine moments of everyday life with those who see the world through the lens of a different culture, and through that experience discovering touchstones of common humanity. Now, 'discovering touchstones of common humanity' sounds like a phrase from a PhD dissertation in one of the softer social sciences. But really, aside from the desire to finally see what my wife looked like in a bikini after seven years of marriage, it was the idea of Getting Down With the People in beautiful, out-of-the-way bits of Oceania that convinced me that moving onto a sailboat with my family might be a better idea than spending the last years of my thirties sitting in an office.

The plan was to meet A'tai at four the next morning. I woke at three thirty, and was on deck twenty minutes later. A flashlight was already shining from the wharf, pointed at *Pelagic* and swinging back and forth impatiently. I flashed my headlight back in response and rowed to the wharf. The night was purest black, with no moon. The mountains above were indicated only by the negative space they created in the field of stars, steep spires of nothing that reached into the sky.

I followed A'tai down the dark street, keeping track of his where-abouts by the sounds of his walking. He coughed and spat, and the sound took on a strange intimacy in the stillness of the night. At his house A'tai made me instant coffee, the fluorescent light above us making the whites of his eyes a dull blue, accentuating the hollows of his cheeks and his hooked nose. His face was lined and his skin was pulled tight around his eye sockets. It was a desiccated Arab-looking face, not the face of someone who lived in a lush tropical place like Ua Pou.

Holer pulled up in front of the house in their father's pickup. A'tai went behind the house and came back holding a dog by the scruff of the neck so that its front legs were off the ground, with three other dogs running ahead into the dark street, yelping and snarling with the excitement of being taken to hunt. Amid great commotion A'tai tried to get the dogs loaded into the truck, but he eventually settled for letting three dogs chase after us while we drove up the mountain, the fourth dog who had fought too much staying behind on his chain.

We stopped at a clearing high on the mountain and stood by the truck and waited for dawn. The dogs caught up a minute later, their tongues hanging far out of their mouths in the headlights. When first light came the island of Ua Pou was revealed around us in different shades of gray. The shimmering gray tropical Pacific was beating against the lava cliffs below, the hills and valleys around us were smothered under dark gray vegetation. The high spires above our heads were still hidden in mist. To the north, across the profound depths of the open Pacific, the hulking shape of Nuku Hiva was slowly coming into relief. The morning was cold, and A'tai wore a green army jacket. The smells of the island were slowly coming to life: the smell of panting dog and sweating man, the smell of rotting breadfruit fallen from a forgotten tree.

A'tai unwrapped his rifle from a towel. He pulled a plastic jar from his pack and tipped a pile of .22 cartridges into his hand. With his blunt fingers he selected a dozen bullets from the pile, and loaded them into the rifle.

The eastern sky was now properly lit up, orange and lilac. Dawn was close. Holer drove back down the mountain. I followed A'tai into the bush.

We walked along a ridge as the sun finally rose from the ocean.

The forest on the mountainside beneath became a full green, splashed with amber highlights. The three dogs followed behind A'tai. He explained that the black one would be no good since his brother had been left behind. The second, a bitch, was white with tan spots. An earlier hunt for boar had left her with a hairless pink scar the length of her body and a hole through her right hind leg. The third dog was dirty-white and heavily scarred around its snout. That one did the real work, A'tai said. They were hunting dogs, dogs that existed only to do the work of helping A'tai shoot goats and pigs. All three had chunks missing from their ears.

A few minutes later the dogs rushed off after a goat.

'*Huish, huish*', A'tai called. Go, go.

After the initial rush of motion the dogs stopped on the mountainside below us, out of sight in the brush, and barked. A'tai decided the goat was on a cliff where the dogs could not reach it. '*Mai, mai*', he called after the dogs. Come, come.

After another half-hour of walking, the dogs rushed ahead of us and brought a pig to bay. I say it was a pig merely on the authority of what A'tai told me, since the brush was so thick that I couldn't see it. A'tai couldn't see it either. All we knew was that the dogs were making a furious racket in the brush on the steep hillside below us. A'tai crawled out on a tree limb that gave him a platform over the hillside and shot twice into the brush. Shot, that is, without being able to see what he was shooting at. After he shot, the dogs quieted down.

A'tai came down from the tree and said, 'I think I kill my dog.'

He called '*Mai! Mai!*' into the bush and we walked off along the trail. A few minutes later all three dogs followed us.

After these first unsuccessful run-ins, A'tai got a clear shot at another goat. This goat was part of a group of goats that very foolishly stood on the patch of mountainside they had browsed back to bare earth and stared at A'tai as he crept closer with his rifle. A'tai shot and then ran up and was disgusted to not find the goat lying neatly on the ground. It was left to me to point out the big puddle of goat blood, but A'tai dismissed the suggestion that it might be a good idea to follow the trail of blood in case it led to a dead goat twenty yards away in the bush.

It is inappropriate and dull to judge others through your own cultural prejudices. But hunting was a big part of our life in Alaska. Our annual consumption of wild food in Kodiak included, in addition to twenty or thirty salmon and a few halibut and many gallons of berries, the two deer that Alisa and I shot, butchered, and packed out of the mountains ourselves at the end of every summer. I had my own standards for hunting that were hard for me to forget on the mountain slopes of Ua Pou. Standards like: Only shoot if you know what you're going to hit. And: If you wound an animal, go get it.

Unchecked populations of feral animals spell disaster for island ecosystems. So I suppose that having A'tai ranging around the mountains a few mornings every week, taking potshots at every pig and goat he saw, would have the effect of protecting whatever was left of the native flora of Ua Pou. But I was sour over the style of hunting I had seen. I started thinking of the morning as a tour through Old MacDonald's ecosystem: with a shot at a goat here, with a shot at a pig there, ee-ai-ee-ai-o.

I didn't know the half of it.

We sat down for a break. A'tai was subdued. Then a feral chicken walked by. The three dogs cocked their heads and stared at it, but didn't move. A'tai waited until the chicken had walked up to within fifteen yards of us and shot.

The bird squawked away into the bush, apparently unhurt. This increased A'tai's disgust at not getting anything, and added dismissive feelings towards his marksmanship to my already generally dismissive feelings about the whole hunt. The morning now nearly over, we started walking back towards the village.

That's when we came across the horses.

There were four of them, big bays that were living wild. We found them in a dry stream bed that we were following up a brush-choked valley. The horses made the same error as the goats. They stood still and looked at us with their liquid brown eyes as we walked up to them. A'tai was a step ahead of me. The day was getting hot and flies were buzzing around the dry stream bed. I could smell fresh horse droppings, and past that the fainter dusty-sweaty smell of the horses' coats. A'tai raised the rifle to his shoulder and said to me, 'I shoot one.'

It is hard to exaggerate what a bad idea it is to shoot a grown horse, from a distance of twenty yards or so, with an inaccurate .22 rifle. A horse is a very large animal. A .22 is a very small bullet. You could kill a horse with a .22 from that distance, but based on the shooting I had seen so far, it would take a lot of shots and a long time. Meanwhile there would be a screaming, struggling horse and more unpleasantness than a few horse steaks would seem to justify.

I waited, wondering what A'tai would do.

After a long moment of looking through his sights he lowered the rifle and threw a rock at the horses. 'You lucky!' he called out as they ran away.

A few minutes later we regained the ridge where the morning had begun. I pulled out my camera and took a snap of A'tai holding his rifle with the spires of Ua Pou in the background. He then insisted on taking a picture with my camera of me holding the rifle. I got the feeling he was acting out his part in a script that had been worked out on other hunts with other visitors, and that getting your picture taken holding the islander's gun was a part of the experience that he knew visitors liked.

I hadn't wanted my photo taken with the gun. But it was

instructive to look at the picture later and to see how forced my smile had become by that point in the day.

We returned to A'tai's house and consoled ourselves with his home-grown marijuana. For all the writing about the Marquesas in sailing magazines and sailing books, I have never seen mention of how ubiquitous marijuana is in those islands. After you have been there for a few weeks, you start to get the feeling that the lush green silhouettes of the islands are mostly comprised of marijuana plants. A certain class of sailor finds the absence of social opprobrium surrounding *pakololo* very much to their liking. Fifty-something year old men who had been living respectable lives and climbing career ladders suddenly found themselves wearing beaded Polynesian necklaces and in need of a hair cut. Forty-somethings who had managed to acquire a cruising yacht without ever really entering the straight world let themselves go completely and started to do things like sailing two days upwind to revisit an island they had already been to so that they could trade a surfboard to someone's uncle for a trash bag full of dope. These were the same cruisers who looked up after a completely relaxing two months in the Marquesas and realized how far they had to go before they were out of French Polynesia, and how soon their visas were going to run out.

A'tai and I pulled off our sweaty shirts and relaxed in the privacy of his walled-off yard. He wore traditional tattoos in a great swath across his chest and left shoulder. The sun was overhead, the saturated ground of the yard was steaming around us, and laconic snippets of conversation from the street made their way over the wall. A'tai showed me the stock of his gun, carved with the letters *Hoka*, short for Hokaupoko, his surname, and *Teikimaakautoua*, a Marquesan word that he translated as 'king think war'. He also unselfconsciously explained the symbols in his various tattoos. Under his pointing finger the swirls and geometrical patterns across his chest and shoulders resolved themselves as a series of stylized male and female faces and idealized marine animals: sharks, manta rays, moray eels.

The next day we came ashore and met a man named Ishmael who was settling into a day of drinking beer underneath a tree with his friends. He gave me a bottle of cold Hinano beer and we were finding our way into a slow conversation of bad English and no French when Etienne drove up in his truck with his daughter Belladonna.

'We are here to pick you up', said Etienne.

'But we're just visiting with these people.'

Etienne looked over the top of his glasses at Ishmael and his friends, then back at me. 'Holer is making you a chicken', he said.

Ishmael wasn't surprised to see the visitors plucked away from him. I drank the rest of his beer riding in Etienne's truck. When we reached the house Holer was grinding coconuts to make coconut milk. He gave us his big loose grin.

A few days later we were invited to dinner at the house of A'tai. Later Holer explained that the invitation meant we would pay 500 francs each instead of a 1000, and we begged off. It began to feel that we were building up unspoken obligations with Holer and A'tai and Etienne, that they were professional friends to sailors who would eventually want to be compensated. From a local's perspective in Hakahetau, this sort of relationship makes all the sense in the world. There is a steady stream of people visiting their village in yachts. There are few sources of cash income in the village. The people on the yachts are much much wealthier than anyone in the village and they want to meet some locals and experience a bit of Ua Pou. So why wouldn't a family like the Hokaupokos get involved in a little informal tourism business.

Except that I never felt like paying money as a shortcut to friendship in a new culture. It also felt that our visit was being managed to some extent, that we were sometimes plucked away when we tried to meet someone outside the family. So we simply decided we would invite Holer out for a goodbye dinner and then leave the next day.

Holer loved the pizza that Alisa made. He asked if she had made it in the boat in the same way that he had made Marquesan food for us at his father's house, and when I said yes he said it was the best pizza he had ever tasted, much better than the pizza he used to buy in Tahiti. During the day his big stoner sunglasses gave him a distant look. But now under the red nightlight of our cockpit, without the sunglasses, Holer's eyes were young and engaging.

'To live in Tahiti, not possible,' he explained. 'I am crazy. No land, no business, no mango tree, no breadfruit tree. Here I can eat without buying. In Tahiti it cost me 5000 francs each day to eat.'

We were eating in the cockpit, under a skyfull of stars. After we were done eating Elias came up to the cockpit and I gave him a horsey ride on my knee.

'What song you sing?' asked Holer. It took me quite a while to realize that he was asking me what I was saying to Elias as I dandled him on my knee. I hadn't thought of 'giddyup, giddyup, let's go' as a song, but I suppose it is. I explained cowboys and the etymology of 'giddyup'.

'I like this very much, learning life of American peoples', said Holer.

Not too much later I rowed him back to the wharf. If we had left that morning I would have told myself a story about Holer as an informal operator in an out of the way village, friendly towards us while he waited to see if we would pay a couple thousand francs for some fruit from his father's yard. But after our dinner on *Pelagic* I had a different story. That story ended with Holer as a straightforward island guy who was naturally friendly and curious, spoke four languages, didn't know much of the world outside of French Polynesia, and just wanted to be friends with the people who came to visit his bay.

31

YOU WOULD KNOW

'WHICH ATOLLS ARE you visiting in the Tuamotus?'
That was the great question among sailors in the
Marquesas.

Like many of the other first-time cruisers who were making the
trip across the Pacific, we had been so engrossed in preparing the boat
beforehand that we hadn't learned much about the islands that we
would be visiting. The Marquesas are the logical first stop if you're
coming from Mexico, but when we left La Paz we hadn't even been
sure which island in the group would be our first stop. We figured we
could learn enough from our library of reference books to make that
decision on the way. It was only when the ham radio began carrying
stories of the miserable experiences of cruisers arriving before us in
the inadequate anchorage at Atuona that we decided to check in at
Taiohae, the other port of entry in the group.

The Marquesas were easy to choose among – there are only nine
major islands. The next island group on the downwind route through
French Polynesia is the Tuamotus. There is nothing easy about the
Tuamotus. This begins with the simple question of picking a few
atolls from among the forty-odd that have passes big enough to allow

yachts access through their fringing reefs. The cruising guides we had on hand were fairly useless in helping us make the choice, since they mostly avoided making any concrete recommendations. And if they did make a recommendation, they guaranteed the favorably-mentioned island would be swarmed with visiting yachts. Cruising sailboats exhibit an indefatigable herd instinct. For whatever reason, boats concentrate their visits on the same islands, congregate in the same anchorages on those islands, and even cluster tightly around each other within those anchorages. We expected that herd effect to be even stronger in the Tuamotus, given their reputation.

The Tuamotu Archipelago is a vast swath of coral atolls scattered in a southeast–northwest direction between the Marquesas and the Society Islands. They are low atolls that cannot be seen from a great distance, with strong tidal currents among them that can sweep an unsuspecting boat onto a reef. In the pre-GPS era, when yachts navigated by eyeball, dead reckoning and imprecise celestial navigation, the combination of difficult-to-see hazards and uncertainty in a vessel's location made the Tuamotus a deadly place, and they were known as the 'Dangerous Archipelago'. Back then most yachts just passed the islands by. Now, with the everyday miracle of GPS, the Tuamotus are open to the run-of-the-mill yachtie, and the treasures of that incredible place are available for all to sample. But there are still the strong tidal currents through the passes, and the chance of position errors in pre-GPS charts that can bring a vessel relying entirely on GPS to grief. The place still has a wicked reputation, and there was an edge of nerves in the question 'which atolls are you visiting?'

We had the good luck to meet Pierre in Taiohae, who was heading to Alaska on his yacht *Kea*. For years he had been managing a fleet of charter boats in the nearby Society Islands, and he had lots of experience cruising the Tuamotus. He came over to *Pelagic* and we shared a great session of trading local knowledge: we showed him all of our favorite haunts in the Gulf of Alaska on the chart, and he gave us his insider's guide to the best of the Tuamotus. We told him about bears on the beach, and glaciers, and hot springs. He told us about skin-diving in passes, and picking coconuts from the trees, and using floats to hold our anchor chain off the bottom, so that it wouldn't wrap around coral heads. In case we were missing the point of what sort of experience awaited us, he occasionally pointed at a favorite anchorage on the chart, kissed his fingertips, and said, '*Magnifique!*'

'That was great,' I said to Alisa after Pierre left.

'I know,' she said. 'Let's not tell anyone else what he recommended.'

We returned to Daniel's Bay on Nuku Hiva for our last stop in the Marquesas. We knew this was a place where we could stock *Pelagic* with fruit and water and prepare for the sail to the Tuamotus. We figured that a couple of days would be adequate to address the usual list of tasks before we put to sea. But then Alisa, bless her, realized that it was Wednesday afternoon, which meant that by the universal conventions of both sea and land the next day would be Thursday, and the day after that Friday. And *Pelagic* didn't start any long trip on a Friday. When we told other cruisers that, we often heard responses like, 'Oh, you're superstitious.' Alisa and I didn't think of it that way. Knocking on wood three times when we talk about something bad happening is superstition. Not leaving port on Friday is more of a maritime tradition, one that was strongly established on many of the commercial fishing boats that we had been aboard in Alaska. We both had tremendous respect for the fishermen of the Gulf of Alaska and Bering Sea, and one of the ways that we showed it is by observing the ban on Friday departures. Plus, it's fun to have a few little rules to organize your life around when you're out on a sailboat, immersed in Personal Freedom.

So we just got the dang barky ready and put to sea on Thursday, rather than cooling our heels until Saturday. It was just as well, too, as the list of pre-departure jobs is invariably padded with wish items that are fit tasks for someone's dream yacht, but don't have much to do with a boat that is sailing places.

Nuku Hiva is such a tiny landmass that it has no chance of changing winds and currents much in all the oceanic vastness, so the big-ocean sailing begins as soon as you clear the lava cliffs guarding whatever little bay you're leaving from. One hour we were anchored up in Daniel's Bay, and the next we were back on passage, sailing down the trades, eighteen knots of wind in the sails and boisterous seas on the port quarter. We set a course for Makemo Atoll, 450 miles away.

We didn't realize it at the time, but we were in for a Memorable Passage.

Events began to unfold as we were leaving the lights of Ua Pou to port, when the pump on the head quit working. That is, the pump that takes whatever is in the head and pumps it out into the sea. I maintain, and there are few who will argue, that opening up the head pump is *the* worst job on any boat. We had just spent forty-two consecutive nights comfortably at anchor in the Marquesas, when I would have at least had the convenience of an even keel for tackling the awful job of fixing the pump if it had gone bad. Apparently realizing this, the pump waited until our first evening offshore to stop working.

I grimly set to work. The head door was closed to deny Eli access, and the sweet-sick odor of the pump filled the little compartment. I had the head fan blasting down on me but I was still saturated with sweat. It pooled in the hollows of my clavicles and my feet left little sweat puddles on the shower grate. Meanwhile the boat was heeling fifteen or twenty degrees and rolling along at seven and a half knots. After more than an hour I gave up for the night. I joined Alisa in the cockpit, a little seasick from working in the closed compartment, chilled from the drying sweat, and grossed out by the mess.

The next morning I was back at it, determined to get the head working. The various flaps and valves inside the pump were so covered with scale that I was surprised it had worked for as long as it had. When I finally emerged victorious from the head after three hours or so, I was dehydrated and cross-eyed with frustration.

Alisa had coached Elias to clap his hands and say, 'Yeah, Daddy!'

'It says a lot that you haven't even had a cup of coffee yet', Alisa said. 'I was ready for you to just decide that we would have to wait until the Tuamotus to get it working.'

I ate a victory lunch of eggs and bread and coffee.

An hour later I puked it all into the ocean. I was suddenly very sick, sick enough that I wanted nothing more than to just lie on the cockpit seat and let the world go by. I rallied enough to go down to the cabin and lie down. A few minutes later I took a sip of water. That sent me scrambling back to the cockpit as the sip of water came back up, immediately and painfully. I dry-heaved over the lifelines until there was nothing in my stomach whatsoever.

I went back down below and lay down. Alisa looked at me with a frown of concern. I just wanted to go to sleep. She got out a quart of pedialyte, the oral rehydration mix that we carried for Eli (knock on wood). Alisa held a teaspoon of the stuff up to my lips and let me slowly sip it down. It came back up so violently that I gave up on trying to reach the cockpit and just sprinted for the head sink.

When I had rinsed my mouth out and retreated to the bunk Alisa sat down next to me.

'I'm worried about you', she said.

'I can't stop sweating', I said. The pillow under my head was squishy with my perspiration. I was conscious, in a fairly abstract way, of how much it was asking of Alisa to handle both boat and baby while I remained on my back. My more immediate concern was the feeling that I just wanted to disappear into the cushions beneath me.

'I'm going to call your sister,' Alisa said. My sister is a doctor.

Alisa went up to the cockpit with the sat phone. Elias started screaming for her, 'Mommy! Mommy! Mommy!' in a one-year-old's unadulterated outpouring of grief and longing, while he was standing about a foot and a half from my head. I had him hold my hand, but that didn't stop him from screaming for Alisa. The best measure of how rotten I was feeling by this point is that Elias was in full tantrum that close to me, and I basically didn't care.

Alisa relayed a few questions about symptoms from my sister and then ended the call. When she came down she picked up Elias and said to me, 'Jenny says you should start taking anti-nausea meds'.

'But those are rectal suppositories.'

'That's right.'

'Am I that sick?'

'You're that sick. I'll get them out for you.'

I must admit that they did the trick. Even if they had melted in the tropical heat. After an hour I was able to keep down an antibiotic. The kicker is that the anti-nausea meds are also tranquilizers, so I went from listless to catatonic. For the next few hours Alisa woke me up every five minutes to give me two teaspoons of pedialyte, per my sister's instructions, until I had a whole quart down. Meanwhile the wind had built to twenty-five knots and *Pelagic* was beginning to round up and fall off, as the windvane had less and less success keeping us on course.

Alisa and I talked over the steps to take. The tradewinds were booming behind us, so rather than heave to and wait until I got better, we elected to keep travelling towards our landfall. 'First thing is to put another reef in the main', I said.

Alisa clipped Elias into his eating chair and set his dinner in front of him – a bowl of cold cereal. After feeding me another two teaspoons of pedialyte and putting on her headlamp and deck harness, she was ready. The whole scene seemed distant to me – after I got down my ration of pedialyte I just collapsed back onto my stinking pillow and retreated into myself. It was only when I saw Alisa taking a deep breath at the bottom of the companionway steps and saying out loud, 'Come on, you can do this, Lis', that I realized how deep she was digging to simultaneously care for me, Elias and *Pelagic*.

By the next day I was better. Simple as that. We had no idea what incapacitated me so severely, though the hypothesis that I got sick from exposure to the inside of the head pump enjoyed favor. I sat in the cockpit for much of the next day, eating a little and drinking a lot of water and regaining my strength. The whole episode reminded me of what a challenging proposition it was to sail our little ship across the Pacific. I knew that I would let out a huge sigh of relief when we reached Oz. But I also suspected that I would feel a huge letdown.

Getting better meant that I was able to enjoy some of the sweetest sailing that we ever had on *Pelagic*.

We were aiming to get just a little further south in the archipelago than was absolutely convenient from the Marquesas given the prevailing southeasterly winds, reasoning that putting up with a little windward sailing on the passage would reward us with time in some less-visited spots. So we had the wind on the beam or forward of it for the whole trip, which kept *Pelagic* heeling over. This made life a little inconvenient for Elias, and kept Alisa and me worried and vigilant on his part. But it also made the trip more exciting, as we could feel *Pelagic* working gracefully to carry us into wind and sea, straining her fibers to do what she was designed for, instead of just drifting downwind with the trades like a log raft.

And so we carried along for a bit more than three days, keeping an eye on our course to make sure we didn't sag down to leeward. The wind kept up in the lower twenties the whole way, which is plenty. Waves crashed across the bow and water poured out of the starboard scupper. If the person on watch stood in the back half of the cockpit they would be doused by the spray that kicked up high in the air. But getting wet didn't matter, since we were in the heart of the tropics and the wind and sun would have us dry in ten minutes. The little hammock under the solar panels was full of *pamplemousse* from Daniel's Bay, the giant, sweet, pine-tasting citrus fruits of French Polynesia. We had two stalks of bananas lashed to the overturned dinghy, one green and one yellow, and the sunset every night was as fine as anything you could ask for. At night the stars were revealed in their true intensity, without the interference of any artificial light anywhere, and we beheld the heavens illuminated as brightly as they had been for Copernicus. Once I was well the trip became something that I would not shuffle off this mortal coil without having experienced, a memory that will be my consolation in old age. There is nothing like being alone with your family in a small boat far out to sea for showing you just how vast the world is, and how magnificent.

If you had been there, you would know.

32

SOMNOLENT AND
SUN-BEATEN

THE NOTABLE THING about our arrival in Makemo was how badly we screwed up the anchoring. We transited the pass and pulled up in front of the village of Pouheva and dropped the hook, savoring the new feeling of anchoring *inside* an island, in the protected atoll lagoon that was surrounded by a nearly continuous ring of coral reef and low sandy islands. Tradewind clouds towered over the scattered white buildings of the village. Coconut palms rattled in the wind. Light seemed to glow upwards from the turquoise water.

The moment when the anchor went over the bow was always the moment when a passage officially ended, when *Pelagic* became fixed in place and we began reorienting ourselves from the joys and vicissitudes of ocean sailing to the novelties of the new bit of land that we had reached. This time, though, the anchor dropped until it was just touching the bottom and then came to a halt. The anchor chain had fallen over itself in the chain locker during the passage and tangled. Alisa and I both jumped below to untangle the mess, but by the time we had the chain running free it was obvious that it had been a mistake for us to both work on the chain while *Pelagic* was left to her own devices. In the steady tradewinds the boat had dragged while we were working on the chain and we were now way too close to a big anchored catamaran whose crew was ashore. When we tried to pull the anchor to move away from the cat we found that our anchor had hooked under their chain, so that their boat and our boat were now bound to each other. We tried pulling our chain as tight as we could with the windlass, until *Pelagic* shuddered with the strain and our anchor was holding the cat's chain up off the bottom. Then we let go of our chain all at once, hoping that our anchor would swim out from under their chain as it fell to the bottom. We tried this a couple times without success. And each time the tradewinds pushed us closer to the cat's bows.

Elias, meanwhile, was hollering his head off in his car seat in the cockpit. I was tired from being up most of the night before. And, well, everything generally sucked. But on the third try our anchor swung free.

It must sometimes seem that Alisa and I spent our sail to Australia lurching from minor crisis to minor crisis, though it rarely felt that way to us at the time. But this was one moment when things aboard were tense enough that when we finally had our anchor back, Alisa looked up at me and said, 'Maybe the Tuamotus aren't for us. Maybe we should just go back out the pass and keep going.'

Luckily Alisa took Elias below to try to get him to nap. I took the opportunity to throw the anchor in again, this time a long long way upwind of the cat. But even though the chain ran free this time, the anchor just dragged across the bottom without setting, and we ended up dragging down on the cat again. We pulled the anchor once more, with Alisa at the wheel to keep us away from the cat while I worked the windlass up on the bow. Elias meanwhile was going through a total meltdown in his bunk.

The bottom was sprinkled with coral heads that had the potential to snag our chain, and we had been trying to anchor in relatively shallow water so that we had a chance to dive down and free the chain if we did get stuck.

'Screw it', I said to Alisa. 'I'm just going out to ten fathoms and dropping it. If we do get stuck, at least we're next to a village where half the men can probably dive that deep.'

Prophetic words, as it turned out.

On the chart, Makemo, like the other Tuamotus, looks like a necklace that has been dropped carelessly on the floor. The Tuamotus are atolls, which is what you get when a tropical volcanic island is old enough that nothing of the original volcanic island remains. The mountainous, lush island that once stood with its feet in the surf and its shoulders in the tradewind clouds has eroded away so all that is left is the coral reef that used to encircle the island, and now encircles a lagoon of protected water where the island once stood. In places a little coral rubble has piled up on the reef to make a *motu*, a tiny island resting on the coral necklace. And in fortuitous cases, the places where river mouths used to drain water from the original island have become passes through the reef that allow boats to travel between the open sea and the lagoon. It was Charles Darwin who first observed tropical islands in various stages of this process and put together the theory of atoll development.

After we were finally anchored, Elias went down for his nap and we began regaining our equanimity. Alisa canned meat from a short-billed spearfish that we had caught on the last day of the passage, and made a fish curry that we shared with Dave and Julia from *Macy*, a boat from Rhode Island that had also made the trip from Nuku Hiva. Dave and I snorkeled the pass we had entered on our sailboats, jumping out of the dinghy at the seaward end, letting the flood tide carry us past walls of coral forest and nations of gem-colored fish, while an occasional shark cruised in the ink-blue water below us. The next day Alisa and Elias and I went ashore in Pouheva, rowing across clear water that was indigo-colored in the deeps around *Pelagic* and changed to turquoise as it shoaled. The landscape, and seascape, that surrounded us was overwhelmingly flat. The *motu* that Pouheva was built on never rose to more than a few feet above the ocean. The calm waters of the lagoon, innocent of the unceasing ocean swell that reigned outside the pass, stretched to the far side of the lagoon, three miles away, where another line of coral reef and low *motus* drew a close horizon. Even the coconut palms, the tallest things on the islands, leaned away from the tradewinds and seemed to be trying to imitate the horizontals all around them. We began to feel the spell of the place. The islands that we had just left behind in the Marquesas were physically superlative: *so* steep, and *so* impenetrable in places, and covered with *such* a riot of plant life. And the people, inevitably, mirrored something of the superlative and the rugged of their land. For all the kindness of the culture, the Marquesas were a place where young men, their faces covered with warriors' tattoos, galloped bareback along beachfront roads. Our trip ashore in Pouheva probably wasn't representative, since we visited in the afternoon, and if the Tuamotus are like the Marquesas in this regard, they are very much a morning place. But Pouheva conveyed itself as somnolent and sun-beaten, a place where nobody was likely to gallop by, and certainly not with the tattoos of a warrior splashed across their faces. The village felt deserted, even though there were lots of kids in the schools that we walked by, suggesting that there must be a corresponding adult population somewhere. In his Really Big Idea book, *Guns, Germs and Steel,* Jared Diamond compared the geography and social development of various Polynesian islands. He concluded that high volcanic islands such as the Marquesas, which provide raw materials like basalt for tools and land suitable for irrigation, fostered the growth of hierarchical societies with entire classes of people who did not produce food, like chiefs and priests and artisans, while low atolls like the Tuamotus, without the rain or soil for intensive agriculture or many raw materials, produced more loosely organized societies where everyone worked at producing food. Seeing somnolent Pouheva, and remembering the vibrancy of a small Marquesan village like Haukehetau, it was easy to imagine that strong cultural differences persist between the two archipelagos, despite their close proximity and recent shared history.

But we didn't stick around long enough to get to know Pouheva. We smiled at a few people and bought a juice at a little store that sat off the road next to a tiny channel through the *motu*, the channel tidal and clean blue and full of interesting fish, with a bridge over it that little kids apparently jumped off for the better part of the day. I wondered how many generations it had been since little kids jumped off bridges into the creeks of Ohio, where Alisa and I grew up. We spent just that one afternoon ashore and the next day we shoved off for the uninhabited western part of the atoll.

Or at least that was our intention. But before we tried to pull the anchor I dove on it and found the chain completely wrapped around a head. We tried driving the boat around in a circle to free the chain while we pulled with the windlass. After an hour of trying this we were as stuck as ever. I had to dive pretty deep to even be able to see the chain, and what I could see wasn't good – after all our effort, the chain was more tangled than when we had started. A big chop was blowing into the anchorage from across the atoll and *Pelagic* was rearing and snorting at the chain and we could hear the chain grinding against the coral and we were stuck there, unable to move – a very bad feeling in a boat, which owes everything to its abilities for motion.

So I rowed into the village looking for help. And in an odd way that turned out to be a good thing. I went to the little store by the side of the channel, looking for the friendly clerk who spoke English. I found out that his name was Augustin, and as soon as he heard my story he locked the store and took me in his truck to go find a diver he knew. In a small village where you are utterly a stranger and don't speak either of the languages in currency, there are few things that are more satisfying then riding around in the truck of a local. Suddenly the veiled glances and restrained smiles with which humanity greets an outsider are replaced by the warm grins of friendship from the people who shout out to the car as you drive by, and you see the villagers revealed as they see each other.

The diver was named Ludo – a curly-haired, lithe Frenchman who had lived on Makemo for seven years and ran a little dive operation that catered to the few tourists who arrived at the Makemo airport. His day job was as a sports teacher at the professional school in Pouheva. He and Philippe, another French sports teacher who had befriended us earlier on Ua Pou, both made excuses for their poor English, but both were conversant in the language. This impressed monoglot Alisa and me to no end – gym teachers who speak foreign languages! On the spot I decided that the problems of our own country would largely solve themselves if America were the sort of place where gym teachers could routinely speak a second language.

As I was rowing Ludo out to *Pelagic* I asked if we could pay him for his time. He said simply, 'No, I am doing this to help you'. He ended up being under water for quite a while, and when he came up he reported that our chain had been wrapped two times around the same head. So much for our efforts to free ourselves. Alisa and I were ecstatic to see our twenty-kilogram anchor finally come out of the water and onto our bow. Ludo rode with us to another spot closer in where we would be able to free ourselves if we got stuck again, and then dove after we were reanchored to make sure that the anchor was set and the chain was free of obstructions. He wouldn't let us show our appreciation with a meal or even a beer, but his face did light up when we offered him some of our Marquesan fruit, giving us a little insight into life on that fruit-poor atoll.

We finally got going the next day and sailed to the other end of the atoll. When we started reading up about the Tuamotus before our arrival, we had decided that while the Marquesas were about the people that we met, the Tuamotus would be a chance for us to reduce the size of our social universe and tend our own gardens. To get down with ourselves, and the reefs and the birds, as it were, and not with the people. To live for a few weeks in one of the more spectacular places on the planet, as a family, self-sufficient, on our little boat. On the west end of Makemo, that vision began to come to life. We looked around, and put together our understanding of the place, one detail at a time. There were the huge storm berms of dead coral on the windward side of the *motus* – millions and millions of pieces of dead gray coral, which had been cast up by cyclones to create dry land. There were the coconut palms everywhere, rustling constantly in the tradewinds and providing the copra that gave the islands the base for their slender cash economies. There were the black-tipped reef sharks, cruising the pellucid shallows. And there was our little rowboat, pulled up on the beach, and our son, who had been walking for less than a year, running along the deserted beach, showing one parent and then another the latest shell he had found, and there was our little boat, bobbing peacefully in the offing, waiting for us when we needed to take our boy home.

33

THE VERY FINEST THING

TRAVELLING CONSTANTLY, AS we were, there was plenty of opportunity for surprises in our lives. Back in our routine in Kodiak, snuggled into our offices for forty hours a week and sleeping every night in a house that was permanently affixed to a foundation and never moved anywhere, Life had to really put in an effort to throw us a curve ball. But now, whenever we pulled the hook and pointed the bow to some other place where we'd never been before, we had no idea exactly what might be in store for us. Normally, when people say things like, 'we had no idea what might be in store for us', they're signposting the imminence of something unpleasant – something momentous, but bad, that will make for a good tale. Human nature being what it is, it's rare that anything happy and pleasant can hold much narrative power, so it's an infrequent moment indeed when we can say, 'we had no idea …' as an introduction to one of the happier occurrences of life.

Pulling the hook in Makemo, it turned out, was one of these rare moments. And, so: As we prepared to shoot the pass at slack water and sail to Tahanea Atoll, we had no idea what lay in store for us.

The fun began as soon as we left the pass on the morning tide and got our sails up. The wind was blowing a steady twenty knots gusting to twenty-five and when we made sail our boat speed shot up to seven and a half knots. In land units that's *nine miles an hour*, which, for people who were taking a year and a half to get from Alaska to Australia, might as well have been Mach 1. Tahanea was forty-nine miles away and we had seven hours until the afternoon slack tide would make the pass safe for *Pelagic*.

'Damn me', I said to Alisa, 'but we just might make it in one day.'

We put up more sail than we normally would and our speed stayed well above seven knots, at times even hitting eight. I watched the GPS count down the distance to the atoll and when each hour had passed we had made exactly seven nautical miles good towards our destination. I got a great feeling of suspense from seeing that we were just on the cusp of making it, and we were excited by the possibility of a night of deep slumber at anchor instead of being hove to off the atoll, each of us up half the night, waiting for the morning tide to give us safe entrance through the pass.

We sailed fast and the waves were big. Two of them even broke right over our quarter one after the other, splashing about a foot of water into the cockpit, the first water that we had ever taken there. Elias was strapped into his car seat at the time. Alisa and I had often wondered how he would react if we took a wave aboard while he was above decks. Now that it had happened, we kept our expressions carefully neutral to avoid coloring his response.

'Mess'! Elias yelled, laughing and pointing at the warm saltwater that was slowly draining away. And that was the limit of his concern – pointing out the mess in the cockpit. He was unburdened by the dark thoughts of breaking seas and rogue waves that adults who sail across oceans with one-year-old children always carry, somewhere in the depths of their psyches, no matter how cheery they seem.

We made it to the pass on Tahanea just in time to catch the tide and just before the sun was too low in the sky for responsible navigation among the coral. We anchored right next to the pass, feeling like we had pulled something off, smug in the knowledge that we could both sleep the night through.

Then after a day we moved to the southeast corner of the atoll. And there we found the very finest thing of all, the thing that we had been looking for, in one way or another, ever since the work harness of our old jobs began to chafe and we began to talk seriously about getting a cruising boat and sailing to Australia.

We found that moment when dream and reality contested the field, and reality did not come out second best.

34

WE'LL ALWAYS HAVE TAHANEA

OVER AND AGAIN on our trip, reality failed to jibe with expectation. This is a core experience of travel, of course, and you either are or are not a traveler depending on how you react to the difference between what you expect and what you find. You reach the farthest, most exotic, most beautiful place in the world that you will ever see, for instance, and you find that it is still of the quotidian world that you know so well. You can either concentrate on the potato chip bags you find in the surf and the way that your bug bites are festering, or you can note with a quiet satisfaction that of all the previous travelers' accounts you had read before you arrived, none mentioned the way the island culture had so easily adopted the widespread cultivation of marijuana. You can note how variable a visitor's welcome is in the smaller villages, and how dependent on the approach of the visitor. You can listen with satisfaction to another traveler's story about how it's still possible to see Marquesas fruit doves on Nuku Hiva. You can enjoy the world for what it is, and not worry about the inevitable tales of how it was better in some recent past.

The South Pacific has been burdened with higher expectations from visiting outsiders than any other place in the world. It began with the reality of abundant food, easy climate, and sexual repletion that tempted so many eighteenth-century European sailors into jumping ship. Those same delights are available, in some combination, on various South Pacific islands today. The fruit of the Marquesas gave us a new standard by which we will forever judge. Alaskan climate refugees that we were, we loved living in our bathing suits day after day. And one of our cruising guides mentioned a certain island where young women are still noted for their propensity to sleep with strangers.

I'm not going to tell you which one.

But no matter how fine the realities, they have inevitably failed to keep pace with the expectations. Generations of travel writers have gone to Tahiti and Bora Bora and, rather than admit disappointment at what they actually found, returned repeating the tales they arrived with, of swaying hips and grass skirts and languorous night breezes. The stream of yachts that was travelling downwind with us was full of people who were, with various success, balancing their actual experience against the dreams they had been stoking for all their lives. An American yachtie with a face twisted in disappointment complained to us on the beach in Daniel's Bay about paying five hundred francs for eight mangoes.

The southeast corner of Tahanea did not offer us perfection. It was not a place out of some fantasy earth, in a parallel universe. No dusky maidens swam out to our anchored boat on starlit nights. (Nor were we looking for them to.) Other anchored yachts were always in view during our stay, so the complete solitude that is so necessary for the full experience of the natural world was missing.

But still, seen through our North American eyes, Tahanea showed us as different a version of what the earth might offer as you could find. A place ultimately of the ocean, and Oceania, with scraps of land suspended above the reef that were just large enough, in the days when the atoll was inhabited, to support a people who lived wholly connected to the sea. A place continuously sublime in its beauty. A place where sky and sea defined twenty different shades of what we crudely describe as 'turquoise'.

The southeast side of Tahanea was the place where our dreams of palm-fringed anchorages came, finally and completely, true.

To reach the southeast side we had a spectacular sail across the flat water of the lagoon, without any chart at all, just navigating around the coral patches by eye as the spray leapt over our bows. And after an hour or so of this great sail we found ourselves in a landscape (seascape, skyscape) that looked like nothing that should have actually contained us and the shabby little fiberglass yacht that had patiently carried our household and our dreams from Kodiak and through all the indifferent ports along the way. We anchored in a patch of clear sand among the coral heads a couple of hundred yards from a pair of *motus*. Green coconut palms clustered on the *motus,* which receded in a distant arc on either side of us. The sun was fierce. The sand spit between the *motus* burned white. We smelled salt, and dry sandy soil. The water surface ruffled in the tradewinds and the palms rustled and the clear depths of water promised tranquility. Sculpted white clouds towered above, and everywhere was the heartbreaking-blue sky and sea.

Alisa came up with the perfect metaphor to capture the moment.

'Damn me', she said. 'This is just like the screen savers that people use on their computers at work.'

We spent ten days in that miracle of an anchorage. The diversions that we found for ourselves were many. There were three endemic landbirds on the *motus* near the anchorage, and for the first few days we spent our shore time getting pictures of atoll fruit doves, Tuamotu reed warblers, and Tuamotu sandpipers, three species that are remnants of the rich avifauna that existed before the arrival of rats with the Polynesian voyagers. The beaches of southeast Tahanea were sandy in places instead of the rough coral beaches that dominate over much of the Tuamotus, and they were safe and endlessly entertaining for Eli. It was a huge relief for Alisa and me to find a place where we didn't have to be constantly ready to grab him if he was about to stray into some danger. Each of his hands was occupied with a piece of dead coral or plastic trash as soon as he hit the beach (if you're familiar with the oceans you know that there is plastic trash *everywhere*, on *every* beach), and he loved throwing coral chunks into the water.

After we had been taking pictures of birds for a few days we started thinking about the little coral reef next to the beach nearest to *Pelagic*. The first day that we rowed by it we remarked that it was probably great snorkeling. Then we forgot all about it for a few days. After an afternoon of snorkeling on the scattered coral heads in deeper water I finally gave the shallow reef a try. What I found blew my mind. The reef was only in waist-deep water. It was high tide on my first visit, with about a foot of water over the coral, and there were fish *everywhere*. I slowly drifted around the edges of the reef and looked out over the top of the coral where feeding drifting darting fish receded into the blue-green distance. Alisa and I came back the next day. It was ideal – we could take turns in the water and watching Eli, who was completely content on the beach. We brought along our field guide to Pacific reef fishes and we got way into identifying what we saw. The diversity was fantastic – I once saw five different species of butterflyfish in a single view. At first we both had a hard time remembering enough distinguishing features to identify anything. We'd come out of the water and look up the white and black striped damsel fish that we had seen and find a dozen possible species in the book. But after a while we got a feel for the bigger taxonomic groups and important diagnostic features and we were able to identify handfuls of new species every time we got wet. It was a great mental game to train ourselves to remember sets of details from particular fish well enough to look them up in the book and not let our impressions get muddled by all the pattern and color, the diversity and similarity of the fish constantly parading before us. Having an appreciation for biology is a huge plus in a place like this, as it gives you a bit of perspective on what's really going on in front of your eyes, the taxonomy and ecology and evolution.

As we were rowing back to our dinner on *Pelagic* after one of these sessions I said to Alisa, 'Damn, don't you just want to live four lives so you can fit everything in? Wouldn't it be great to do some kind of coral-reef ecology study using all these coral patches as replicates?'

'And the cool thing is that fish diversity will only increase as we go west', she said.

'Remind me', I said. 'What was I doing studying cod-shrimp interactions in the Gulf of Alaska, anyway?'

Seeing first the Marquesas and then the Tuamotus gave me my best-ever insight into how long geological time scales really are. It was nothing but time that removed the immovable mountains that were once the Tuamotus, removed them one grain of sand at a time and turned them into placid lagoons. Nothing but time enough to strain the bounds of my imagination. Human societies in the Marquesas have a strong post-apocalyptic feeling, where valleys that used to support thousands of people now support a dozen. But the Tuamotus are post-apocalyptic on a whole other scale. The land is gone, the plant and bird communities are gone, and only the passes through the *motus* mark the places where rivers once flowed to the sea.

This is the kind of insight that gives you a dangerously realistic perspective on the questions of natural history that should do a lot more to frame our worldview than they actually do. Questions like the age of the earth, and the amount of change that landscapes and living communities continually undergo, and the novelty of our tenancy here.

Days of unsettled weather interrupted our tradewind delight – days when black clouds drifted above us and waterspouts appeared in the distance, snaking up into the clouds from the lagoon surface. Days when it rained hard enough to make Tahanea unavailable to us, days when we stayed on the boat. But we were glad for the water that we collected from the rain. When we bought *Pelagic*, the gear aboard had included a watermaker, a 12-volt machine that forces seawater through a membrane so fine that the dissolved salts are stripped out, producing potable water for our tanks. The watermaker had been helpful on the three-week sail to the Marquesas, giving Alisa plenty of water to wash diapers every other day. But it also required regular maintenance, and, in the way of these things, it stopped working while we were at Ua Pou, letting us know that it would require a new feed pump before it would deign to fill our tanks again. With no new feed pump in the offing, Alisa used a scrap of material left over from our sun awning to sew a raincatcher for *Pelagic*, a little awning that would hang between the mast and the staysail while we were at anchor and funnel rainwater through a hose into the water tanks. When the first downpour began at Tahanea I dashed out on deck with the new raincatcher under my arm, wearing only my bathing suit, the sharp raindrops surprisingly icy against my bare skin. Working with my eyes half-closed against the deluge, I soon had the awning suspended from the rigging, and I was gratified to watch a trickle of water flowing steadily through the clear hose to the tanks. By the end of the day our tanks were completely full. In the short term, that meant we had no concern of being forced to leave

Tahanea for want of water. And the watermaker stayed in mothballs for the rest of the trip, discredited as a finicky gizmo that didn't fit with our approach to sailing.

Between showers we let Eli play in his little inflatable pool in the cockpit. When the rain was through, the dinghy was so full of rainwater that we were able to wash clothes in it, the bow and stern sections serving nicely for separate wash and rinse cycles. Once that chore was over, we discovered the joy of feeding table scraps to the half dozen remoras that had attached themselves to *Pelagic*. Elias, still not yet two, could not contain his joy at this new game. He stood on the cockpit coaming in his lifejacket, holding onto the lifelines, a halo of hair wafting out around his over-large toddler's head. Alisa opened one of the cans of corned beef from Nuku Hiva that suffered from less-than-favorable comparisons with dogfood and threw a chunk into the water. And, look, suddenly they're there! The cadaver-gray, torpedo-shaped fish with the oddly flattened heads came out from the shelter of the hull to compete for a meal. Elias pointed at the swirl of fish and looked up at us, breathless in laughter, to make sure we saw them. And look, he pointed when he looked down at the water again. Now they're *not* there. And *look!* Mommy threw another piece of corned beef into the water and the fish are there again!

Alisa and I said, collectively, 'What could be better than this?', and we ripped up the list of other atolls that Pierre had recommended visiting.

There were still fish to be identified on the reef. We found a colony of nesting red-footed boobies on one of the *motus*, the chicks sitting singly in their nests in the shrubs, adult-sized but still covered with bone-white fluffy down, patiently waiting for a parent to arrive with their next meal. And then a boat we had known since Baja arrived in the company of like-minded boats we hadn't yet met, and we suddenly had the society of new friends at a bonfire on the beach, people who gave us the chance to realize the true size of our delight as we described our stay to them.

Finally we left that heavenly place and moved to an anchorage near Passe D'Otao, the easternmost of the three passes into the lagoon. There was an old village site at the pass, now occupied only seasonally by people who came to cut copra, and we used water from one of their cisterns to do another round of laundry and get ourselves ready for the big city of Pape'ete, the administrative center for Tahiti, and the Society Islands, and all of French Polynesia. Our visas for French Polynesia were only going to last another month, and we had several thousand miles still to go before cyclone season would chase us out of the tropics in November. So we set a day to leave for the two-day sail to Tahiti. Luckily when the day arrived the wind had died completely so we got an extra day to spend in Tahanea. It was a day when we looked out of the portlight and saw billowing tradewind clouds suspended over their perfect mirror images on the still lagoon. It was a day when the water was so clear that I got vertigo walking around on deck and looking at the bottom 45 feet below. It felt, with little imagination required, that *Pelagic* was suspended in nothing but a bluish haze of air. I could count the drag marks of our individual links of anchor chain in the sand bottom, and when parrotfish swam along we watched the shadows of their pectoral fins flitting back and forth on the lagoon floor.

I used the gift of this extra day to snorkel in the pass on a flood tide. Dropping into the pass was a bit like something from Aldous Huxley: I felt the biological doors of perception swinging open. There was at least an order of magnitude more fish than there had been at the little reef at the last anchorage, and also more diversity. I was suddenly in a thicket of biodiversity, a blue universe of life and adaptation and predation and coexistence that was entirely foreign and novel.

When I got back to *Pelagic*, I found that Alisa had taught Elias to say, 'Dad, let's party!' The saloon was decorated with crepe paper and ribbons, Eli was wearing a crepe paper necklace, and he had learned to say 'necklace', too. It was June 23rd – one year since we sailed out of the Kodiak harbor. Alisa had baked a chocolate cake and was wearing the little black dress I had given her on her last birthday.

We ate the cake and looked at photos taken one year before. Alisa immediately noticed that her eyes were puffy in the pictures, still affected by our tear-washed exit from town. The difference between the puffy-eyed picture and the exuberant wife who sat next to me in her little cocktail dress, feeding bites of cake to her one-year-old son in the middle of tropical nowhere, did a lot to encapsulate our experience in that last year. Leaving Kodiak might have been the most difficult thing that either of us had ever done. And doing that one difficult thing had only begun a whole year of unexpected gut-wrenching moments as we made the fits-and-starts transition away from the Alaskan life that we loved so much. And yet, here we were now, happy in Tahanea, thoroughly engaged in an incredible new way of living that might turn out to be just as hard to give up when the time comes.

We put Elias to sleep in time to enjoy one last Tahanea sunset from the cockpit, cocktails in hand. The sun set behind the surf crashing on the distant reef and the sky went swiftly dark. I kissed my wife and I tasted the salt on her lips that was always there no matter what chocolate cake or gin and tonics might do to hide it.

The next day we did leave. The world is very big and, practically speaking, we would have to sail around it, or at least all the way around the Pacific, to see Tahanea again. We might sail for the rest of our lives, but that first year of setting out with a baby and learning the ropes was something rich and vivid that we could only do once. And an experience like the one that we had in Tahanea, when we had no idea what lay in store for us, is something that will be very difficult to replicate. We shot the pass in the morning under a blustery sky, getting through a little late so that the ebb tide had built into a race out on the ocean swell. We steered around the race and turned to the west and unrolled the jib and let it do the work of pulling the boat along, with wind and sea behind us. Alisa and I held hands as the pass faded behind us, and the seaward sides of the *motus* spooled by.

'You know', I said, 'we'll always have Tahanea'.

35

THE MOSTLY GOOD AND
THE OCCASIONAL BAD

WE MADE FIFTY-SEVEN miles during our first day, and
only ninety-five during the second. With good winds we
normally counted on making 130 to 160 miles noon-to-noon. But
the winds stayed light, and then when they did come up they were
headwinds, out of the west. We were happy to sail along without
turning on the motor, making two or three or four knots, letting the
windvane do the work of steering, and we gave up all thoughts of
doing the 700-mile trip from Raiatea in five or six days.

Our reluctance to motor was evidence of a progression. We had
become much more sailors than when we left home, and we didn't
mind sailing slowly. Even if the autopilot were working flawlessly
and diesel fuel had been cheap in Tahiti, we would have preferred
to sail than motor.

Especially on a trip like the one we were having, where the
Pacific was flawless day after day. There were always enough clouds
to be interesting to look at during the day without being so many
that the Milky Way was hidden at night. The sun was far too strong
for us in the cockpit during the middle of the day, but the sea was

gentle enough to leave hatches and portlights open, so we could retreat down below to the shade and breeze of the saloon. Every day the sea was empty. For six days we saw no ships, no birds, no mammals. The world contracted to the size of our boat. We woke up each day and settled into a routine of just being together. Alisa and I talked for hours about the past and the future.

Elias was suddenly easier to handle on passage. His imagination grew and grew. A seat cushion dragged onto the cabin sole became the motor boat that he and his stuffed animals took fishing. We looked down at this miracle, a child who could entertain himself. Freed from his constant care, Alisa took a turn playing foredeck ape, swinging the whisker pole through a jibe, the maneuver on *Pelagic* that most resembles waving a red handkerchief at a bull.

Passages had become a regular part of our life. For days our ears were filled with the murmur of water parting at *Pelagic*'s bows, the slap of waves on the hull, the rustle of sails that caught barely enough wind to hold their shape. We got another view of how inexhaustibly large the world is, more so than anyone who stays at home and looks outwards through the internet can ever know. Every night I sat in the cockpit as we slowly moved west, west, west. I looked upwards at the perfect celestial canopy, a sight that simultaneously smites us with the unimaginable scale of creation, and thrills us with the idea that our imagination might after all be the tool adequate for grasping at it. Every morning I awoke to the wonder of nature that is an almost-two-year-old who has been refreshed with ten hours of continuous rest and is ready for everything to happen now, immediately, the moment he awakes, and simultaneously to the more soothing sound of Alisa whispering to him, 'Quiet, Dad's still sleeping!'

Sea travel is generous with time to digest what you have just seen, and the people you have met, with none of the too-quick transitions of jet flight. During the three weeks we had just spent in the Society Islands, in Tahiti and Raiatea and Taha'a, we mostly put our noses down and took care of business. Those islands still offer a lot to a traveler: good people to meet and beautiful places. But you have to pick and choose when you're crossing as much ground as we were in our single cyclone-free season jaunt across the Pacific. So we held ourselves back from the Societies, and concentrated on installing a new oil cooler on the engine, and taking care of other boat jobs, and I finished up revisions to the very last research paper to come out of my old job in Kodiak. After three weeks of this, and having a bit of fun too, we felt prepared to continue into the vastness of the Pacific, ready to be delighted by whatever places we might find like Hakahetau and Tahanea, places that retained some innocence in the way they greeted outsiders. If you're lucky enough to be travelling just for the hell of it, it's good to have a standard for what you find to be really valuable. A standard that explains why one place makes you wish, for as long as you are there, to be absolutely nowhere else on the whole spherical globe. Better to have the frustration of not meeting that standard over and over, and then valuing those rare instances when the standard is met, and reinforced, than to just be vaguely satisfied with every place that doesn't actively piss you off. In other words, I would rather once stumble on a red-footed booby colony that I had no idea existed than a hundred times follow the directions in the cruising guide to the place where the hotel employees feed the stingrays so that you can pet them.

Every boat visiting French Polynesia is meant to check in at Tahiti, which is why Pape'ete, the main city of Tahiti and the administrative center for the Societies and all of French Polynesia, is particularly heaving with yachts. We enjoyed the crowds during our stay there, though, as we weren't in any way looking for an experience beyond the Yachtie Scrum. We saw lots and lots of boats that we had seen previously in French Polynesia, and we got into the excitement of all these people embarked upon the same dream trip that we were engaged upon. We also enjoyed some of the benefits of having, if

I may say so, one of the coolest hailing ports possible emblazoned on our stern. We were lucky enough to meet Richard and Michelle, the French/South African wonder sailors aboard *Thélème*, who came over one day to say hi because they had spent a winter in Kodiak on their boat ten years before. These two were additions to a short list of really interesting long-term voyaging sailors whom we met in French Polynesia, people who had been sailing the world for *decades*, and who had a twinkle in their eyes announcing that they were still enjoying it very much. When we met them, Richard and Michelle were refitting *Thélème* for a two-year stint in Patagonia. And I learned two things from Richard: that it is impossible to count on having any tropical anchorage to yourself outside of hurricane season, and also that thing that French sailors say about boats like *Pelagic*: 'It's so American, if it were any more American, it would be dead'.

The next stop on the tradewind route after the Societies is the Cook Islands, a self-governing Polynesian nation that is in close association with New Zealand. The Cooks are composed of northern and southern archipelagos that are separated by about five hundred miles of open ocean, and many of the islands are without good anchorages, which makes the nation more of a place to pass through than a real cruising destination. The main cruising route from the Societies goes through Rarotonga, the administrative center in the southern group, and then on to the nations of Niue and Tonga. A smaller number of boats go to the northern group, and thence typically to Samoa. With the cyclone-free season rapidly waning, we weren't interested in giving up time in Tonga and Fiji in order to visit Samoa. But there is an island in the northern Cooks that we were very keen to see. So we chose to make the 700-mile passage from Raiataea to the northern Cooks and then another 700 miles onwards to Tonga, an increase of several hundred miles in distance over the standard southern route to Tonga.

The draw for this extra travelling was the island of Suwarrow, an

is now a Cook Islands National Park and inhabited outside
the season by two caretakers and their kids, and during the
season by nobody at all. Suwarrow was uninhabited for most
of the twentieth century, and then for a while was the home of a
lone Kiwi, Tom Neale, who was keen enough, and skilled enough,
to actually pull off the dream of living alone on a deserted tropical
island. He spent three long stints on Suwarrow during the fifties,
sixties and seventies. The world has changed enough that it would
now be impossible to experience such an enticing setting in the utter
isolation that he found. He wrote a very good book about his life
on the island, *An Island to Oneself*, that both Alisa and I had read.
The Tuamotus had left us as confirmed connoisseurs of atolls, and
reading Tom's book stirred our imaginations enough that we weren't
going to pass through without a visit to Suwarrow.

The western tropical Pacific has a reputation for generally worse
weather than the eastern, and the area west of the Society Islands is
known for 'enhanced' trade winds in July and August. The stories
we heard on the ham radio from the boats leaving the Societies
in the week before our departure weren't very encouraging. Boats
reported knockdowns, damaged rigging and generally unpleasant
sailing. Luckily for us, by the time we were ready to leave, the bad
weather was gone. On a beautiful sunny day, we had the pleasure of
sailing off our mooring and transiting the pass through the fringing
reef around Raiatea without resorting to the motor.

Our eighth sunset since leaving Raiatea found us just twenty-five
miles short of Suwarrow, though the low atoll was still out of our
sight. A whale circled the boat and Alisa, Elias and I wordlessly
watched its immense form swimming past us on one side and then
the other, moving very fast just under the water. After the whale
disappeared we hove to and waited for dawn. The wind was coming
up and wind waves began to run. Heaving to normally guaranteed
us a smooth ride, but for some reason the swell and jerk of the

waves had *Pelagic* rolling uncomfortably. I tried to balance the boat at an angle to the wind that would be more comfortable while still controlling our rate of drift down towards the island. Alisa fought against the unpleasant motion while she led Elias through a toddler's whole evening litany of dinner, diaper change, books read aloud, nursing, consolation, and finally, sleep. When I made trips below to plot our position, I felt myself getting green, and I retreated to the open cockpit as soon as my task was finished. I didn't envy Alisa's long stint in the cabin.

When Elias finally was asleep she came up to the cockpit and said, 'I don't know if I'm cut out to live on a sailboat long term'.

I spent an anxious night. In the early hours I made sail so that we might be at the pass into Suwarrow when the morning light would be good for seeing coral. But then, my head musty with sleep, I caught myself in a navigational error that, uncorrected, would have cast us up on the merciless reef. Meanwhile the windvane had somehow lost a critical little plastic bushing for which we had no spare, so that all-important device was temporarily held together with vicegrips. We had left Raiatea feeling that we were at the top of our game, but on the final miles of the passage it felt like we were limping.

And that's how it went, the mostly good and the occasional bad hand in hand all the way across the Pacific. When it was good there was nothing else that we wanted to do, ever, and when it was not so good we reminded ourselves that nothing lasts.

36

TOMORROW AND TOMORROW AND TOMORROW

I DON'T KNOW ENOUGH Shakespeare for him to inform my everyday thinking, except in that background way in which a writer can structure your opinion about important things, even after you've forgotten the stories and characters. So I don't usually go around quoting him. But Suwarrow was a place that we understood directly through the soliloquy from *Macbeth* that rode across the Pacific with us, taped above the chart table.

The three Cook Islanders whom we met all pronounced Suwarrow as 'Soo-WAH-roh', rhyming with 'tomorrow.' And that brings me to the only bit of Macbeth that I know, besides 'out, out, damn spot':

Tomorrow and tomorrow and tomorrow
Creeps in this petty pace from day to day
To the last syllable of recorded time;
And all our yesterdays have lighted fools
The way to dusty death. Out, out, brief candle!
Life's but a walking shadow, a poor player,

That struts and frets his hour upon the stage
And then is heard no more. It is a tale
Told by an idiot, full of sound and fury,
Signifying nothing.

Cheerful stuff, you might say, but there it is. 'Tomorrow and tomorrow and tomorrow / Creeps in this petty pace from day to day' is a big part of the reason that Alisa and Elias and I found ourselves living on a sailboat in the South Pacific, far from kith and kin. What we had been doing for that year, acting on a dream, was our best collective answer to the question of what we *should* be doing with this life that we find ourselves in the middle of. Whenever I felt oppressed by the idea that sailing along for months and years on *Pelagic* might represent abdication from a serious life, I reflected that the default model of job-house-mortgage was, for me, a more serious abdication, a refusal to decide, actively, what life might be. What a simple allure there is in the idea of living a life that will be worth the telling. It might have been a certain French respect for dreams, and for lives organized around self-evident principles, that had informed our recent Francophilia. And it was definitely the example of one man's dream realized that makes Suwarrow such a unique place. Whatever his inevitable faults and frustrations, Tom Neale had been fortunate enough to know what he wanted, and strong enough to guide his hour upon the stage, to wrest some measure of his own meaning, and his own satisfaction, from this tale told by an idiot. And Suwarrow is where he did it.

The magnitude of recent change in the world is really brought home when you read Tom's book and see how much lonelier the South Pacific was during his years on Suwarrow. Tom had no communication with the outside world after a trading schooner dropped him off, and during his first stay, in the 1950s, he went thirteen months without seeing any ships or boats or airplanes. Even during his final stint on the island, in the 1970s, when news of the friendly hermit of Suwarrow made the atoll a sought-after destination for yachts, the most yachts to visit Suwarrow in an entire *year* was seventeen.

There were more yachts than that anchored up in Suwarrow on one *day* in 2008, and *Pelagic* was one of them.

At first this relatively crowded state was a bit of a let-down. We were just finishing an idyllic passage, which always set us up for a buzz kill when we finally reached land. And then of course Tom Neale's book had turned Suwarrow into a symbol of solitude. So even though we expected there to be a lot of boats, arriving still made us miss Alaska, where we could count on having some of the more spectacular places of the world all to ourselves.

Among the vessels sharing the anchorage was the *Søren Larsen*, a Baltic trader built in 1949, 105 feet long on deck, now converted to a brigantine rig and carrying paying passengers, or 'voyage crew' around the western tropical Pacific. Sitting off by herself in the deep blue water of the lagoon, with her square-rigged foremast and three furled headsails sitting on the jaunty angle of her bowsprit, the *Søren Larsen* gave the anchorage a touch of golden nostalgia, the feel of the South Pacific in the age of sail. By our great good fortune, the *Søren Larsen* also happened to have on board Tom Neale's daughter Stella. When we first went ashore we found Stella working at an outdoor table in the little compound formed by her dad's low house and the new house occupied by the island caretakers and their children. Surrounded by a milling group of crew and passengers from the *Søren Larsen*, she was preparing for a party that night, cooking a meal in an *umu*, an underground oven heated by a fire covered in volcanic rocks. The meal featured yellowfin tuna and *uto*, which is the meat from a sprouted coconut, and *pana uto*, or bread made from *uto*.

'I hate *pana uto* when it's too hard', she said to us, her hands covered with the dough. She had the curly hair of the islands, set atop an Anglo Kiwi's broad friendly face. She looked like someone's favorite aunt, or the best sort of school librarian. 'But then I always go and make it too soft. I'm a bit nervous, this is the first *umu* I've done without my mum around. The island ladies never really tell you how to do it, they just expect you to follow their example.'

Stella turned out to be an easy person to get to know, perhaps in contrast to her dad, who, though apparently very friendly, was, after all, a hermit. 'Are you coming tonight?' Stella asked us when we made our goodbyes and headed back to *Pelagic*.

We rallied that evening, despite our short sleep the night before, and we rowed back to the island with a bowl of Alisa's peanut sauce pasta to contribute to the meal. We had expected to be subsumed in the yachtie scrum, but found that only one other yacht crew was in attendance. Otherwise it was just people from the *Søren Larsen* and John and Veronica Samuela, the island caretakers, and their four kids, and a Kiwi who was on the island to count birds. So it was a great chance for us to meet the owners of the *Søren Larsen*, Steve and Rosie, and to talk with Stella and John and Veronica. I also chatted with Rhys, who had been doing the bird counts for the previous two weeks. He told me that the most numerous birds on the atoll were sooty terns, at sixty to seventy thousand individuals, and that between five and seven per cent of the global population of lesser frigate birds and red-tailed tropicbirds also nested on the atoll.

Alisa and I had been waiting for a long time to run into a biologist working in one of the fantastic places that we had been visiting. Even though Rhys protested that he was actually a micro-biologist, and only doing these bird counts as an avocation, he fit the bill perfectly, as he and I drank a beer in front of the fire and chatted about this or that weird evolutionary strategy. We stayed long enough to join a little of the knee-swinging dancing that broke out after dinner, led by Stella and John. And then it was time to get

Elias to bed. When we had him successfully transferred to his bunk, Alisa and I took stock.

'That was *fun*', Alisa said.

'What a difference from last night, when we were hove to and a little queasy and all alone on the big big ocean.'

'Who'd think we'd have fun hanging out with passengers on a glorified cruise ship?'

It was the start of a fun social week. Who would have guessed that Suwarrow, famous for its former isolation, would turn out to be such a social place? It helped that most of the boats in the anchorage were new to us, so we got to meet some fresh faces after having been with many of the same boats all the way from Mexico to the Societies. And it really helped to have the spirit of Tom Neale about the place. His experience continues to make Suwarrow special. If it were just another tropical island for us yachties to visit, we'd all process our experience separately, either doing the work of discovering the place for ourselves, or glomming onto the conventional wisdom about the quality of the fishing, or the beauty of the coral relative to the Tuamotus, or whatever. But because of Tom, we all tacitly agreed that Suwarrow represented something: the chance that still existed, within the lifetime of almost everyone in the anchorage, to reclaim a bit of the Garden of Eden, to experience the world innocent of the grosser impositions of our fellow humans, a chance that is now either gone or very much more difficult to find. For all of us who had put together enough power of will to get ourselves all the way out there on our little plastic sailboats, his example of a dream realized was a powerful one.

The next few days were too windy for us to venture out to any of the other *motus*, so we spent our time on Anchorage Island. Alisa and Stella hit it off, and Stella told us how on her mother's side she was a Marsters from Palmerston Island, a direct descendant of William Marsters, an Englishman who ran a copra operation on Palmerston in the late nineteenth century, and who proceeded to populate the island with the descendants of himself and his three Polynesian wives. We also spent time talking with the caretakers, John and Veronica. John looked like a Cook Island version of an American Colonial gentleman, with his curly hair pulled back in a stubby pony tail and tied off with a green silk ribbon; a receding chin, splayed teeth, and a habit of blinking when he talked. John took an obvious concern over the conservation of Suwarrow. He carefully explained his approach to enforcing the national park rules. 'The last caretaker showed people how to catch birds, but we don't do that. No touching the birds, no touching bird eggs, not at all. If someone needs a fish to eat that night, I tell them OK, go fishing. But there was a boat here before, they caught a lot of fish, they knew the method for catching grouper very well, they caught seven or eight big grouper in an hour, and I went out and told them, that's it, no more fishing. I don't want Suwarrow to become a sport fishing park.' He also told us about the six big commercial fishing boats ('Korean, we think') that Google Earth photographed in Suwarrow during the last cyclone season, when there was no caretaker on the island.

Alisa formed a quick friendship with Veronica, and learned a lot from her about Cook Island life. She took the chance to expand upon her cross-cultural survey of breastfeeding habits, and found that Cook Islanders wean late; Veronica nursed her first son until he was five. We were always a little unsure how breastfeeding in public would be seen in the various places we visited, and this news made Alisa's life on Anchorage Island very relaxed, as no one thought twice about a nearly-two-year-old nursing. Veronica and Elias also formed an immediate bond; for days he carried around the (hookless) fishing lure she had given him, a mutual interest in fishing being one of the foundations of their connection. At a barbecue on the beach I looked at him sitting in her lap, the two of them completely at home with each other, and I got a glimpse of a different world, where there were aunts and nieces and grannies around who gave us a break in raising Elias, and who gave Elias a family experience wider than that of his two parents.

The time came for the *Søren Larsen* to leave. She weighed anchor and headed towards the rushing water of the reef pass. We walked to the other side of Anchorage Island to watch the ship go through the pass and to the open sea beyond. She motored out to sea with little canvas up, and we were surprised to see how violently she pitched and rolled. We could, too easily, imagine the distress of some of the voyage crew aboard.

'They'll feel better after they throw up', said Alisa.

The passengers and crew of the *Søren Larsen* could mostly look back at Suwarrow the same way that we would when we left, as a delightful diversion, a little-visited corner of the world at its very best that they, and we, had been fortunate enough to visit. But Stella, who was also on the *Søren Larsen*, was leaving behind something much more important: a place that was central to her life although she had been there less than a handful of times, a place that held the memory of a father whom she had barely known.

The *Søren Larsen* disappeared into the open Pacific. We continued our walk around Anchorage Island, crunching along a beach of dead coral. Back on the lagoon side of the island, we saw the fleet of anchored boats, *Pelagic* among them. The Cook Islands flag flew from a flag pole near the place where Tom Neale nearly killed himself with the inhuman effort of building a dock by hand so that boats visiting Suwarrow would have a place to tie up. The effort of building that dock haunts *An Island to Oneself.* At the same time he was living on an inadequate diet of fish, tortured by visions of red meat, he worked his stressed body beyond the breaking point to roll man-killing blocks of coral into place, naked in the sun but for his hat and a loincloth. The story of his futile attempt to build that dock is so poignant because it reveals something so universal – the way that we get what we want, and then want something a little different. Behold the man who has succeeded in the task of achieving splendid isolation, working desperately to build a facility for visitors.

We walked past John and Veronica's four boys at play next to the path leading from the modern dock up to Tom's house. And, at the start of the path, we came to a monument stone that read

1952–77

TOM NEALE

Lived his dream

on this island.

That stone was left by the French sailor Bernard Moitessier, who visited Suwarrow several times in the 1970s and became friends with Tom. While James Cook is commonly a hero to English-speaking yachties, we on *Pelagic* found ourselves drawn to Moitessier as a figure to emulate. Cook, though his achievements were greater than any other explorer's, and though he was a man who can remain remarkably sympathetic when judged under modern ethical standards, is nonetheless a figure from remote history. Moitessier, on the other hand, was alive during our lifetimes, and is therefore a role model for swimming, with whatever grace a person can muster, through the rushing flood of the modern era. Moitessier's life is a long story, most enjoyed as he chose to tell it, through his books. Suffice it to say that his peers admired him as the finest of seamen, he had, in spades, the Gallic knack for the Grand Poetic Gesture, and he cultivated a mystical relationship with the sea, and its solitudes, that contrasts mightily with the more practical writings of English sailors. His friendship with Tom Neale, and the regard that is embodied in the monument, only cemented our opinion of Suwarrow as somewhere special in all the world.

The next day the tradewinds eased. John and Veronica, knowing that Alisa and I were very interested in the nesting seabirds of Suwarrow, offered to organize a visit to Brushwood Island, a *motu* near Anchorage Island that is the site of a bird colony. They kindly made room for us in the park skiff, along with the crew of *Momo* and their two girls, in addition to their own four boys, while all the other yachties followed along in their own dinghies. When we got to the island we enjoyed the initial sensation of being overwhelmed by the number of birds, and the noise, and the stench of the colony, which I was glad to find was nearly identical to that of a North Pacific seabird colony. There were sooty terns everywhere, thousands and thousands of sooty terns on the ground and on the wing, small sleek black and white adults and the less sleek mottled brown juveniles from this year's nests, already the size of adults. They either begged for food from passing adults, or hung in the tradewinds on their new wings, or stood huddled in still groups on the ground. Along with the other yachties we enjoyed the curiosity of these young terns, the way they would fly up to investigate if we held a hand suggestively in the air, and we noted also the cold hard reality of seabird colonies everywhere, and the way that dead tern chicks were scattered around the landscape.

Alisa and Elias and I separated from the group and sat down at the edge of the colony to enjoy the show. The *motu* was flat of course, and therefore very different from the cliff-girdled colonies that we were used to in Alaska. John had explained that this low elevation was key to the island's suitability as a nesting place, as outside of the nesting season cyclone-generated waves occasionally washed completely across the island, and so controlled the rats that would otherwise eat their way through entire populations of nesting birds. The only relief to the island, and the only segregation to the nesting habitat, was offered by the bushes and low trees. The red-tailed tropicbirds nested under the bushes, the boobies (brown boobies we think, though we saw only chicks and not adults) nested in the open away from the bushes, and the lesser frigatebird chicks, looking very much like the dinosaurs that they are, sat in their throne-like nests in the tops of the bushes. We also saw adult fairy terns on bare branches inside the low trees. I looked around for their eggs or chicks – among the great sights in natural history since this species is famous for laying eggs in the crooks of slender tree branches, without building any nest at all, and raising their chicks in these precarious spots. I saw neither eggs nor chicks, and had to be content with the sight of two adults, purest ivory white in the green shade of the trees, facing each other across a narrow branch and each flapping their wings to hold their place on the wobbling perch.

Elias practiced his running, the way he always did while we were ashore, and he practiced falling face-first in the coral rubble of the island, which he also did every time ashore. Alisa and I entertained him, and let him enjoy the freedom of running away from us. We sat on the ground in the sun-baked landscape and enjoyed the over-whelming concentration of life.

'I'm trying to imagine places like this before the Polynesians brought rats', I said. 'Every *motu* in the South Pacific would be covered with this many birds.'

Eventually we saw that the various dinghies had left, and we walked back to join our group at the park skiff. Walking across the coral flats towards that group of figures clustered around a small boat at the water's edge, the high tradewind clouds rushing through a sky so vast, the landscape before us perfectly flat, I had a strong sense of the timelessness of Polynesian atolls. How they were all places that had, in the last few thousand years, seen the arrival of people by boat, people who either arrived beyond relief at the fortuitous appearance of land when they could no longer keep the sea, or confident after having made a known landfall. How these people of Oceania had a worldview so different from that of continental peoples – a view of an amorphous, flowing world, the sky and the sea vast beyond vastness, larger than a lifetime of voyaging in any craft would ever see. A vastness measured by generations. And in the middle of it, these scraps of land, land enough to stand on, places that supplied coconuts to eat, and coconut crabs, and seabirds, and, just beyond the land, reefs teeming with food. These islands became places to mark the time from one generation to the next, places to tell stories, and to keep the knowledge of currents and stars and islands alive, and to stare, every generation or two, with quivering wonder at the arrival of a strange sail, coming from a place that was known only through songs.

Soon after our visit to Brushwood, we left Suwarrow. We left after another day of visiting at John and Veronica's house, and trying the strange delicacy of raw *uto*, with its taste of green living styrofoam. We left on a day when the trades were booming, after John had surprised us with his evident unhappiness at the news of our departure.

'He was sooo nice', Alisa said later. 'He sees so many people coming and going here and he treats us all so well.'

'I think he really appreciated how much we liked the seabirds', I said.

We had kisses all around with John and Veronica when we made our goodbyes, and John picked a flower for me to wear behind my ear. We really enjoyed their company, and we like to think that they enjoyed ours. We got a great feel for the Cook Islands from these three Cook Islanders that we had met: Stella from Palmerston, John from Manihiki and Veronica from Puka Puka. Many of the Cook Islands are very difficult to visit with a yacht, as the anchorages tend to come in two kinds, poor and non-existent. But of course that also makes them all the more alluring, as yacht visits are rare events in those places, and not the constant parade of short-term visits that other islands get. Suwarrow was our only visit to the Cooks on this time around, and as we rowed from Anchorage Island to *Pelagic* for the last time Alisa and I talked about sailing a loop through the western tropical Pacific, during some cyclone-free season in the future, as a way to visit some of the other Cooks.

'You know what we're doing?' Alisa asked as I leaned back for another stroke of the oars.

'No, what?'

'We're talking about a sailing trip after we reach Australia. It's the first time we've ever done that.'

37

EVERYONE SHOULD TURN FORTY IN TONGA

THE SKIES WERE overcast, and ominous, the seas troubled, coming from several directions. There was a bit of suspense in this passage from Suwarrow to Tonga, the possibility that we might get a smacking from the South Pacific convergence zone. This is another area, like the ITCZ over the equator, where rising air creates squalls and thunderstorms, and generally nasty spots of local weather. But unlike the ITCZ, the location of the South Pacific convergence zone isn't so carefully tracked by weather services, and its exact location and strength were mysteries to us. After days of fast sailing and less-than-placid conditions we did finally see the convergence zone, a long band of dirty-gray clouds hanging low over the ocean, directly in our path, and vanishing beyond the curve of the earth in either direction. *Pelagic* sailed for two days and a night to pass under those clouds, but we never got anything worse than a downpour, though the radar returns from squalls kept us from using the radar alarm to warn us of ships, so we stayed up through the night, keeping watch. The wind stayed fresh behind us, pushing us towards Tonga, insistently.

For days we had been explaining to Elias about presents, and cake, and singing, and the other components of a birthday party. Then August 5th rolled around, and we celebrated his second birthday, still on passage from Suwarrow to Tonga. Alisa made a chocolate cake, which he found even more to his liking than the carrot cake she had made for his first birthday, half of his lifetime ago, and it seemed half of ours as well, in distant Haines, Alaska. For presents he received a plastic airplane, made in China and bought at the Raiatea grocery store, emblazoned with the legend 'Super Jet Flighter', and also a copy of *Make Way For Ducklings*, which we read to him again and again and again, and of which he almost instantly had long passages by heart. And so he passed that milestone in his short, accelerating life, and left behind the second year of his existence, in our little birthday party in the cabin while the windvane steered, with his little face that was so good at showing delight, and his curly hair sweat-caked to his skull, and a film of sweat on his bare little torso, his two-year-old's body with suddenly recognizable muscles and the slender chest like the prow of a ship, and very little of the baby to it at all.

We almost made it to Vava'u, our target island in Tonga, on August 9th, the day before my birthday. But the twenty-knot trades that had made the passage so fast finally died on us. We spent one final night at sea, a still, velvet-black night, and Alisa and I stayed up late and had a gin and tonic each and celebrated the turning of my birthday at midnight. I stayed up through most of the night, catnapping in the cockpit and guiding *Pelagic* through a jibe and two long downwind legs that brought us to the north side of Vava'u just at dawn. I was amazed how much this tropical island looked like Afognak Island, in Alaska, at least from a distance.

August 10th was a Sunday, so we couldn't check into the country. In this situation we were supposed to proceed straight to the Customs dock and wait there, without leaving the boat, until we could check in on Monday. But sailing past all the beautiful tropical anchorages of Vava'u to tie up at the rusty, dirty Customs dock in the main town, Neiafu, was not how we wanted to end our 700-mile passage. So we went on stealth mode and tucked into a beautiful little anchorage, in 15 feet of turquoise water just next to an uninhabited island in the little world of high limestone islands and intervening channels that nestles within the arms of Vava'u. We felt honor-bound not to go on shore before checking in, but Alisa and I did each go snorkeling right from the boat, over a little fringing reef that was home to some fish species that we had never seen in French Polynesia. I came out of the water and let the saltwater dry onto my skin in the heat. Birds were singing in the trees on the island, which made me realize how much I had missed birdsong in French Polynesia, where extinction has made landbird communities so poor. It was a lush and beautiful spot, completely new to us and particularly sharp to our senses after six days at sea.

'Everyone should turn forty in Tonga', I said to Alisa.

Then it was time for the main event. I had been up since three am bringing the boat to land, and I was having trouble keeping up with Elias, who was, as always, perfectly rested. But when Alisa set a cake in front of me, considerably more ablaze than Elias' had been, I rallied to blow out the candles. Eli couldn't believe his good fortune when he saw Alisa cutting him yet another piece of cake, so few days after the leftovers from his own cake had finally succumbed. I got the Speedos that I had been wanting ever since we reached the tropics, which Alisa had carefully hidden aboard since Tahiti. And I tumbled into bed early and enjoyed the secure slumber of a sailor at anchor. It was a great birthday.

The next morning we tried to figure out what the local time was, so that we would be sure of presenting ourselves to officialdom during working hours. Tonga is thirteen hours off GMT, we read in our *Lonely Guide to the South Pacific*.

'That doesn't make any sense', I said to Alisa. 'How can any place be more than twelve hours away from any other place in the world?'

We consulted a cruising guide that told us that Tonga's motto is 'The place where time begins', or some such thing. And even though we were just shy of 174° W longitude, and thus far from 180°, where you might expect the dateline to be, we had in fact crossed the dateline when we entered Tongan waters. So we went straight from August 9th to August 11th.

'So we were hiding out on a Monday, and we could have checked in right away', I said to Alisa.

'So we celebrated your birthday on the wrong day.'

'We missed it completely! I'm forty years old, but I've only had thirty-nine birthdays!'

Everyone should turn forty in Tonga.

38

THE HANDS OF THE NOBLES

BEFORE WE ARRIVED Alisa and I knew that Tonga was the only nation in Polynesia to never be colonized, and that it was governed by one of the few strong monarchies remaining in the world. What we didn't know is that we would have a chance to see the trappings of Tongan royalty and independence on display.

We tied up at the Customs dock in Neiafu, the biggest town in the Vava'u island group in the northern part of the kingdom, and the first thing we heard was that the king was coming. Lofi, the nice old man who meets every yacht that he can, took our lines and sold us a loaf of bread for US$5, which turned out to be five times what it cost at the bakery.

'The king is coming on Sunday', Lofi said. 'There will be festivities and feasts and you are welcome to join in. You are very lucky to be here now.'

A parade of officials followed: the health inspector, the Customs officer, and a third man who I think represented the quarantine service. They all enjoyed coffee and leftover birthday cake in the cockpit, charged us a few bucks, and accepted smokes from our stash of cigarettes for trade and gifts and sailing-across-the-Pacific-with-a-toddler-is-more-than-I-can-take moments. All three officials agreed that we were lucky to be visiting at this time. The word 'coronation' came up a few times, and I realized that a new king was being installed. The last king, Taufa'ahau Tupou IV, had reigned for forty-one years, one of the officials explained. After an interregnum of two years following his death, his eldest son, Siaosi, or George, Tupou V, had just been crowned in Nuku'alofa, the capital, and was travelling to all the island groups of the kingdom for celebrations of the event. The three officials left, and, after I had visited the immigration office and fetched local currency from the bank to pay our quarantine fee, we were cleared into the country.

Before leaving the quarantine dock we wandered into town to buy beer, which was mercifully affordable after the painful restraint that had been imposed on us by French Polynesian prices, and vegetables, which we hadn't seen since leaving Raiatea. People smiled at us in the street, evidently reacting to our just-arrived euphoria, since we never got such warm interactions again. Our quick use of *malo e lelei* for 'hello' went far. And our first look showed Neiafu to be a very rural town. The business district was a humble couple of streets that quickly gave way to rambling neighborhoods of breadfruit trees and chickens and houses with corrugated roofs. Pigs ran free everywhere. Clothing was somber, trending towards the black. Men wore *tupenu*, or skirts, to the knee, women wore *tupenu* to the ankle. Both sexes, women especially, wore *taovala*, woven mats wrapped around the waist like a second skirt on top of the *tupenu*. Color was provided by school uniforms – boys in green or sky-blue *tupenu*, girls in blue dresses.

I bought a crate of one of the local beers, Mata Maka ('Friendly Islands Lager'), which turned out to be brewed in New Zealand, but still tasted fine. The produce market was a highlight. There was good produce, cheap, and a half dozen vendors sold chilled drinking coconuts, at the equivalent of US$1 each, which quickly became our favorite Neiafu treat. Alisa waded into the center of the market to get us greens for dinner. Eli and I stayed on the periphery. It was afternoon, and we were the only customers. More than half of the vendors were asleep behind their wares. Alisa took a quick tour of the available stock on hand, then began asking prices from a woman selling tomatoes. No smiles from the seller, a middle-aged woman wearing a *taovala*. The discussion seemed to go on longer than might be necessary to communicate the price of tomatoes. I overheard Alisa saying, 'but we were just at the bank, and the exchange rate is 1.9 for a dollar'. She was gesturing and speaking slowly, clearly invoking her best experienced-traveler-needing-to-communicate persona. I glanced at the seller, wondering what her response might be. Just a little shake of the head, like someone trying to get a fly off their cheek. Nothing else. Alisa tried another stall, too far away for me to eavesdrop, where a man sat behind a pile of melons. Another long conversation ensued.

'That was *so* confusing', Alisa said when she finally emerged fifteen minutes later clutching plastic bags full of produce. 'A lot of the people were telling me prices in dollars. But when I tried to work out the conversion rate into *pa'anga* with them, they didn't want to talk about it. That was *so* confusing.'

Our confusion abated the next day, when we realized that Tongans used both '*pa'anga*' and 'dollar' to refer to the local currency.

'And how confused were those people in the market?' I asked Alisa. 'When this *palangi* woman starts trying to tell them that the conversion rate is 1.9 *pa'anga* per dollar, so she should get six tomatoes for the price of three?'

Neiafu boasted a lively little expat scene built around the needs of tourists and yachties, and we enjoyed the experience of going out for cheap drinks and cheap meals, delighted by how well Elias did in the unfamiliar setting of a restaurant. For days after our first night out he declaimed 'Lobsters got *away!*' to any who would listen, the warmly received rumor of economical lobster dinners proving, when we put it to the test, to be hypothetical.

With a few days in hand before the coronation celebrations, we spent some days away from Neiafu and visited the most improbably situated Spanish restaurant in all the world, alone on a Tongan islet, without obvious access for anyone without their own boat. And when we came back to Neiafu we met up with our good friends Julia and Dave on *Macy*, whom we had last seen in Raiatea. Expecting us, they had been sitting in a waterfront bar waiting for *Pelagic* to pull into the harbor. Seeing them tearing out to meet us in their dinghy, with big grins on their faces and their hair pushed back by the wind, was one of the best people moments that we ever had on *Pelagic*. The friendships between people on travelling boats can be so quick and so intense, with the chance of meeting up again after the inevitable separation so uncertain, and the intervening time spent in such an intense way of living, that a reunion becomes a moment of over-the-top joy, triggered by seeing someone whom you met for the very first time only a month before. We caught up on each other's news, and I told Dave and Julia the story of my missed 40th birthday. They returned for dinner with a birthday gift, a bottle of Panamanian rum that we put away in the proper manner for sailors, in one sitting. They told us about their visit to Niuatoputapu, in the far northern part of the kingdom, during that island's Coronation celebrations.

'We waited at the airport for four hours', Dave said. 'And we didn't see the king for more than two minutes. There was another event we went to, all these kids from the school were dressed up and ready to perform, and the king never even showed.'

That, it turned out, was a foretaste of the general attitude towards the coronation celebrations among the yachties we spoke to. The chief complaint was that there was no telling when the various events would happen, since nothing in Tonga could be counted on to begin on time. There was also more than a bit of knowing cynicism among resident expats about the new king. He was a little simple. He was a sixty-year-old man who still played with toy soldiers. The local people couldn't take him seriously, he lacked the common touch. The Tongans I spoke to maintained the king was a savvy businessman. He had already signed the papers to institute democracy in two years. Or, in two years he would abdicate in favor of his younger brother, who had children, so that the continuity of the monarchy would be guaranteed.

Armed with a schedule of events from the visitors' bureau, we managed to find our way to two instances of celebration. First, the kava celebration for the new king, held in a field at the local college. One hundred men dressed in white button-down shirts, ironed crisp, and white *tupenu*, with sashes of dry leaves over their shoulders, necklaces made of fresh-picked leaves, and aprons of leaves hanging down over their formal *taovala*, were sitting in a huge circle in the field, with the king sitting under a canopy at one side of the circle and officiants, and the kava bowl, at the other. In the center of the circle were gifts to the new king: twenty-odd hogs, woody clusters of kava root, and a couple of hundred baskets, woven from leaves for the occasion, full of food.

We were waved away from the area behind the king's canopy by an army officer, and we sat down with other spectators far back from the kava circle. One man was singing or chanting the same phrase over and over on a loudspeaker, and a few people were coming and going at the far end of the circle, by the kava bowl. We had no idea what was going on. We had arrived late, and soon the king got up and left. Walking away with an army officer one step behind him and a security guard on his flank, he was a man reaching a pinnacle late in life, wearing a fine *taovala* and walking with a cane.

The ceremony was over and the security relaxed. I wandered

over to the pile of gifts, where the men in white were milling around. I met two of them, who introduced themselves as Tuamololu and Mafilauncave. They explained that they were *matapules*, the 'hands of the nobles', who serve at ceremonies such as this. The title of *matapule* is hereditary, with a son assuming the office only after his father has died.

After they sat for a group portrait, the *matapules* began dividing up the gifts: the hogs (*tuaka toho*), the baskets of food (*umu kaveitau*) and the kava root (*kava tohu*). In the baskets I saw cooked chicken and spareribs, taro, canned sardines and hot dogs still in the wrapper. Tuamololu explained that the food would be divided among the king, the nobles and the higher order of common people.

It was a fun spectacle, but this sort of event is all opaque when you're an outsider who has no idea of the significance of anything. I was provided one little piece of perspective by an account of pre-Christian Tonga that I had been reading. It was written by William Mariner, a fourteen-year-old clerk on the English ship *Port au Prince*, who was stranded here in 1806 after the ship was attacked in the Ha'apai Group, and most of the crew massacred. Mariner was taken under the protection of Finau, a *how*, or king, and spent four years in Tonga, mostly in the Vava'u Group. Mariner wrote extensively about the *matapules*, who at that time were advisors to the Tongan chiefs. Having read that, it became great fun to meet some real *matapules*, and see the continuity of the tradition.

There was an official reception that night that I talked big about crashing, but we settled for rowing by the waterfront hotel where it was being held. A military band in dress uniform was playing old swing tunes from a landing craft that was docked bow-on at the hotel. The guests looked listless – no dancing, no obvious fun. The king was apparently either gone or had never arrived. But the band sounded good ('American music', I said to Alisa as they launched into Glenn Miller), and it was a beautiful and romantic setting, these uniformed musicians playing under the South Pacific stars, with a circle of fires that had been lit all the way around the Port of Refuge in celebration.

The next event that looked appropriate for a couple of *palangi* with a two-year-old was the military parade the following day. We again arrived late, just as various soldiers and sailors were finishing their drill around the parade ground. Soon after we arrived, the king departed from the reviewing stand. We expected that he would be part of a general parade into town, though we had no idea what route that parade would take. It turned out that the king's motorcade was leaving the event alone, and, to our surprise, he took a right-hand turn after leaving the field and headed right for us. We happened to be the only people standing on this section of road. The king approached, standing in the back of a jeep, wearing white gloves and a white Kaiser helmet with a gold spike and a military uniform awash in gold braid and ribbons. As the king passed us, Alisa gave him her biggest uninhibited-in-public American wave. The king looked right at her, smiled, and waved.

And then the moment was over – the motorcade drove into the palace, and the king was seen no more. Alisa was ecstatic. 'Did you *see* that?' she asked me. 'He looked right at me! I didn't know what to do, should I wave, I asked myself, and I thought, *yeah*, that's the king right there, why *shouldn't* I wave? So I gave him a big wave and a smile and did you *see* that little look and that wave he gave me? He was looking right at me, there was no one else there but Eli. *Wow*, I hope you got a picture of that.' And then she laughed, 'ha ha', just like that, and I was suddenly back with the 22-year-old graduate student I first met in Fairbanks fourteen years before, prone to outbursts of unbridled enthusiasm at any moment of the day, before she became a serious government biologist and then an occasionally frazzled mother of a two-year-old. 'Wow!' She punched me on the arm and looked up with a big grin. We were walking down the hill back to town, pushing Elias in his stroller. 'Wait till those other yachties hear about *this*.'

39

'NEW YACHT, NEW YACHT, NEW YACHT'

WE LEFT OUR mooring in Neiafu sailing under main alone. The best part about laying to a mooring is leaving it. There's no messing around with the windlass, no stacking the anchor chain. Just put up a sail, slip the mooring line, and silently leave. Nice. We rode a fine northeasterly breeze out of town. But just as we were leaving the Vava'u Group the wind died completely and we were left riding an oily swell, looking at the little palm-covered islands in the distance. The mixing elbow on our engine had started to leak exhaust fumes into the engine compartment, and I was hesitant to motor all through the night to the Ha'apai Group for fear of it getting worse. We talked about anchoring in one of the little islands in the southern part of the Vava'u Group and waiting for wind, but decided that we might as well risk a little motoring to get where we were going.

We motored into the night, taking turns hand steering. At one in the morning we shut down and drifted to avoid arriving in the Ha'apai before dawn. It was a star-filled, still night, with just a bit of a roll to the ocean. We set the radar alarm and I woke every hour or so to check on things. At one point I realized that a whale was sleeping near us. I could hear the giant gasping breaths, and I could just see the occasional white patch of disturbed water over the beast's back. It was close, and the night quiet enough that the sound of its breath was loud, and a little spooky. I turned the engine on and motored a half-mile away to avoid any unwanted interactions.

In the morning we arrived at the island of Lifuka, and dropped the hook off the little port of Pangai, the administrative center for the Ha'apai Group. At Lifuka we found ourselves at a crossroads of European history in the South Pacific. Lifuka is where the crew of the *Port au Prince* was massacred. It is also the place where in 1777 Captain Cook, who famously called Tonga the 'Friendly Archipelago', was entertained, along with his officers, at a feast ashore in a manner that 'would have met with universal applause on a European Theatre'. Cook was unaware that the feast was part of a plan to massacre him, his officers and marines, and seize the *Resolution* and *Discovery*, said plan failing to come off only due to arguments about tactics among the chiefs involved. And from Lifuka we could look west and see the volcanic island of Tofua, where William Bligh and eighteen loyal crew came ashore in 1789 after the mutiny on the *Bounty*, only to have one of their number killed on the beach by Tongans, forcing the start of their 3,600-mile voyage, in a 23-foot boat, to eventual safety in Timor.

For all these dramatic events that had happened in another age, our first look showed Lifuka as an everyday sort of place. We were fuzzy-headed from short sleep the night before. Lifuka lay before us as another low tropical island baking under a merciless sun, surrounded by turquoise water. It was early afternoon by the time we had the anchoring sorted out, and a consensus was slowly building that we should delay the hassle of putting the dinghy in the water and rowing in to deal with officialdom until the next day; even though we had only travelled within Tonga, we were still expected to check in with Customs upon entering the Ha'apai.

Then a voice came over the VHF.

'New yacht, new yacht, new yacht, this is harbormaster, harbormaster, harbormaster, do you read me over.'

'They beckon', I said to Alisa. Then, 'Harbormaster, this is sailing vessel *Pelagic*, sailing vessel *Pelagic*'.

Unintelligible.

'Could you repeat that, over.'

Unintelligible.

'Could you repeat that again please, over.'

'What I am saying is I am asking you to call me.'

Quizzical look to Alisa. 'Um, OK, Harbormaster, this is sailing vessel *Pelagic*.'

'No, I am asking what time you will come to see me.'

'Um, how about in two hours, we still have to get our dinghy in the water, over.'

'I think, one hour, over.'

And so, our sense of enterprise was rekindled. We got the dinghy in the water, child and adult crew in the dinghy, and rowed the quarter-mile to shore, all within the given hour. But once we got to the village nobody could direct us to the harbormaster. Everyone was reserved, but friendly when approached.

The first man I asked was standing on the wharf.

'I have no idea where he is', he said to me, successfully conveying his absolute ignorance concerning the harbormaster's whereabouts.

I tried again, rephrasing my question like any experienced traveler. 'Do you not know where the harbormaster man is, or do you not know where the harbormaster office is?'

'I have never heard of that person or that office', he said, putting any lingering doubts to rest.

Another man knew exactly where the harbormaster was. He walked me to a vantage point in the middle of the staging area between the harbor and the military barracks and pointed down the coast. 'There', he said with great authority. 'The office is right by that blue boat.'

When we arrived at the blue boat we found a mix of offices – the electric company, the revenue service, the Customs service, but no harbormaster. Feeling the *palangi*'s burden of an appointment neglected, I stuck my head in the first office and startled a very sleepy bureaucrat by saying hello.

'Do you know where the harbormaster's office is?' I asked.

He looked at me with perfect perplexity, and I realized that I likely represented the most surprising event to occur during office hours in recent memory. After pausing to parse his phrasing, the young man said, 'I have never heard of that before in my life'. This was a response so airtight against any further enquiry, and so similar to the denials of the first man I had asked, that I began to doubt the harbormaster's existence myself.

I figured that I might as well check in with Customs while I was in the neighborhood. And the Customs man directed me to the harbormaster's office, which proved to be on the wharf, thirty yards from the first two men I had asked.

I found the harbormaster inside an open-walled room under a galvanized roof where passengers waited for the inter-island ferry. Two women sat in a corner next to piles of baggage. The harbor-master was in his mid-twenties. He had a big halo of curly hair and dewy eyes and wore a plastic port security badge with his picture and name on it. He was talking into a handheld VHF: 'New yacht, new yacht, new yacht'.

We had found English to be universal in Tonga, and the harbor-master was the only person we had trouble speaking with. I struggled to understand anything he said, but he seemed used to that, and just produced a sign-in sheet for me to fill in. The previous entry from a boat checking in was five days old, which made me very happy. After I was done filling in the sheet, the harbormaster made me understand that he hadn't heard from the other yacht that was anchored off the town. 'They must check soon', he said. 'Overtime charges.' And as I left he got back on the radio, his voice an insistent drone. 'New yacht, new yacht, new yacht'.

The thing that had most excited us about the Ha'apai was the favorable comparison that one cruising guide made with the atolls of the Tuamotus. Vava'u had been a high limestone island with its arms wrapped around a little galaxy of protected reefs and anchorages, a self-contained world of intermingled land and water so completely protected from the open sea that it offered one of the region's few havens from cyclones. The Ha'apai Group was totally different: a 30-mile long string of low islands and reefs running north to south and providing indifferent protection to a universe of islets and reefs lying to the west. The next day we sailed south from Lifuka, in the lee of the barrier system, bound for one of the many uninhabited islands. We passed a red yacht motoring north towards Pangai, and were gratified an hour later to hear a familiar voice on the VHF, droning on at great length without any response: 'Red yacht, red yacht, red yacht. Red, red, red, red …'

We sailed past a humpback calf swimming just behind its mother's long pectoral fin, their distant Antarctic feeding grounds the business of another season. We dropped the hook off Tofanga Island, a little heaven of sand and coral five hundred yards long and only thirty yards across. We rowed ashore and explored – Alisa and I checked out a bird we hadn't seen before (wattled honeyeater), Alisa found an exquisite shell the size of an apple, we took turns walking the beach that completely encircled the island, and Elias got busy picking up pieces of coral and digging in the sand. A yacht was anchored about a mile away, but it left the next day and it was ten days until we saw another.

This is exactly what we had come for – a deserted tropical island. It was amazing how infrequently we had the experience of an entire island, or even just an anchorage, completely to ourselves on our way across the Pacific. We made the most of this experience at Tofanga, spending whole days just reading and playing with Elias and working on the boat and going to the beach and snorkeling and generally letting the problems of the world take care of themselves for a while.

When Saturday rolled around we jumped five miles north to the village of Uiha so that we could attend church the next day. We were feeling very short on the Getting Down With the People side of our stay in Tonga, especially after the effortlessly warm interactions we had enjoyed with people in the Marquesas, Tuamotus and Cooks. At this latitude, at least, Tonga is the western outpost of Polynesia, with Fiji, and Melanesia, just next door. We wondered if the reticence towards outsiders that we sensed had something to do with the history of being so close to the Polynesian–Melanesian cultural border. In any event, we were keen to meet some people in the Ha'apai, and since Tongans are famously church-going, we figured that church was the place to do it.

On Sunday morning we forayed ashore and found Uiha as a hamlet – sandy roads, breadfruit trees, loose herds of pigs, goats tied up in the yards of scattered houses. No stores that I can remember, and the endlessly renewed parade of tradewind clouds overhead. There were at least two churches to choose from, and the one we ended up at, the Free Wesleyan Church, was a remarkable building, really a small cathedral of the tropics, built of bricks and concrete and coral, painted white with jolly red trim and a green corrugated roof, the entrance flanked by two spires, one of which had tumbled into the churchyard, and two high towers, one crumbling, about the middle part of the long building. The interior was dim, the service informal and entirely in Tongan, which spared me exposure to any theology. The singing was strong, and crisp, and resonant, and different from anything I had ever heard. A music leader gave the pitch before each song with a mouth organ and the little congregation of maybe thirty adults launched into two – and three-part harmonies and pulled them off very well. Men and women sat apart and little children wandered from relative to relative while old ladies dispensed smacks to keep them in line. The young men wore boldly printed shirts with ties and their *tupenu*, and on the backs of the pews they rested corded forearms, broad palms, splayed fingers. The older men wore dark jackets and ties and *tupenu*. The women wore dark blazers and dark shirts and red scarves and *tupenu* and everyone wore the mats around their waists, the *taovala*.

After the service everyone walked together down the road, we guessed towards lunch, but we weren't invited along. The vibe was very guarded, though friendly. The people who did talk to us tended to say things like, 'Are you going back to your boat now?' Alisa did manage a great interaction with two old women and we both talked to Matetau, a big gray-haired man whom we had met after he rode up to church on his bike from the pre-service kava ceremony with the minister.

We went back to the boat for lunch and printed up pictures as gifts for people we had met. Our return that afternoon was a mixed bag – Matetau smiled at the picture we had taken of him with his three grown kids, but then explained that his wife had died in 2006 and he was a poor man and did not have anything that he could give us in return. But Alisa found one of the women she had been interacting with and completely bowled her over with the picture she had taken of her and her friend. She was a small bent woman in black with the impish smile of a little girl, a smile that owed nothing to the resignation and wisdom of age. She was on her way to the second church service of the day when Alisa found her and she turned straight around and walked back home with the picture, holding it up in front of her face with both hands and smiling at it in disbelief.

We kept scolding Elias not to pick up the dried pig turds that were here and there on the road and on the way back to the boat Elias wouldn't stop putting his hands into his mouth, in fact when I yelled at him not to do it he smiled at me and took a two-year-old's obvious joy at putting the turd-handling hand right back in his little mouth. Oppressed at the idea of the parasites that were going to colonize my sweet boy's poorly-defended little body as the result of my selfish desire to do something besides the natural routine of spending my life safely behind a desk, I completely flipped out. I got angry at Elias with the unfiltered sort of rage that parents sometimes feel at the innocent failings of toddlers, unreasonable little creatures that they are. So I completely, inappropriately lost my temper at little Elias in the nesting dinghy that had already been the source for so much trouble between Alisa and me. And then, when it was all over, I had all the time in the world to regret my failed self-control.

Later, when Elias was safely down for his nap and I had calmed down, I said to Alisa, 'I'm not sure how many more poor villages I feel like visiting with our two-year-old.'

40

TONGA STYLE

THE WIND HAD been blowing strongly for a couple days. Ready for more deserted tropical isle delights, we left the anchorage at Uiha with the wind gusting over twenty-five knots and the dinghy towing behind us. This soon proved to be a big mistake, as the dinghy flipped over in the waves and could not be righted until we reached our next anchorage, ten miles away. We both assumed that the loads generated by dragging the dinghy upside down would be too great for the painter or the dinghy itself, that the dinghy was a goner. It's hard to overestimate what a blow this would be to the trip – without the dinghy we could get nowhere, as it was the only link between *Pelagic* and the places we visited. But when we finally pulled into the Limu Island anchorage hours later, the dinghy was still with us. There was some fiberglass damage to the joint between the two halves of the dinghy, but I was able to fix that the next day, though it was a bit of an adventure working with fiberglass and epoxy in the thirty-knot winds. And we both had a new appreciation for that troublesome little dinghy, the wellspring for moments of marital tension in anchorages across the Pacific as the two of us, exhausted by sailing and child-rearing, were forced into the highly collaborative effort required to assemble or disassemble the nesting dinghy, usually in the pitch dark after Elias was asleep.

'I wonder if we should give the dinghy a name now to show her how much we appreciate her?' I asked Alisa.

'I guess *Fair Dinkum* never really stuck.'

'No, it didn't. It seemed like such a good name, but it never did stick. Maybe a dinghy is such an everyday bit of gear that you shouldn't give it a formal name, but just use whatever nickname sticks to it.'

'So you think we should just call it the "dinga-linger"?'

'Well, it does kind of fit. And there is something so sweet about hearing Elias say "dinga-linger".'

So we made it official, and that night we drank a toast to the second life of our old nemesis, the *Dinga-linger*.

It blew hard for the first three days we were at Limu Island – we saw our first steady thirty-five knot winds of the whole trip, and our first forty-knot gusts. Limu is a tiny islet of sandy beach and impenetrable low forest sitting at the apex of a ninety-degree angle in the Ha'apai barrier reef. While the gale was still blowing, it was a lonely place, with the surf exploding onto the reef to either side of us, and all eight tons of *Pelagic* pulling back insistently on the anchor chain, over and over. We were anchored over a patch of sand, a maze of little reefs with sharp coral teeth just off the stern, waiting to catch us if the anchor dragged. But we had everything set up correctly: the proper type of anchor, much larger than the size recommended for our boat, properly oversized anchor chain, and all the details of seized shackles and chafe-guarded snubbing gear well taken care of. I dove on the anchor every day and was happy to see that the wind load was burying it deeper and deeper in the sand, without creating any drag. And just to be sure, I swam out a second anchor at a thirty-degree angle to the first. So we knew that everything was fine, and we just relaxed until the blow would ease enough for us to brave the 300-yard row to shore.

When the wind did abate we found incredible snorkeling on the reefs around *Pelagic*, and then we rowed ashore to find another fantastic deserted tropical isle experience. Our world was reduced to a new set of elements: the soft sand that completely encircled the little island, the turquoise water beyond that, and the white clouds above. And we had this slice of creation all to ourselves to discover, to reflect upon, and to enjoy. In the week we were at Limu we once saw a local fishing boat in the distance, and never any other yachts. Meanwhile, less than a hundred miles away in Vava'u, hundreds of cruising yachts were congregated. It felt like the cruising route across the Pacific was a six-lane highway, and we had found a little cul-de-sac without any traffic at all. I figure that everyone out cruising in a sailboat makes the itinerary that most interests them, and there's no cause to criticize other people's selection of routes as better or worse than anyone else's. But it was remarkable to find a place that offered everything that fuels the South Pacific dream, with so few other yachts venturing down from the well-travelled environs of Vava'u to check it out. Alisa and I agreed that our time in Alaska might have made it easier for us to be alone in a wild anchorage in the Ha'apai when a gale was blowing, since we were at ease with the psychological demands of solitude and independence. And I also think that as much as people might say they want a deserted beach all to themselves, many are more comfortable with a tropical experience that has been interpreted and validated by other visitors, and a beach that has been raked clean by the staff of the local resort.

After our week at Limu was over, and we were rowing away from the island for the last time, the three of us sang the new mantra that we had created to entertain Elias on our long rows back and forth to the beach. While I kept time with the oars, he sat on Alisa's lap in the stern sheets and sang along with us in his two-year-old's piping voice:

'Tonga Tonga Tonga … doin' it Tonga style.'

We found Tonga taking on the role of our new Favorite Place. From Limu we sailed to the island of Ha'afeva. A man diving for sea cucumbers for the export market snorkeled past our stern and, with the same lack of preliminaries that A'tai had displayed at Ua Pou, invited us to lunch the next day. When we arrived, with Alisa wearing her long skirt that was appropriate for conservative rural Tonga, we found that our host was out working for the day and would not be joining us, though his wife and two sisters and all their children were there. The table in the front room of the house was set with three plates, and Alisa and Elias and I sat down to eat lunch while everyone else watched from the couches around the periphery of the room. The women all wore shorts and t-shirts, *tupenu* and *taovala* not being in evidence, and, isolated as they were, were very glad for gifts of outgrown children's shoes and aspirin and an extra pair of swim goggles when they came out to meet us at the dock later in the day.

41

FIJI IN TWO WEEKS?

'WELL', I SAID. 'It's September 12th.'

Pelagic bobbed in quiet waters off Pangai, where we would get our outward clearance from Tonga. Elias was asleep, and Alisa and I were using the sudden peace and quiet to plot out the rest of the trip.

'So', Alisa asked, 'we want to be in Bundaberg in … six weeks?' Having heard that the Customs agents in Bundaberg were used to dealing with yachts, we had selected that port as our entry point for Oz.

'I guess so. *World Cruising Routes* says that the Coral Sea cyclone season can start early. I'm sure that we could push it quite a bit later, but I'd really rather be home and hosed once cyclone season has begun, even if the risk is low early on.'

'The last thing we want is to be a little late in Noumea and then to find out we need a new engine part shipped in, or a shroud replaced, or something like that.'

'That's right', I said. 'So we've got some travelling ahead of us.' I ran the dividers over the small-scale chart of the southwest Pacific. 'It's four hundred miles to Fiji, then two 700-mile passages to get to New Cal and onto Oz. Add in a couple of hundred miles for stopping in here and there and it's two thousand miles of sailing.'

'Good thing we took the time to enjoy the eastern Pacific so much.'

'Good thing.'

Our trip began to fly away from us, the end came rushing near. As we sailed away from Pangai the next morning, the world around us was an exalted horizon. The barrier islands of the Ha'apai clustered behind us in the east, all of them as flat as Texas and barely above the water when viewed from a few miles away. To the west was the open ocean. We picked our way past a few reefs, relying on charts drawn from an 1880s survey by the British Navy. A beautiful golden mahi mahi took our lure as we approached the two volcanoes that are the westernmost limit of Tonga. I slowly reeled the big fish in, the yellow forked tail flapping against the blue waves that were overtaking us. Alisa and I were already talking about how we would cook it. It had been so long since we'd caught a fish. And then, just as I was about to gaff the fish, it slipped the hook and was gone.

The undersea area that we would cross between Tonga and Fiji is a nasty piece of work, a subduction zone where the Pacific tectonic plate is forced under the Fiji plate, and lots and lots of energy is released from the subsurface earth in a really unpredictable way. For people living in Tonga and Fiji and Samoa, this means the continuous possibility of seismically-generated tsunamis that may come sweeping over their shores. And for vessels transiting the area, the subduction zone creates the potential for bits of magma to come to the ocean surface as hazards to navigation so new that they've never been properly charted. On *Pelagic* we had a list of possible uncharted obstacles in the area that had been passing around the yachtie community. The list ran to sixty items. We took the time to pencil them all onto our chart, and they made a nice shotgun pattern of possible dangers to be concerned about.

As the passage progressed the tradewinds failed and were replaced by light westerlies. These westerlies grew and grew, until we spent the final two days beating into twenty knots of wind. *Pelagic* put her shoulder into the sea, and we were made aware that the leaks between caprail and deck were reasserting themselves. Then we changed our course to pass between the Fijian islands of Totoya and Matuku, heading northwest for the capital, Suva. With the change of course the wind was no longer in our faces, the ride became more civilized, the rail was no longer in the water, the spray no longer came over the bow. The ugly low overcast that had come with the westerlies gave way to sunshine. Elias took his nap. Alisa and I lounged in the cockpit for an hour, enjoying the peace and privacy and perfection that yachties without children might find routine, but was a rare treat for us. The sweat pooled on our skin, we stretched out in the cockpit without for once being too concerned with UV levels. The beautiful tropical islands slid past us, forbidden to *Pelagic* until we first checked into the country at Suva. Somewhere on the two little islands on either side of us there might well be people. But we saw no evidence of their presence, the sea was innocent of other boats, the skies above empty of planes, the world was ours and ours alone, to be enjoyed only by the two of us and our sleeping son, all of us cast far out from home on this 37-foot fiberglass artifact of our civilization.

Then the spell ended. Elias shouted from his berth forward.

'I'm all done sleeping!'

Alisa unhooked the netting that held him in the bunk, and he came running back into the cabin, dressed for the tropics in just shorts, his hair tousled with sleep. Alisa made him a cup of powdered milk, then asked if I wanted tea.

'Oh hey', she called up a minute later. 'Butane's out. Can you switch over?'

In North America we had cooked with propane, but in Tahiti we had filled our two tanks with butane, the version of cooking gas that is available in French Polynesia. We had been using just one five-kilogram tank of butane ever since Tahiti, and we had been amazed at how long it had lasted – two months, twice as long as the same tank would have lasted if we were cooking with propane. We still had a nearly-full bottle in reserve that, at the rate we seemed to be going through the butane, would last us all the way to Australia.

'I guess butane just lasts longer than propane', I had said to Alisa the last time we talked about it.

I opened the vented locker in the lazarette, where the tanks lived. And when I tried to open the reserve tank, the mystery was solved. The valve was already open.

'Hey Alisa', I said. 'You know how that tank of butane lasted twice as long as we expected?'

'Yep?'

'It's because I left both valves open. So we were drawing off both tanks.'

It was four in the afternoon, we couldn't expect to reach Suva until the next morning, and we had no gas for cooking. Oops.

That evening Alisa made Elias a fine repast of crackers, canned olives, canned corn and uncooked tofu. We luckily still had half a mahi mahi in the fridge, and so Alisa and I had sashimi for dinner that night and for breakfast the next morning too. Thankfully we had wasabi and soy sauce and pickled ginger on board. We agreed it was the best meal possible for people unexpectedly deprived of the ability to cook.

We each stayed up half the night as we coasted in towards Suva, keeping our speed as low as possible with heavily reefed sails. We still arrived outside the harbor in the wee hours, and Alisa tacked us back and forth in the company of freighters and fishing boats while I enjoyed a coma-like three hours' sleep.

At dawn I ran the Fijian courtesy flag up to the starboard spreader and ran *Pelagic* in through the opening of the reef that guards Suva Harbor. First light showed a thick layer of smoke hovering low over the waterfront. The big buildings clustered along the shore made Suva look like more of a city than anything we had seen since San Diego. Shipping dominated the waterfront. Modern foreign-flagged freighters unloaded at the King's Wharf downtown and a line of smaller ferries and local trading boats crowded the shipyard docks that stretched north. The hammering of steel hulls undergoing repairs was constant. The harbor water was covered with the rainbow scum of spilled petrochemicals.

We checked in with port control on the radio and proceeded to the quarantine anchorage, where we raised the yellow quarantine flag. I collapsed into a nap while we waited for our visit from the health inspector, then I woke to find the morning mists replaced by a blinding tropical day. Elias was antsy in the way that a two-year-old who is trapped on a 37-foot boat with two parents who can barely keep their eyes open is antsy. Lunchtime came and Alisa bravely produced another cold meal. Our stores were low, though, since we were planning on a big provisioning in Suva, and we were quickly running out of no-cook options. And we couldn't make coffee or tea, a real blow to the person (me) who had been in the cockpit approximately twenty of the last twenty-four hours, conning *Pelagic* to shore, and also to the person (Alisa) who had been conning Elias through the reefs and shoals of a two-year-old's routine during the same hours.

The health and agriculture inspectors finally showed up on their big orange launch seven hours after we had arrived. We promised the agriculture inspector that we would not land our coconuts and limes from Tonga. For the health inspector, I filled out a wonderfully anachronistic form that appeared to be left over from the age of clipper ships. Among the questions I had to answer were: 'Has there been on board during the voyage any case or suspected case of plague, cholera, yellow fever, smallpox?' and 'Has plague occurred or been suspected among the rats or mice on board or has there been an unusual mortality among them?' On the back of the form was a declaration for the 'particulars of every case of illness or death occurring on board', including a space to note the disposal for each case: 'State whether still on board; landed at (give name of port); buried at sea'.

More to the point, the health inspector, a smiling woman in her thirties, said, 'I must tell you that there is an outbreak of dengue fever in Fiji'.

'Oh,' I said. 'Where is that happening?'

She gave me a diffident look. 'Mostly in the west and central regions.' Suva is in the east. No worries, I thought.

Our health clearance granted, we re-anchored outside of the quarantine area and rowed in to the Royal Suva Yacht Club. Even though we reached the shore after four, I still managed to hop in a cab and get both butane bottles filled before Fiji Gas closed at four thirty. Any place where cooking gas is so quickly available wins very high marks from the cruising sailor, and this was an early plus for Suva to counter all the negative things we had heard.

Most westbound yachts clear into Fiji in Savusavu, but we had decided that the best place to get some needed engine parts shipped to us was the capital, Suva. Once we had ordered the parts from Tonga and arranged to pick them up in Suva, thereby committing to that port of entry, it seemed that every yachtie we met was suddenly ready to tell us what a festering hole Suva was. Our cruising guides noted that thefts from anchored yachts were a real problem, and that the number of yachts visiting Suva was down markedly following the violence that attended coups in 2000 and 2006. And once we ran our wifi antenna out onto the dodger in Suva Harbor and caught up on email, an online search revealed that the region affected by the dengue outbreak did include Suva (something that will concern any parent travelling with a two-year-old) and that the Australian embassy had evacuated dependent personnel because of the continuing potential for political violence and a decline in law and order that had seen a rise in violent crime aimed at foreigners. Our *Lonely Guide to the South Pacific* noted that, for fear of crime, locals in Suva always take cabs after dark, even for trips of 300 meters. Ugh.

But we ended up having a fine time. First of all, the taxis were plentiful and cheap. While this was a problem for the cabbies, who drove for thirteen or fourteen hours a day to make a go of it on a series of $2 and $3 fares, it made Suva a logistical breeze for us. Usually we spent a lot of time getting to know our way around new towns, but in Suva we just jumped in a cab and said, 'King's Wharf, please!', or 'Fijian Affairs Board, please!', or even, 'Can you take us to a good curry restaurant?' From the perspective of the cabs we watched the pageant of the city reel by. The cabs drove us past the Suva Market where shoeshines and cobblers and peddlers of pirated DVDs jostled for trade. We drove by the bus station, where threadbare porters sprinted behind their wheelbarrows to claim a place by one of the baggage compartments of each arriving bus. Pedestrians waded out into the traffic, alternately stepping into the way and holding back, scowling, in obeisance to implicit rules of the road that I did not understand. And it all happened with the disorientation that came from sitting on the left-hand side, where the driver should have been, and observing the continuing string of surprises and violations of good sense that is city traffic in a drive-on-the-left country. I became concerned for our chances once we began driving in Australia.

I had great chats with cabbies. My enthusiasm for a new place was obvious, and a series of drivers roused from the waking dream of their endless days behind the wheel to answer my questions about Suva and ask their own about Alaska. A Melanesian driver in sunglasses bemoaned the loss of ethnic Indians from Fiji. 'If it goes like this for three years or five years, my friend, there will be no Indians left in Fiji. This is a very big problem.' The Indians in Fiji are the descendants of laborers imported in the early days of the twentieth century. Generations later, they have generally made a success of themselves in their new country, but they are still called 'Indians' instead of 'Fijians', are prohibited from owning land, and have been the victims of political persecution following the recent coups. An Indo-Fijian driver with eyes red-rimmed for want of sleep told me, 'All you can do is go with the flow. If they want to charge you two more cents, you cannot fight over this two cents or you will go crazy. Go with the flow, that is all you can do. If you eat two meals a day instead of three, go with the flow.'

The Melanesian and Indian populations gave Suva the combined feel of Africa and Asia. The view of the other side of the harbor from the waterfront was incredibly beautiful, high silhouetted mountains disappearing one after the other into the mists of distance on the island of Viti Levu, which is continental in size when compared to the South Pacific islands we had been visiting. The constant traffic of ships and fishing boats on the harbor was mirrored by the struggle and fury of the crowds on shore. And over the whole scene hung the stench of unstable politics and possible violence.

Alisa and Elias and I waded into Suva to provision the barky. We pushed shopping carts through a gleaming fluorescent-lit super-market, and wandered through the ancient, dim warren of the Suva Market, a two-story building offering every sort of produce we could want, the vendors standing behind their tables of wares and greeting us warmly, but also with the wary excitement of people in the long course of another day at a marginal business in an uncertain time who suddenly find a family of foreigners peering at their cabbages. Outside the Market building an overflow of vendors stood behind their tables beneath old blue tarps that provided insecure protection against the recurring torrents of tropical rain. We returned in a cab to the Royal Suva Yacht Club, our refuge and our home base, a faded relic of British colonial days now reduced to making a living on its bar and its facilities for various functions and events, the grounds gone tatty and the gleaming yachts that were once maintained by cheap indigenous labor gone forever. We met a great South African family, a mom and dad and sons, four and six, circumnavigating from their adopted home on the US East Coast on board the yacht *Tiger*. They became instant good friends with whom we enjoyed a fine meal aboard *Pelagic*, yarning and drinking Fiji Bitter as the kids fell asleep one by one, and then we waved goodbye to them forever the next day as they set off for Vanuatu. And Elias got mosquito-bitten in Suva, stunning Alisa and me with our failure to keep him safe from the threat of dengue.

When we arrived in Fiji on September 17th we had found ourselves again facing the strict math of getting out of the tropics before the start of cyclone season. Staying on pace to make our goal of arriving in Australia by November 1st meant we would only have two weeks in Fiji. After months and months of wandering through the South Pacific mostly at our own pace, we were suddenly on a schedule.

We had thought, Fiji in two weeks? No problem. We would just take care of a few chores in Suva and then identify a completely fantastic locale to visit for a week or so before we started thinking about heading west. We chose Kandavu Island, about fifty miles southeast of Suva. Our *Lonely Guide to the South Pacific* said that Kandavu would be a great place to visit if only you could get there, and even better if only there were anywhere for a tourist to stay once there. For much of the trip we had used the *Lonely Guide* as a tool for deciding where *not* to go. If a place had a big write-up in the guidebook, with restaurant and accommodation choices organized by price, we figured that was a place to leave to those who weren't travelling the South Pacific by yacht. So Kandavu passed that test.

Another yacht crew who had visited said it was great. Our bird field guide listed tons of interesting species as resident there. And just north of Kandavu is the Great Astrolabe Reef. Just say that name out loud – Great Astrolabe Reef. Doesn't it sound like the perfect place to park the yacht, mix up the rum punches, and catch up on your snorkeling?

What actually happened reminded me of what happened to my mountain-climbing career after I got a real job and began trying to squeeze Alaska Range climbs into two-week vacations. Although a spell of light winds was forecast, when we motored out of Suva Harbor the winds were blowing hard from the southeast – directly from Kandavu.

We were not going to tack back and forth into a near-gale, getting soaked and trying to feed, maintain and entertain a two-year-old in a world that was tilted over twenty degrees and bashing up and down ten feet every ten seconds. So we eased the sheets and fell off for our back-up choice, Bengga Island (or Bega or Mbengga, depending on which reference you consult), figuring we'd spend a few days there and then head down to Kandavu once the weather was better.

We dropped anchor in a narrow bay that was shaped like an Alaskan fjord, but surrounded by low mountains covered in thick tropical foliage that were completely unlike anything in Alaska. There was a village down the coast, and we rowed ashore to present *sevu-sevu*, the gift of *yaqona* (kava) that outsiders traditionally present to a senior man of a village when requesting permission to visit the surrounding area. We were met at the beach by a woman named Elizabeth. Everyone we saw was very friendly. Elizabeth took me to the proper man and I presented him with *sevusevu* as we sat on the floor of his house. While my intentions were excellent, my ignorance of good manners proper to the event were doubtless shocking. Alisa and I then explained to Elizabeth that we were hoping to walk around and look at birds. Our expressed desire was clearly outside of

Elizabeth's experience of visitors to the village. 'What kind of birds do you want to see?', she asked. 'We have chickens. And pigs.'

We walked around the village with our binoculars and got a tour of the poverty of the place as much as a view of the local avifauna. Then we got back in the rowboat and retreated to *Pelagic*. We stayed on board for a few days, blowing in circles around the anchor and listening to the rain fall while the weather sorted itself out.

Bengga Island is home to a tradition of firewalking, a tradition that is now restricted to performances at a resort on the other side of the island from our anchorage. We had managed to avoid resort demonstrations of 'traditional culture' all the way across the South Pacific. But when Monday rolled around, which was firewalking day at the resort, it was also our seventh wedding anniversary. So who could resist? We prepared to pick the hook and head over for a night out.

But then someone had a Human Moment. Like most American yachts, *Pelagic* was equipped with one battery that was dedicated to just starting the engine, a separate bank of house batteries that was dedicated to everything else, and a switch to determine whether the starter battery or the house bank was connected to the electrical system. While Alisa was trying to change us from the starter battery to the house batteries she moved the circular switch from battery #2 to battery #1, but went clockwise, through OFF, instead of counter-clockwise, through BOTH. This was a feature of our electrical system that British sailing magazines call 'fail dangerous': if you switch the battery switch to OFF while the engine is running, even for a teeny moment, the electricity generated by the alternator has nowhere to go, and the alternator blows up.

So the alternator blew up.

We could have motored to the resort without the alternator and enjoyed our anniversary anyway. But that would not have been consistent with what we were beginning to call The *Pelagic* Way.

We saw a broken alternator as the first step in a hypothetical chain of events leading to Something Bad happening. So the next hour of our anniversary was spent installing one of our two spare alternators while any possible consequences remained hypothetical, and afterwards we had noodles and white wine for our anniversary meal. And we listened to the rain fall. The next day we gave up waiting for the weather to improve and sailed back to Suva.

In Suva we checked out of the country. On a blustery afternoon we left for New Caledonia.

42

STUCK IN THE ETERNAL NOW

A MENTAL PICTURE COMES to me whenever I try to remember the long tradewind passages of our trip. A mahi mahi has just come aboard, the captain is smiling and holding the beautiful fish for a photo. The wind is behind us and we're sailing on an even keel. We are completely divorced from the larger world, all we know is what we see within the horizon that encircles us, and all is well.

Time and again, our passages were strings of moments like that.

But our trip from Fiji to New Caledonia turned out to be the *other* kind of passage.

As we motored away from our final anchorage in Fiji, it was blowing hard enough to send sheets of spray over the dodger and into the cockpit, soaking me. The passage to New Caledonia would be almost seven hundred miles long. We had an initial forecast of twenty-five knot winds out of the southeast. That kind of wind on the open ocean makes for rowdy conditions on a 37-foot boat. But, travel-hardened as we had become by this point, we didn't mind. We reasoned that the wind would be behind us, and it had been blowing twenty-five knots for most of the two weeks that we had been in Fiji. If we waited for perfect conditions we would likely never leave.

When we reached the reef pass that gave access to the ocean, a critical flaw in our pre-trip reasoning asserted itself. I pointed the bow towards New Caledonia, and the wind wasn't behind us. There was just enough south in the wind direction for it to be a little forward of the beam – in non-sailor talk, we would be sailing into the wind just a little bit. This would mean that the ride would be significantly less comfortable. We would be heeling over and travelling into the waves instead of with them, which would make the ups and downs of the sea harder to bear. We would have to be super-careful with Eli to guard against the chance of him hurting himself in a fall as *Pelagic* charged up and down wave after wave, day after day.

But again, we weren't too concerned. So we'd be going a bit to windward. That's life on the big blue Pacific. As the sun sank to the west and we cleared the breakers on the reef I made sail. My first task was to unroll the jib, which got us underway and allowed me to set up the windvane to steer the boat. As soon as the jib was out *Pelagic* heeled away from the wind and threw up a bow wave. We started making time towards our destination. Alisa was down below, immersed again in the hundred provocations and frustrations that routine tasks of cooking and cleaning and getting a two-year-old to use a toilet become on a sailing yacht in a seaway. After clipping in my deck harness and clambering up to the mast I wedged myself into the low side granny bars, a secure spot where I could use both hands to prepare the main to go up. And then I did nothing for a few minutes, I just felt the sloping deck moving beneath me and the occasional blast of spray shooting across my face while I looked at dusk falling over the wild ocean that would be our home for the next six days. Some of my favorite parts of ocean sailing were the hypnotic moments like this one, when I became effortlessly mesmerized by the interacting pattern and chaos of the ocean's movements.

In the midst of this reverie I saw a big torpedo shape moving down the inside of a wave, heading for the windward side of

Pelagic's bows. It was a cetacean too big to be a dolphin, the color of pewter beneath the black water of dusk. It swam under *Pelagic* and a few minutes later I saw two of the animals on our downwind side, swimming back towards us, big black melon heads and falcate dorsal fins revealed each time they came up to breathe. Pilot whales, I thought. Something I'd never seen before. I wanted to tell Alisa to come up and look, but figured they'd be gone before I could get to the cockpit. But then she did come up to the cockpit to check on me. I told her about the whales and she just missed seeing one of them breach behind us, its long kettle-black body suspended almost completely out of the water, hanging for a perfect moment above the spray of the tossing sea surface. And then they were gone. The breach gave me the perfect look that is so often missing when you're trying to identify an unfamiliar marine mammal. Elias and I checked the field guide after dinner and the animals turned out to be false killer whales, *Pseudorca crassidens*.

For days it was a wet ride. *Pelagic* sent sheets of water up into the air each time we crashed into a wave and the wind carried the spray horizontally across our decks. Every surface forward – jib, rigging, anchor windlass, lifelines and stanchions – ran with flowing seawater. The scuppers on the low side of the boat gurgled with gallons of clear water that were constantly flowing through them. And when the wind and waves came together to put all their force at once onto *Pelagic* she reacted with an animal's instinct for the proper time to bow before superior force, rolling away from the clawing sea and dipping her low side rail deep beneath the waves until the moment passed and she could swim upright again. This went on, hour after hour, without any reprieve.

And then the problem revealed itself – the fly in the ointment, the worm at the bottom of the bottle. A few drips had made their way below on the sail from Tonga to Fiji, giving us notice that the caulk I had applied to the caprail after the miserably wet sail from Alaska to Washington was giving up its grip on the oily teak. But we hadn't spent much time going to windward on that last trip, and the rail hadn't been buried too deep in the sea, so there had really just been a bit of dampness below. And so, in the natural course of things, we forgot all about the caprail during our time in Fiji.

Then this windward passage came along. The double bunk forward where Elias slept at sea became soaked and unusable. The starboard bunk in the saloon where Alisa slept at sea became soaked and unusable. My clothes locker got soaked, and, since I couldn't leave the door to the locker open without all its contents spilling out, the door stayed shut and my soaked clothes mildewed in peace.

Just as on the passage to Washington, we retreated to the half of the boat that was usable. Being more travel-hardened now than we were then, we were able to shrug the situation off to a certain degree. I was reminded at one point of the terminology of my mountain-climbing days. Back then my friends and I were in the habit of setting off into unvisited corners of the Alaska Range in groups of two, with no communication to the outside world and no more gear and supplies than we could easily carry. Thus dubiously positioned for success in a notoriously inimical environment, we would attempt to climb some mountain or another that no one had ever heard of, by a route that no one had ever tried before. Sometimes this was a lot of fun, and other times boots froze, storms raged and tent poles snapped. Being crazy enough to get ourselves into these situations in the first place, we had a name for these not-fun times that reflected the devil-may-care bravado that we hoped to bring to the whole affair. We called them 'suckfests', and we developed a certain connoisseur's appreciation for them, especially when they happened to someone else.

Our passage from Fiji to New Caledonia would have been a

routine trip, but the deck leaks turned it into a suckfest. A suckfest with a two-year-old. A suckfest with a two-year-old that was happening to us, not to someone else.

As I've noted before, there was a timelessness to these passages. At sea things ceased to happen one after the other in a linear way. Time just became another ocean that we were sailing across. We were somewhere in that ocean of time at the present moment, we had been at the beginning of it at some other time, and likewise we would find ourselves at the end of it, sometime. But for the long 'right now', we just found ourselves afloat on that shifting surface of time, with the shores of the 'beginning' and the 'end' out of our sight. When things were going well, this was the most sublime aspect of our whole sailing life, as close as a skeptic might ever get to something like a spiritual experience. But when things were going poorly, we found ourselves adrift in timelessness. We could imagine the horizon we needed to reach before time would start flowing again, but we couldn't see it. We hoped for it, but despaired of ever reaching it. And meanwhile we were stuck in the eternal 'now'.

The events of that passage were hard to keep straight, they just happened now and then as we lived through timeless day after timeless day. Once I watched Elias, who was looking at picture books on the cabin sole up forward while Alisa made our daily radio call to the Pacific Seafarers' ham net. The boat was closed and airless. The bow was an anti-gravity chamber. Elias read his books. I got sick. After Alisa was done with the net I went upstairs and vomited. A convenient thing to do under those conditions, as it turns out. No need to actually lean over the lifelines and hurl into the ocean – I just slumped on the cockpit seat, comfortable in my misery, leaned over the coaming, and was sick on the side deck. The waves that washed over the deck every fifteen seconds had things cleaned up four times over by the time I was through, all evidence of my infirmity efficiently removed by sparkling saltwater.

The next day on our timeless round of days I spent collapsed in the portside saloon bunk that was still dry. I didn't feel quite seasick – no nausea, none of the relief that I usually found from seasickness when I hit the refuge of the rack. I just lay there, big strong dude that I am, arm over eyes, bereft of all strength, content to be ill and useless. I listlessly thought back to my one experience of commercial fishing, which, as it happens, was Bering Sea crabbing in really really bad weather. During that season we watched a 120-foot boat near us roll so violently that we looked down its stacks at one moment and the bottom of its keel the next. I had been seasick on the trip from Kodiak out to the Aleutians before the season, but once the crabbing began there was nothing that would keep me from doing my part to work through the season with the rest of the crew. I wasn't sick for one second of that five-day season.

I thought back to that time and wondered, did I rise above myself for the five other men on that boat in a way that I am not doing now for my own wife and son in this boat? Alisa looked at me with concern and then got onto the business of managing boat and toddler, alone, far from land.

I stayed sick, and started to think of all the times I had been laid out on passage since we left Mexico, some of them in conjunction with the symptoms of seasickness, others clearly not. Something seemed to be going on, Alisa and I later agreed. Something that we would have to figure out before that passage from New Zealand to Patagonia that we were starting to talk about doing some day.

We sailed between the islands of Aneityum and Tanna in Vanuatu, a Melanesian nation with an almost legendary reputation among cruising sailors. Having decided that we had pushed our luck travelling with a two-year-old far enough, we passed Vanuatu by, not wanting to expose Elias to any malaria risk.

The day came when nightfall found us only twenty miles or so out of Lifou Island, where we would make our preliminary clearance formalities into New Caledonia. I shortened sail and went to sleep in the quarterberth. Two hours later I woke up, just before my watch alarm was set to go off, and also just before the radar alarm would have warned me that we were ten miles from land. If you sail the open ocean you start to feel the danger and approach of land keenly enough that your subconscious mind can wake you at precisely the right moment in a situation like this, although setting a couple of alarms to back up the subconscious mind is certainly a good idea. Completely befuddled with sleep, I crawled out of the catacomb slot of the quarterberth and climbed into the cockpit. I looked automatically at the sails, then snapped awake when I looked at the horizon and saw the light on the southern end of Lifou Island winking away on the beam, well back from where our bow was pointing. The east side of Lifou is a large bay, and sailing within ten miles of shore meant that land was surrounding us on three sides, and we were sailing directly away from the safety of open water. Alone while Alisa and Elias slept trustingly below, I marveled at the new sea sense that had me awake at precisely the right moment and simultaneously felt the dread at realizing how much depended on the combination of my internal clock, the radar alarm and my watch alarm to wake me on time. Otherwise *Pelagic* was sailing, surely and blindly, towards her destruction at the base of some wave-washed cliff.

I turned the boat around and hove to. We crept away from the island at a knot or so, waiting for the sunrise before making landfall. I stayed up to watch our progress, making sure that sails were balanced with helm and we were moving away from land. I then slept for two more hours and woke as the eastern sky was just turning gray and resumed our course towards Lifou. One part of passagemaking that I found was getting easier and easier was the sleep deprivation. When squalls or landfalls allowed me only four or three or two hours of sleep in a night, I now found that I still did OK the next day.

The marina in Lifou turned out to be the best marina in the world. The harbormaster was named Lulu, to start with, and the local village was named Wé. All good so far. The water was turquoise and clean enough that coral was growing inside the marina and we could watch reef fish right from the dock with Elias. Pretty cool. And there was a great mix of travelling yachts who were checking into New Caledonia, like us, and local French yachts. So we chatted with the other visitors and walked the docks looking at the very cool aluminum and steel French sloops. We washed everything that had gotten wet on the crossing, taking full advantage of our first dockside hose since Mexico, and then festooned all the rigging and lifelines with clothes and cushions to dry in the sun. We made brief forays into Wé and availed ourselves of the cheap baguettes, and then we left for Noumea.

43

SAILING TO AUSTRALIA

'IT'S OCTOBER 14TH', said Alisa. 'Almost my Dad's and brother's birthday. I was just saying to myself, wow, it's October 1st. And now all of a sudden it's two weeks later. It's *crazy* how fast the time is going.'

'It would've gone faster if we'd stayed at home', I said.

'You think?'

'Sure. If we'd stayed home we'd be sixty by now.'

Until 2006, the only port of entry for New Caledonia was Noumea, the capital, which is on the western side of Grande Terre, the main island. Boats making the tradewind passage from Fiji or Vanuatu had to sail past the Loyalty Islands and the Isle of Pines, two of the premier cruising areas, to go check into the colony, and then were faced with an upwind trip to get back to those places. So it was a change for the better that we could check into Lifou, in the Loyalty Islands on the east side of the archipelago. But the rules required us to make our final clearance at Noumea within a week, so we weren't completely at liberty. During the couple of days we spent in Lifou drying out *Pelagic* we talked about going up to Ouvea, an atoll in the Loyalty Group, for one last hit of the atoll living that we had loved so much in the Tuamotus.

A quick look at the distances on the charts, and reflection on how a strong southeasterly would make it so hard to get from the Loyalties to Noumea, put that plan to rest. With Ouvea out of reach, we realized that atolls were suddenly a thing of the past for us, at least until our next set of tropical passages would come along. Dear Reader, let this be a metaphor for everything that you find beautiful or worthwhile in life: for a while there, in the misty recesses of time (you know, *three months ago*), we had been living an atoll-to-atoll existence. The Pacific stretched out endlessly before us. We had plenty of time to learn about harvesting coconuts, and there would be lots more times when we would sit on the beach, salt water drying on our skin, and look through the reef fish field guide with Elias to identify the multicolored wonder we had just seen. And then, suddenly, it was all over.

Our consolation would be the Isle of Pines, which was conveniently on the way from Lifou to Noumea, and is meant to be one of the jewels of New Caledonia. We had a great overnight sail to get there, close reaching into a whisper-smooth twelve-knot breeze. In the morning we woke to accompaniment – flocks of thousands of either short-tailed or sooty shearwaters (I never learned to tell them apart). These two species, the most abundant birds in Alaska, migrate to the Bering Sea for the Austral winter, where there are contemporary accounts from reliable observers of flocks so big that they take days to fly past. The birds return to Tasmania and New Zealand for their breeding season, where they feed their chicks in the nest with a strategy of alternate short local foraging trips and massive 1500-kilometer foraging trips to Antarctica. Very cool birds, in other words. This flock was congregating over the turbulent water in the reef passes between Grande Terre and the Isle of Pines, black-gray-silver birds that were continually coming together in long strings, looking for a meal after the ordeal of their migration all the way from Alaska. They had followed a southwards path similar to our own, first down the west coast of North America and then across the Pacific. Seeing these familiar birds in such an unfamiliar place was a great confirmation of life lived at a global scale.

Our goals for the Isle of Pines were simple: a beach for Elias and a coral reef for us. We ended up with just the beach. We found the anchorages in our cruising guide full of yachts, so settled for a spot off a little deserted island with no other boats at anchor and a nice beach for the family, but no coral. So suddenly snorkeling was a thing of the past for us, too.

We settled into a lazy routine, going ashore every morning with Elias, getting him back in time for lunch and a nap, and spending the rest of the day on the boat. 'It's embarrassing how quickly these days go past', Alisa said. We reveled in the slow pace, knowing that we'd get busy again once we hit Noumea and started preparing for our last passage of the trip. There were some natural history delights to keep us entertained. We saw our first sea snake, swimming along next to the hull as we were dropping the anchor, and several more after- wards on shore. And there was great birding on the island, reflecting the presence of the large landmass of Grande Terre just a few miles away, as well as the east–west gradient of landbird diversity in the tropical Pacific.

And there was the endlessly fascinating natural history of our little boy, who was now firmly in the stick phase of life. The instant we were on the beach he had a stick in hand, generally the longer the better, and he went around smacking every bush and dead leaf and bit of sandy beach that he could possibly smack in our brief time ashore. When he got tired of running around and smacking things he would find me in the position I had staked out on a beach towel and use my recumbent body as a seat from which he smacked the bit of beach at his feet with the stick, over and over again. At the end of every beach visit there were sticks to come back with us, and, since we drew the line at bringing them on board *Pelagic*, the bottom of the dinghy showed a new tendency to become stick-cluttered.

We moved on to Noumea, making the trip in two easy days. The earth of southern Grande Terre was red and the brush was silver-gray, reminding us of the vast Australian landmass ahead. We found the harbor at Noumea thick with yachts, many of which were joining a scheduled cruising rally to Bundaberg. These events are becoming more and more popular – pre-scheduled group passages ranging from a single leg, like this one, to complete round-the-world voyages. What the allure might be I cannot begin to guess.

We talked to the crews of some boats we knew and started hearing things like, 'The wind's supposed to peak at twenty-four knots in five days, but that'll probably be thirty', or, 'There's going to be a westerly swell, and the period is supposed to drop to six seconds four days from now, so it's a bad time to leave'. How they could know the weather in such detail so many days out, we hadn't a clue. We could feel a big round of group psychology coming along as all the Bundaberg-bound boats in the rally started attempting to choose the very best time to leave on the 790-mile crossing. There's something about leaving a safe harbor that gets very difficult once people start trading weather rumors. At this point in the trip across the Pacific everyone knew a boat or two that had run into weather bad enough to break rigging or rip sails, so it was only natural for people to feel a bit of suspense over this last passage before the cyclone season hiatus, wondering if they'd get away with an easy trip just one more time.

We wanted to avoid that scene, mostly because we knew we were as susceptible to group psychology as anyone else. And we didn't want to be trying to check into Bundaberg while all the rally boats were arriving. And the harbor in Noumea stank of sewage and the local Melanesians, the *kanaks*, gave us the same greasy eyeball that they give to the French. The racial tension and urban dislocation of traditional culture in Noumea were palpable. While tension between Melanesians and Indo-Fijians in Suva was obvious, it didn't have anything to do with us. But in Noumea being white was enough to get us involved – nothing overt, just that unspoken tension and a very noticeable reluctance for any Melanesian to make eye contact.

So we just left. Let other boats go through the indecision of 'should we go or shouldn't we?' Let other people stare at weather faxes and GRIB files and worry about squalls and lows and squash zones. Let the tourists pay the high prices for the dubious honor of staying in this colonial city. We were going sailing.

We made one final pre-departure push, much like the pre-departure pushes that had kept us working late at night after Elias was asleep in every port we had left since Kodiak. Alisa provisioned the boat and I dealt with the bureaucrats and laid a new bead of caulk inside and outside the caprail, hoping to staunch our recurring indoor Niagara Falls if we ended up in sloppy weather. Alisa took Elias on his long-promised visit to the aquarium that we had read about in the *Lonely Guide*, and he ran around in front of the shark tank, holding his hand over his head like a dorsal fin and scaring little girls with his 'dun-dun-dun-duh' imitation of the theme from *Jaws*. I pulled the dinghy around the perimeter of *Pelagic* and gave the waterline one last scrub, mindful that the Australian quarantine authorities could require a fouled boat to haul out and repaint upon arrival in order to limit the introduction of exotic organisms to Oz. I watched other skippers in the stinking harbor water, scrub brush in hand, and enjoyed my moment of smugness over having already given the bottom a thorough scrub in the clean waters of the Isle of Pines.

Friday was coming, and we still didn't like to leave port on a Friday, so one final push on Thursday saw Alisa grabbing some final food items and me speed-walking the rounds of officialdom in the punishing tropical humidity, and then both of us winching the dinghy onto deck while Elias took his after-lunch nap.

'I'm exhausted', I told Alisa. 'Maybe we'll just get out of town and anchor up somewhere.'

'Fine with me', she said. 'As long as we leave Noumea today it counts as starting the trip on Thursday.'

The harbor patrol came by and made outlying yachts squeeze into the already-crowded anchorage outside the marina. We picked the hook and gave thanks that Elias didn't wake up, then steered through the anchored fleet, waving to boats we knew.

And then the excitement hit us.

'I can't believe we're sailing to *Australia*!', Alisa said.

Elias came up into the cockpit and watched Noumea disappearing over the stern. We would have just enough time to get out through the reef pass before dark. We were energized, all thoughts of anchoring for the night forgotten. I cracked a beer and picked our way around the shoals between Noumea and the open ocean.

We pulled out through the pass. A sport fishing boat went the other way, hurrying to be back in town by nightfall. The water was gray beneath the western Pacific overcast that had been following us since Fiji. Shearwaters swarmed over prey schools in the current. I unrolled the jib and Alisa went below to feed Elias his dinner. The sun disappeared in front of us. I set the windvane, *Pelagic* cleaved the night-time ocean. We were sailing to Australia.

44

EACH OF US TO THE OTHER

I LOUNGED UNDER THE dodger, out of the occasional spray. Every twelve minutes my watch alarm beeped and I roused myself to scan the horizon for ships. Duty done, I reset the watch and slouched back full length on the cockpit seat. I dozed, not even doing the minimal work of entertaining any thoughts. When my brain did flicker to life, it was to reflect on my talent for bringing indolence to active adventures like ocean sailing. During my climbing career there were few who enjoyed a good storm day as much as me: long tent-bound days with nothing on the agenda but cups of tea and a paperback and endless naps in my muggy sleeping bag. I tasted some of that old magic on the first few days of our passage to Australia, as I kept a lookout for hour after hour. The trip was starting off under overcast skies and with rough seas, just like all of our trips in the western Pacific. *Pelagic* rolled and pitched. Water came sweeping over the windward rail and went streaming out of the low side scuppers. It was a good day to keep my ambition firmly in check, to doze in twelve-minute intervals and to just let time, and miles, pass by.

The wind models from the Australian meteorological service had predicted light and variable winds parallel to the coast of Grande

Terre, the main island of New Caledonia, and then a sharp shift into the twenty-five knot southeasterlies that would carry us all the way to Australia. Exhausted from our hard push to get out of Noumea, and deflated after the exhilaration of departure, I skipped the production of rigging ourselves wing-and-wing and let the ship find her way under jib alone. I set up the windvane to steer us to the south of our desired course. That kept the wind a little forward of the stern, enough for us to maintain speed and self-steer. The winds were still light, and if they had been right on the stern we would have moved slowly, the windvane would have had problems keeping us on course, and I would have stayed up half the night adjusting things. Getting a little farther to the south would also put the southeasterlies aft of our beam when they came, guaranteeing us a fast and comfortable ride.

The next day we did reach the trades, but found they were south-southeasterlies instead of southeasterlies. This meant that we had the wind forward of our beam, just as we did on the sail from Fiji to New Caledonia. And, just like the sail from Fiji to New Cal, the decks were awash and the cabin got soaked forward and to starboard by our old friend the leaking caprails. My band-aid caulk job in Noumea evidently hadn't done the trick. *And*, just like the trip from Fiji to New Cal, I found myself with the numb feeling in my face that is my first symptom of seasickness, and then I was on my knees in the cockpit, spewing downwind like a good sailor spews.

'Oof', I said to Alisa after regaining my equanimity. 'I think the lesson may be that we shouldn't be so cavalier about setting off into twenty-five knot winds.'

'I don't know', she said. 'We knew it would be like this. It really isn't that big a deal.'

Even though we had had a fairly miserable time on the passage from Fiji, with a soaked interior and sea conditions that required constant vigilance over Elias' safety, Alisa had been completely unfazed by the imminent passage to Australia, bringing to bear the 'get 'er done' attitude to seafaring that she picked up from her time on commercial fishing boats in Alaska. It had been Alisa who had been the main driver for overcoming port inertia in Noumea and getting us back to sea quickly. We knew several boats that were finishing their cruise across the Pacific with the wife flying ahead to New Zealand and the husband sailing the passage with friends or casual crew. It's hard to overstate how different this was from our approach on *Pelagic*. Different things work for different people, but we couldn't imagine setting out on a trip that we knew in advance wouldn't be sailed by both of us. *Pelagic* only went where both of us wanted to go. With the boat being so much our home, and the adventure so much the current version of our shared lives, there was no other way.

Which brings me to the answer that I had rehearsed for anyone who might ask for advice on sailing the world on a small boat. You *could* do it without my wife, I would say. But I wouldn't recommend it.

After a couple days of uncomfortable sailing, the wind backed from south-southeast to southeast, and everything changed for the better. With the wind further behind us, *Pelagic* was able to stand up and sail on her feet. We picked up a westbound current that boosted our speed by as much as a knot, and found ourselves back in the effortless passagemaking that we first experienced sailing from Mexico to the Marquesas. *Pelagic* danced over the seas. The waves, tamed by the following current, gave the boat just enough back and forth motion to lull us, ease us, soothe us. Storm petrels fluttered off the stern. The GPS showed our speed as anything between six and a half knots and an otherworldly eight and a half. Elias went down for his nap and Alisa and I enjoyed the rare freedom of relaxing in the cockpit without worrying over his safety. Everything was sunny and blue, the world was perfect and it was ours.

The shortwave radio carried news of a worldwide financial crisis. It sounded impossibly abstract – toxic debt, bailouts, credit lockup. Somewhere, on some computer, we had investment accounts that were suffering. But that was all part of a pretend world, a parallel universe for people who didn't get outside much.

Night found us only three hundred miles away from our landfall in Bundaberg. Our previous noon-to-noon run had been 160 miles, a stellar pace. I began doing the arithmetic in my head to calculate what it would take to get us into port in time to clear in during business hours in two days' time. Liking the answer I got, I began tweaking sails in search of an extra quarter knot to give us a cushion against dying wind. With the end of the trip at hand, I was surprised to feel the coming end of a tension that I hadn't always been aware of. Ever since we had left Kodiak on a rainy afternoon, our own particular brand of superstition had kept me from speaking my greatest fear aloud, even to Alisa: that Elias might be injured when we were far from help. It wasn't storms that scared me, or tidal passes, but a stumbling two-year-old, a broken ulna and a broken radius, and a week of travelling on a pitching boat to reach a doctor. Now I found myself counting down the hours until the passage would be over and I could stop living with that one particular worry.

The next day the trades failed. The wind speed dropped and the wind came right onto our stern, where it did us little good. We left the favorable current and sailed into a giant eddy that pushed against us. We were making four and a half knots through the water, and a dismal four over the ground. We began motorsailing, picking up an extra couple of knots. For a while the windvane was able to steer us, but then the wind became too light and I started to handsteer. Elias went down for his nap and Alisa gave me a spell.

She took a moment to get the feel for the motion and the rhythm of responding to the waves with the wheel and then looked at me and said, *apropos* of nothing in particular, and everything in general, 'You know, I'm not ready to stop sailing. We've got to keep going for a few more years'.

I had always been conscious of the fact that it was my dream we were following. And though Alisa bought into the dream completely, and thrived in our life aboard, I always knew that our new life hadn't been bought cheap. Alisa gave up a lot to go to sea. Which is why it was so great to hear her, unprompted, say that she wanted our family life to continue afloat.

On the whole trip from Alaska, we had never seen average wind speeds of thirty-five knots at sea. We never braved a real gale, much less a storm. We had no answer ready for the people who were forever asking us to describe anything 'really hairy' that happened on the trip. On the fifth day out of New Caledonia, Alisa and I talked about the upcoming Litzow family reunion in Australia. 'You know,' I was saying, 'we're going to have to come up with some good stories from this trip. My Australian relatives are natural story tellers, the kind of people who come up with hilarious adventures to relate whenever they do so much as go grocery shopping. When they really branch out and come to the States to see us, they end up with all kinds of great stories about the funny things that happen to them. Stories that they tell each other for *years*. I'll feel so lame if we sail all the way from Alaska to Australia and all I can come up with is, "The sunsets were *really* beautiful."'

Ask, and be careful what you ask for.

That same night the three of us were relaxing down below after dinner while the windvane steered *Pelagic*. I was wearing headphones in an attempt to put some distance between myself and the two-year-old who for some reason seemed to be accompanying us across the Pacific in our not-overly-large sailboat. So the first time I heard the sound it didn't make much of an impression. It was a loud 'wham!'

that, with the headphones on, sounded a lot like the jib backwinding and then filling. A lot like, but not exactly like. The second 'wham!' was unmistakably the sound of something breaking. When you're in the middle of the ocean on a small boat, sudden noises like this get your attention in an absolute way. Alisa and I both dashed into the cockpit to investigate. As soon as we reached the cockpit there was a third 'wham!' and we saw the windvane jumping on its mounts. I moved aft and saw something big splashing in the water just behind the boat. My first thought was that we'd hooked a fish that was way too big and that it had somehow gotten wrapped around the windvane.

But both fishing lines were slack. My sluggish post-prandial brain tried to figure out what the big thrashing presence in the water might be, and how we might get it away from the delicate and oh-so-important windvane. But then whatever it was left. The windvane hung limp in the water, no longer steering us. With no one at the helm *Pelagic* jibed and the preventer held the main backwinded, slowly pushing us back to New Caledonia. Alisa took the wheel and got us back on course. I went back down to the saloon and reassured Elias until he stopped crying. Then, after a little struggle against the force of our wake I pulled up the windvane rudder. And then things started to make sense.

We were about 170 miles from the nearest point on the Queensland coast, moving through the water at six and a half or seven knots. The moon wasn't up yet, so the night was dark. There was a little bioluminescence in our wake. The windvane rudder was criss-crossed with bite marks. Something, we figured a shark for lack of any better candidate, came across *Pelagic* out on the dark ocean and took a fancy to the shiny stainless windvane rudder that was swinging provocatively back and forth behind the stern. Enough of a fancy not to give up until it had hit it three times.

A central linkage on the windvane had blown out under the

load. This was a pretty serious deal, since having no windvane meant we'd have to handsteer the last two days to reach our port of entry. Handsteering around the clock is no joke for a two-adult crew with a two-year-old, especially with the conditions we had – a broad reach in about twenty knots of wind. It took work and concentration to handsteer a course with the rig we were travelling under (full main, full jib), and it renewed our respect for the windvane to remember how well it had been steering us in those conditions, hour after hour.

We took a reef to make the steering easier and after Alisa put Elias to sleep I managed to fix the windvane with a few spare parts we had on board. And that's the real joy of the windvane compared to the more modern electronic gear that infests yachts these days – if something goes wrong with the windvane, you can actually fix it at sea.

Once the windvane was steering us again Alisa and I sat in the cockpit, watching the stars overhead swinging back and forth every time a wave swept under us.

'The territorial waters of Australia extend out two hundred miles', I said. 'So that was the very first thing that happened to us in Oz. A shark attacking our boat and all. Welcome to Australia.'

'Welcome to Australia', said Alisa. 'Hopefully things will look up from here.'

It wasn't until we hauled the boat out six months later that we realized the shark had taken a bite at *Pelagic's* hull, too.

We spent one more day of living as a family on our boat crawling westward across the vast Pacific. Then the sun set on our last day at sea. It silhouetted the freighters that were parading up and down the shipping lanes along the eastern seaboard of Oz, then fell over the vastness of Australia, still out of our sight to the west. I got out the camera and started snapping pics of the sunset like a tourist. Having watched the sun disappear out of sight of land a hundred times, I was suddenly not sure when I would see this simple miracle again. For sixteen months we had lived with the constant company of our next passage: talking to other sailors about it, plotting it out on the chart, considering patterns of wind and weather, making lists of tasks that *must* be completed before leaving, working away to get half of them actually done, reading about our destination, considering what the people might be like, how expensive it might be to live, what the history and natural history might have to offer us; everything involved in making another relocation on our endless shift from *here* to *there*. Suddenly, we had no idea when our next passage might be.

At dawn land was still out of sight. But rays of light seemed to spring upwards from the western horizon, through the purple-brown atmospheric haze, giving us an indication of the vast landmass ahead. It was as if the huge desert landscape of this continent were a jewel floating in the ocean and casting its own light heavenwards. What would a lookout at the masthead of Captain Cook's ship have made of the sight? Would he have hesitated before hailing the deck, trying to make sense of what he saw? Or would he have sung out with joy and certainty?

Excitement at our arrival animated every brief conversation between Alisa and me, enlivened every routine task. For years we had dreamed of the day when we would set out from home on a small boat to sail to Australia. It seemed that departure day would never arrive, would never be as real as all the sleepy, half-pointless days of our old lives of routine. But the day did come, and we left. Then we had a new day to dream about, the day we would make landfall in Oz. That day, too, seemed unlikely to ever arrive. As we travelled onwards and onwards it stayed stuck in the unknowable future. And now that day was here, it was today, we were living in the midst of it. But we still couldn't see Australia, and without that all-important visual, our arrival seemed hypothetical and uncertain.

We tried to convince ourselves that we really were reaching the end of the trip, that we really had sailed the boat almost all the way from Alaska to Australia. Neither of us quite believed it. If the end of the trip wasn't actually in sight, it couldn't be in our grasp.

What was apparent, and immediate, was that we were different people from the couple who had left Kodiak. It would be hard to explain how much the trip had changed us in part because it was so hard to remember what it was like to be back home, dreaming about sailing the world and wondering what it would be like to travel far from the beaten track with a toddler. But now we had worked the trick of reclaiming the feeling of endless possibility that hadn't been part of our lives since we each, separately, moved to Alaska in our early twenties. A year and a half earlier we had walked away from two good jobs and a cozy house and the condition of being known quantities among a community of friends. For a year and a half we lived by our wits, keeping one step ahead of a toddler and the deep blue sea. And now we looked back on that departure and realized that we had given up all the security in the world and received, in return, something far better. The world.

Pelagic crept closer to the unseen coast and Elias took his nap below. Alisa and I sat in the cockpit in the sun, together at the end of one year and a half of giving up everything certain except for each other and the needs of our child. With Elias asleep, the privacy of the sea still about us, *Pelagic* carrying us ever closer to the new continent, we celebrated together the discovery that our strength, each of us to the other, had been full to the test.

Nineteen miles from Australia and we still had no sight of that low landmass. With a touch of ceremony I raised the yellow Q flag to the starboard spreader, our request for *practique* in this new country – after all these places we had visited, our last new country for a while, and, for all that might be possible, *our* new country.

I went below to catch up on sleep lost the night before when we had conned our way around the northern end of Fraser Island. While I slept Alisa was the first to see Australia. She called out a *sotto voce* 'Land ho!' to let me rest.

When I woke I peered through the binoculars to find the line of markers that would guide us into the Burnett River. The Queensland coastline was unforgivably flat, and now perceptibly growing closer. The sugar warehouses on the river, marked 'consp' on our charts, lay in plain view. We tidied ship to make our best impression on Customs and Quarantine.

We sailed into Australia.

And everything that happened after that is another story.

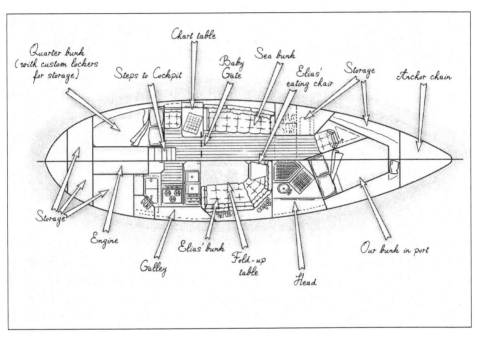

Pelagic
1982 Crealock 37

Designer	Bill Crealock
Length overal	37'11"
Waterline length	27'9"
Beam	10'10"
Draft	5'5"
Displacement	16,000 lbs.

GLOSSARY

I'm sure that for the non-practitioner, sailing language can sound fussy, or worse still, be simply incomprehensible. Here is a short list of nautical terms to (hopefully) clear up any mystery.

aft towards the stern.

beam the side-to-side dimension of a boat, also refers to something to the side of the boat – e.g., a beam sea occurs when waves are hitting the boat from the side.

boom the spar that holds out the base of the mainsail.

cockpit the area above decks where the action of sailing mostly takes place – the place where there are benches for sitting and the wheel for steering, and where the dodger provides protection from spray.

companionway the main passageway from the cockpit to the area below decks.

dodger the fiberglass and plywood shelter over the companionway of *Pelagic*.

forward towards the bow.

freeboard the amount of hull that is above the water.

gunwale the upper edge of the hull along the sides of the boat, the place where hull meets deck

hailing port the home port of a boat, written on the stern beneath the boat's name.

ham net an organized call-in session for keeping in touch via the ham radio.

heeling the action of a boat leaning over from the force of wind.

jib the forwardmost sail, set between the bow and the top of the mast.

jibe to change direction by turning the boat away from the wind. Generally more dramatic than tacking, as the boom can swing madly across the boat if not well controlled.

knot one nautical mile per hour.

lazarette the storage area in the stern of a boat.

leecloth fabric barrier that runs along a bunk and keeps the occupant from rolling out at sea.

leeward away from the direction the wind is blowing from. Pronounced "loo-ward", often shortened to "lee", which is confusingly pronounced as "lee". A "lee shore" is land that is downwind of a boat.

lifelines cables running on either side of the deck, supported by stainless steel stanchions, that help keep the crew on board.

list the action of a boat leaning over from some force beside the wind, for instance from a poorly distributed cargo.

mainsail pronounced 'MAIN-sl'. The sail that runs up the mast and out along the boom.

painter a line for tying up a dinghy when it isn't in use.

port the left-hand side of the boat, as you are facing the bow.

portlights opening windows in a boat.

reef to make a sail smaller in strong winds.

rigging two types – standing rigging is the set of wires that hold up the mast, running rigging is the set of lines ("ropes" in non-sailor talk) that control the sails. (The stickler will object that the running backstays are running rigging that nonetheless hold up the mast, but this definition is generally good enough for our purposes.)

saloon the central living area of a sailboat, where meals are eaten.

scuppers holes that drain water from the deck

settee the bench seat in the saloon that doubles as a bunk at sea.

sheet the control line that trims a sail (adjusts its angle relative to the wind).

sole the floor of a boat, below decks.

spinnaker the big, colorful sail that is flown forward of the mast, in place of the jib, when the wind is light.

starboard the right-hand side of the boat, as you are facing the bow.

staysail on a cutter, like *Pelagic*, the small sail that is aft of the jib and forward of the mast.

tack to change direction by turning the boat into the wind.

whisker pole an aluminum pole that holds the jib out on the other side of the boat from the mainsail when sailing downwind.

winches hand-cranked drums that allow lines with very heavy loads on them to be pulled in manually.

windvane a mechanical autopilot that steers a boat on a constant course relative to the wind direction.

windward towards the direction the wind is blowing from.

ACKNOWLEDGEMENTS

Good first readers are difficult to find, and I am grateful to the people who encouraged me after reviewing early drafts of this book: Diana Bagnall, Melissa Beit, Heather Furey, Gillian Gill and Tom Van Pelt. Two of these people (Diana Bagnall and Gillian Gill) acted to turn manuscript into book, and I thank them for it. Jane McCredie had the confidence in what she read to set in motion the wheels of publication, and Tim Fullerton edited the book into its final form – thank you both. I am also forever grateful to Joan and Merv Litzow for giving a habitually wayward son more affirmation than he could reasonably expect. And finally Alisa Abookire, in addition to everything else, worked hard to make time in our shared life for me to write this book. Thank you.

Mike Litzow lives with his wife and two sons on a 45-foot sailboat. *South from Alaska* is his first book. Follow Mike at thelifegalactic.blogspot.com.

Reviews are a writer's gold! If you enjoyed *South from Alaska*, please log onto amazon.com or goodreads.com and leave a review to help other readers find this book.

Made in the USA
San Bernardino, CA
23 October 2016